Women in the Story of Jesus

Women in the Story of Jesus

The Gospels through the Eyes of
Nineteenth-Century Female Biblical Interpreters

Edited by

Marion Ann Taylor and Heather E. Weir

WILLIAM B. EERDMANS PUBLISHING COMPANY
GRAND RAPIDS, MICHIGAN

Wm. B. Eerdmans Publishing Co.
2140 Oak Industrial Drive N.E., Grand Rapids, Michigan 49505
www.eerdmans.com

22 21 20 19 18 17 16   1 2 3 4 5 6 7

ISBN 978-0-8028-7303-3

Library of Congress Cataloging-in-Publication Data

Names: Taylor, Marion Ann, editor.
Title: Women in the story of Jesus : the gospels through the eyes of nineteenth-century female
    biblical interpreters / edited by Marion Ann Taylor and Heather E. Weir.
Description: Grand Rapids : Eerdmans Publishing Co., 2016. |
    Includes bibliographical references and index.
Identifiers: LCCN 2016036811 | ISBN 9780802873033 (pbk. : alk. paper)
Subjects: LCSH: Bible. Gospels—Feminist criticism. | Women in the Bible.
Classification: LCC BS2555.52 .W65 2016 | DDC 226/.06082—dc23
    LC record available at https://lccn.loc.gov/2016036811

Table of Contents

Table of Contents

Acknowledgements

The project that resulted in this book, a small part of a larger project on women's interpretation of the Bible, has been very much a collaborative effort. We are profoundly grateful for the generous tangible and intangible support of family, friends, colleagues, and institutions. The institutions at which we teach and work are committed to supporting scholarship, especially Wycliffe College at the University of Toronto. The thoughtful responses of our families, friends, and students who have heard us talk about the writings in this book have been a valuable resource and encouragement. We want to especially thank Dr. Thomas Power, the theological librarian at the Graham Library, for his generous support and practical help during the research and writing stages of the book. Special thanks to Carolyn Mackie for compiling the bibliography in the appendix and reading early drafts of the book. We also want to thank Ashley Bailey, Wendy Amos Binks, Kari Reed, Jasmine Shantz, Beth Robertson, Lorraine Hudson, Meredith Donaldson, David Horrocks, Rick Maranta, Sean Otto, and Amanda MacInnis-Hackney for their helpful feedback, biographical research, and practical work of scanning, editing, and researching. Thanks also to our colleagues who offered helpful suggestions in the early stages of our research: Diane D'Amico, David Kent, Cynthia Scheinberg, Peter Erb, Christiana DeGroot, Tim Larsen, Gillian Mitchell, and Carey Newman.

We are especially thankful for the generous support of the Reid Trust, the Louisville Institute, and the Association of Theological Schools Lilly research grants that funded research on forgotten nineteenth-century interpreters of the Bible.

We also want to thank our courageous foremothers whose lives continue to inspire and encourage us. Responses such as "Wow, I can't believe she thought that!" or "Amazing!" are common when reading nineteenth-century women's comments on Scripture. Our lives have been enriched by the writings and lives of the women who were courageous enough to step out, write, and publish and we hope that your lives will also be richer as you encounter both the authors and their writings.

A Note on References and Editors' Additions

Scripture references in square brackets are editorial additions. For ease of reading, the authors' Scripture references have been modified from the standard nineteenth-century form: for example, Proverbs xv. 25 in the original reads Proverbs 15:25 in these excerpts.

Any text in square brackets is an editorial gloss, modification, or addition.

Numbered notes are the editors' notes. Notes marked by symbols are original to the nineteenth-century authors.

Changing Landscapes: Setting the Stage

In his introduction to *The Cambridge Companion to Biblical Interpretation*, John Barton wonders if there is anything left to discover about the Bible.[1] His answer confirms our own thinking on this question: there is not only primary research still to be done to shed light on the world of the Bible and its meaning, there is also research needed on the interpretation and reception of the Bible. Although each generation and each interpreter asked different questions and discerned different meanings from the text, important family resemblances can be traced in the way succeeding generations of interpreters heard the message of the Bible. The recent interest in the reception history of the Bible reinforces the value of listening to the variety of interpretive voices throughout history.

Women's writings on the Bible have been the subject of increased interest in at least three academic fields over the last few decades. Literary scholars have recognized the influence of the Bible on literature and have studied the ways women interpreted the Bible in their literary output.[2] Historians have argued that European women and men both read and interpreted biblical texts to discuss patriarchal practices.[3] Biblical scholars have looked for women interpreters of the Bible as examples and foremothers for women working in the field today.[4] Building on the early work of literary scholars,

1. John Barton, *The Cambridge Companion to Biblical Interpretation* (Cambridge: Cambridge University Press, 1998), 1.

2. One example of this kind of work is Patricia Demers, *Women as Interpreters of the Bible* (New York: Paulist Press, 1992). Examples have multiplied in the last decade.

3. See Gerda Lerner, *The Creation of Feminist Consciousness: From the Middle Ages to Eighteen-Seventy* (New York: Oxford University Press, 1993), particularly the chapter "One Thousand Years of Feminist Biblical Criticism," 138–66.

4. See Marla J. Selvidge, *Notorious Voices: Feminist Biblical Interpretation, 1500–1920* (New

historians, and biblical scholars, interest in women's writings on the Bible has grown considerably. The reception history of the Bible expands the history of biblical interpretation beyond the traditional interpretive genres. This book is best located in the growing and fruitful field of reception history, in the corner of that field dedicated to hearing women's voices.[5]

There are three stages in the work of listening to women's voices from the past in biblical studies. Women's interpretive writings need to be first recovered, then analyzed, and finally integrated into the history of biblical interpretation. The task of recovery involves raising the existence of women interpreters in the history of the church to consciousness, and making their writings widely available. Initial analysis of women's writings proceeds along-side the work of recovery. While recovery is often exclamatory (Hey! Look at this! Wow!), analysis questions the work in order to understand it well (Who wrote this? Why did she write? Why did she say that?). Scholarly analyses of women's writings are often presented at conferences, then collected into volumes of essays.[6] As analysis continues, the integration of women's voices into wider discussions in biblical studies has begun. One early example of the integration of women's voices into a work of scholarship is David M. Gunn's

---

York: Continuum, 1996). Also see the recovery work done in Elisabeth Schüssler Fiorenza, *In Memory of Her: A Feminist Theological Reconstruction of Christian Origins* (Lexington, NY: Crossroad, 1983).

5. Some representative publications from this corner of the field of reception history include the following works: Marion Ann Taylor and Heather E. Weir, eds., *Let Her Speak for Herself: Nineteenth-Century Women Writing on Women in Genesis* (Waco, TX: Baylor University Press, 2006); Joy A. Schroeder, *Dinah's Lament: The Biblical Legacy of Sexual Violence in Christian Interpretation* (Minneapolis: Fortress, 2007); Marion Ann Taylor and Agnes Choi, eds., *Handbook of Women Biblical Interpreters: A Historical and Biographical Guide* (Grand Rapids: Baker Academic, 2012). *The Bible and Women: An Encyclopedia of Exegesis and Cultural History* is an international interdisciplinary project that includes reception history. The English publisher for this collection is SBL/Brill. For more information see the project's website: http://www.bibleandwomen.org/EN/index.php, last accessed May, 2015.

6. At the annual conferences of the Society of Biblical Literature and the Canadian Society of Biblical Studies, papers are regularly given on these women. New working partnerships with colleagues continue to be formed at these meetings, and several books have resulted from these consultations. Books resulting directly from conference sessions include Christiana de Groot and Marion Ann Taylor, eds., *Recovering Nineteenth-Century Women Interpreters of the Bible* (Atlanta: Society of Biblical Literature, 2007); Nancy Calvert-Koyzis and Heather E. Weir, eds., *Strangely Familiar: Protofeminist Interpretations of Patriarchal Biblical Texts* (Atlanta: Society of Biblical Literature, 2009); and Nancy Calvert-Koyzis and Heather E. Weir, eds., *Breaking Boundaries: Female Biblical Interpreters Who Challenged the Status Quo* (London: T & T Clark, 2010).

commentary on Judges. Joy A. Schroeder's more recent work on the history of interpretation of Deborah demonstrates the importance of integrating women's voices into scholarship.[7] Integration asks scholars what they will do with women interpreters of the Bible: treat them as a curiosity? Or will they read them, engage with them in interpreting the Bible, and include them in theological discussions? All three tasks—recovery, analysis, and integration—continue to be important in the field of reception history.

At the same time as knowledge of women's interpretations of the Bible has proliferated, the landscape of biblical interpretation in the twenty-first century has changed. Modern notions of what constitutes the meaning of biblical texts have shifted away from a primary focus on what the text *meant* to embrace not only what it *means* today, but also what it *has meant* and how it has been *received* and *appropriated* by diverse readers using a variety of media throughout history. This means that the popular voice, which includes the female voice, is valued in new ways.[8] A related shift is the movement towards the recovery of theological readings of biblical texts.[9] This particular change means that women's distinctively "Christian" readings should no longer be dismissed out of hand as having no value; rather they offer a plethora of examples of theological exegesis.

Changes in the landscape of biblical interpretation and new interest in the reception history of the Bible affect how we assess the significance of nineteenth-century women's writings on the women in the gospels. Their writings give witness to women's engagement with gospel women; they model a variety of interpretive approaches including reading texts canonically, theologically, experientially, and critically; they expand the scope of what used to be considered appropriate genres for biblical interpretation. Further, they show women's involvement in all levels of education. They show us how the Bible functioned devotionally and practically in women's lives.

---

7. David M. Gunn, *Judges*, Blackwell Bible Commentaries (London: Blackwell, 2005). Joy A. Schroeder, *Deborah's Daughters: Gender, Politics and Biblical Interpretation* (New York: Oxford University Press, 2014).

8. Note that the *Women's Bible Commentary*, first published in 1992, now includes Carol Newsom's essay "Women as Biblical Interpreters before the Twentieth Century." Carol A. Newsom, Sharon H. Ringe, Jacqueline E. Lapsley, eds., *Women's Bible Commentary*, Twentieth-Anniversary Edition (Louisville: Westminster John Knox Press, 2012), 11–24.

9. Craig Bartholomew, "Theological Interpretation," in *The Oxford Encyclopedia of Biblical Interpretation*, ed. Steven McKenzie (Oxford: Oxford University Press, 2013), vol. II, 387–96. Christopher Roland and Ian Boxall, "Reception Criticism and Theory," in *The Oxford Encyclopedia of Biblical Interpretation*, ed. Steven McKenzie, vol. II, 206–15.

Our goal in this volume is not to present as many of the writings of nineteenth-century women on the gospel women as possible, as fifteen years of retrieval work has shown conclusively that hundreds of women published on subjects related to the Bible.[10] Rather, we feature both typical and exceptional examples of women's writings on ten of the women featured in the gospels. We introduce typical interpretations that illustrate many commonplace assumptions about women and how women interpreted Scripture in the nineteenth century. At the same time, we include more exceptional writings that show women using methodologies they identified as "manly" approaches to reading texts on the one hand and "womanly" approaches to interpretation on the other. We also provide examples of writings that combine these so-called "manly" and "womanly" approaches.

Changing Landscapes:
The Study of the Gospels in the Nineteenth Century

Most Christians reading the gospels in the nineteenth century assumed that they were historically reliable. Attentive Christians have always observed both similarities and differences between the gospel accounts and often harmonized the four gospels into one story. One common example of gospel harmonizing that happens almost unconsciously is the referencing of the story of the "rich young ruler," which conflates Mathew's description of the man as "young" and Luke's depiction of him as "a ruler."[11] While many authors drew on harmonies published by male scholars, some women published their own harmonies.[12] Over the course of the century, questions about the reliability of the gospel accounts and about traditional approaches to such issues as the similarities and differences between the gospel accounts became part of public and not simply scholarly discourse.

Augustine's opinion that the canonical order of the gospels reflected their chronological order held sway until the late eighteenth century when a variety of alternative theories about the ordering and compositional history of the gospels were proposed by scholars.[13] Of lasting importance was the

---

10. See the selected bibliography in the appendix of this book.

11. See John Barton, *Holy Writings, Sacred Text: The Canon in Early Christianity* (Louisville: Westminster John Knox, 1997), 92.

12. One example of a harmony by a woman is Favell Lee Mortimer, *Light in the Dwelling: or, A Harmony of the Four Gospels* (London: J. Hatchard and Son, 1846).

13. For the history of New Testament scholarship see Stephen Neill and N. T. Wright, *The*

work of German scholar Johann Jakob Griesbach who, in 1776, prepared a synopsis of the first three gospels that allowed the passages to be closely compared and contrasted. Griesbach himself continued to support the tradition of placing Matthew as the first gospel, also theorizing that Mark based his gospel on Matthew and Luke. Alternative theories about the origins of the gospel accounts supposed that oral or lost written traditions lay behind the gospels. By the end of the nineteenth century, many scholars had set aside Griesbach's theory in favor of the idea that Mark was the first gospel written, drawing upon a hypothetical source document know as Q (German *Quelle* or source). According to this theory, Matthew and Luke were thought to have used both Mark and Q as independent sources.

Other developments in historical-critical studies of the gospels focused more on questions about the historical accuracy of the events recorded in the gospels. David Friedrich Strauss's *Life of Jesus Critically Examined* (1835) forced scholars to confront the question of how the gospels could be used as biography and history. The ideas of German scholars such as Strauss became well known in Britain and America after the fourth German edition of *Life of Jesus* was translated into English in 1860 by Mary Ann Evans, better known by her pen name, George Eliot.[14] Evans was one of many English women who translated the writings of contemporary German scholars. This translation work facilitated both the spread of biblical criticism and orthodox responses to critical scholarship in English-speaking countries.[15]

Further developments that affected gospel studies in the nineteenth century centered around text criticism, often called lower criticism.[16] For hun-

---

Interpretation of the New Testament 1861–1986 (Oxford: Oxford University Press, 1988), and William Baird, *History of New Testament Research*, 3 vols. (Minneapolis: Fortress Press, 1992). See also Mark Goodacre, "Synoptic Problem," in *The Oxford Encyclopedia of Biblical Interpretation*, ed. Steven McKenzie (Oxford: Oxford University Press, 2013), vol. II, 354–62; Nicholas Perrin, "Gospels," in *Dictionary for Theological Interpretation of the Bible*, ed. Kevin J. Vanhoozer (Grand Rapids: Baker, 2005), 264–268.

14. She was born Mary Anne Evans, dropped the "e" from Anne in 1837, became Marian Evans in 1851, Marian Evans Lewes in 1854 and Mary Ann Cross in 1880.

15. Sophia Taylor, for example, translated one of the volumes of J. P. Lange's German work that was edited by Marcus Dods, *The life of the Lord Jesus Christ, a complete critical examination of the Gospels* (Edinburgh: T. & T. Clark, 1864). For an examination of nineteenth-century women's engagment with criticism in Britain see Marion Ann Taylor, "Women and Biblical Criticism in Nineteenth-Century England," in *The Bible and Women: An Encyclopaedia of Exegesis and Cultural History*, vol. 8.2, edited by Ruth Albrecht and Michaela Sohn-Kronthaler (Atlanta: Society of Biblical Literature, forthcoming).

16. See also N. Clayton Croy, "Textual Criticism: New Testament," in *The Oxford Encyclo-*

dreds of years, scholars had been collecting and analyzing New Testament manuscripts into text types and families of manuscripts, comparing them to the *Textus Receptus*, or received text, of the New Testament, first published in 1516. This text was the basis for most Reformation-era translations. In 1831, a new critical text of the Greek New Testament was published. It was intended to reflect the New Testament as it existed in the fourth century. Other editions of the Greek New Testament followed, including the edition by Cambridge scholars B. F. Westcott and F. J. A. Hort in 1881. Growing awareness that the King James Bible was based upon an inadequate critical edition led to a revised translation of the New Testament in 1881. Discussions about the revision project and the published Revised Version furthered doubts about the veracity of the gospel accounts and traditional teachings about the Bible's inspiration. Important to the women's writings in this collection is the consensus reached by text critics that the story of the adulterous woman in John 7:53–8:11 was secondary, raising the important question of whether this passage should continue to be read as Scripture.

While a number of nineteenth-century women knew Greek and Hebrew well enough to study the Bible in its original languages, and in some cases, to publish their own translations,[17] women did not have the academic training or the support of academic institutions to be text critics. Privately-educated Scottish twins, Agnes Smith Lewis and Margaret Dunlop Gibson, who discovered, photographed, copied, purchased, and later published important manuscripts related to the Bible and its reception history, are exceptions in this regard, as they were veritable text critics.[18] Especially relevant to the text-critical study of the gospels was Agnes Lewis's discovery of a second-century palimpsest of the Syriac Gospels in 1892.[19]

Although with few exceptions, women were neither historical critics nor text critics, their writings on gospel women show that many women

---

pedia of Biblical Interpretation, ed. Steven McKenzie (Oxford: Oxford University Press, 2013), vol. II, 379–87.

17. Julia Evelina Smith translated the entire Bible five times and published her translation in 1876. See Marla Selvidge, "Smith, Julia Evelina (1792–1886)," in Taylor and Choi, *Handbook,* 455–57. In 1885, Helen Spurrell published a translation of the entire Old Testament based on an unpointed Hebrew text. See Samuel D. Giere, "Spurrell, Helen (1819–91)," in Taylor and Choi, *Handbook,* 467–69.

18. See Alicia Batten, "Gibson, Margaret Dunlop (1843–1920), and Agnes Smith Lewis (1843–1926)," in Taylor and Choi, *Handbook,* 210–13.

19. See Agnes Smith Lewis, *Light on the Four Gospels from the Sinai Palimpsest* (London: William & Norgate, 1913).

were aware of current debates about how to read and interpret the gospels. Women's thoughts on gospel scholarship are found in novels, poetry, essays, commentaries, and a variety of other educational materials. Their views on biblical criticism were not uniform. Many followed tradition and harmonized the gospels, assuming one gospel story rather than four.[20] Others popularized the views of moderate or liberal biblical critics and clergy in educational materials, including books for children and young adults. In 1887, for example, English educator Anne Mercier introduced teenagers to the challenges of reading the gospels and provided them with a thirteen-page harmony of the gospels.[21] In 1892, university-educated author and educator Mary Petrie informed the more than three thousand women enrolled in The College by Post, that "all good authorities agree . . . that an exact harmony of the four gospels cannot be constructed." The gospels were not to be read as a complete history, but rather "as memoires containing infinitely beautiful pictures of the infinitely beautiful Life [of Jesus]."[22]

Changing Places: Gendered Roles and Expectations

Shared stereotypical views of gender roles and attitudes permeated nineteenth-century culture. While these stereotypes did not always reflect the nuanced truth of life during this time, they represented ideals held up for women and men to follow. Women were generally held to be more spiritual and emotional than men, who were more material and logical beings. In this kind of thinking, women were heavenly, whereas men were worldly. Women by nature were thus closer to God than men. American physician and poet Oliver Wendell Holmes expressed these differences between men and women in a poem found in his collection *The Poet at the Breakfast Table*:

Oh, that loving woman, she who sat
So long a list'ner at her master's feet,
Had left us Mary's Gospel—all she heard,

20. Brevard S. Childs, *The New Testament as Canon: Introduction* (Philadelphia: Fortress, 1985), 143–209.

21. Mrs. Jerome [Anne] Mercier, *The Story of Salvation: Thoughts on the Historic Study of Scripture* (London: Rivington's, 1887), 244–78.

22. Mary Louisa Georgina Petrie, *Clews to Holy Writ or, the Chronological Scripture Cycle: A Scheme for Studying the Whole Bible in Its Historical Order During Three Years* (London: Hodder and Stoughton, 1893), 244.

Too sweet and subtle for the ear of man!
Mark how the tender-hearted mothers read
The messages of love between the lines
Of the same page that loads the bitter tongue
Of him who deals in terror. . . .
Would that the heart of woman warmed our creeds!
Not from the sad-eyed hermit's lonely cell—
Not from the conclave where the holy men
Glare on each other as with angry eyes.
They battle for God's glory—and their own—
Ah, not from these the list'ning soul can hear
The Father's voice that speaks itself divine.
Love must be our master; till we learn
What he can teach us from a woman's heart,
We know not His, whose love embraces all.[23]

Josephine Butler, a British social activist, quoted these lines of poetry with approval in an interview with Sarah Tooley on "The Sex Bias of the Commentators."[24] She longed for "Mary's gospel," to hear the stories of Jesus from a woman's point of view. Holmes was convinced that women would hear "messages of love" where men heard anger, and would teach men to better know God as Father.

The quotation of Holmes by Butler helpfully illustrates a number of things about the nineteenth-century context of the writings in this collection. First, the poem Butler quoted illustrates some gender expectations held by both nineteenth-century men and women. Holmes, an American man, expected women to understand love and tenderness better than men. He saw holy men as angry warriors battling for God's glory and holy women as tender mothers who saw love "between the lines" of Jesus' teaching. Butler, a British woman, endorsed this view; she also saw men and women in this way. While men might set up and reflect common expectations for women (as Holmes did), women did not always reject those expectations. Butler shared the understanding of women and men reflected in Holmes's writing, and both

23. Oliver Wendell Holmes, *The Poet at the Breakfast Table* (Boston: James R. Osgood, 1872), 365–67.
24. Sarah A. Tooley, "The Sex Bias of the Commentators: An Interview with Mrs. Josephine Butler," in *The Humanitarian* V, no. 6 (December 1894), 420. An excerpt from this interview is included in chapter 7 of this book.

the American man and the British woman thought that the gospels would be enhanced if a female point of view were available.

Second, from the lines of the poem it is clear that women, particularly mothers, were held up as ideals of love and self-sacrifice in the nineteenth century. This ideal was embraced and used to different degrees by women writing at that time. The ideals of love and self-sacrifice were particularly Christian, as shown in the life of Jesus. Women could be seen as naturally closer to the Christian ideal and thus qualified to give spiritual advice to others in their teaching and writing. The love and self-sacrifice of women could become an argument in favor of hearing women's voices, as it did in the lines of poetry by Holmes. Similarly, women of the nineteenth century were quite capable of turning other culturally imposed ideas and ideals about gender to their benefit. For example, mothers were seen as powerful influences on their children's lives, thereby influencing the future of nations. Women could therefore encourage mothers to become very well educated so that they could teach their children well. Women's expected care for those in their households was also extended to include care for those in need outside of their immediate households.

Third, the poem illustrates the transatlantic exchange of ideas that took place between North American and British thinkers and writers: a British woman quoted an American man. Nineteenth-century women did not write in isolation. They had access to the ideas of others, including writers and thinkers who might be at a geographical distance. Holmes's *The Poet at the Breakfast Table* was published in Boston and London at the same time. Similarly, the works by Sarah Hale and Harriet Beecher Stowe excerpted in this book were simultaneously published in the United States and Great Britain.[25]

Finally, the quotation by Butler of the poem by Holmes in an interview on the sex bias of biblical interpreters illustrates that simplistic categories, such as public/private or sacred/secular, do not adequately describe the lived reality of nineteenth-century culture.[26] Gendered ideals and ideas about women were used to empower women as well as to silence them. The recovery and recognition of women's voices in biblical interpretation provides data for the ongoing reconsideration of how nineteenth-century gender ideals, such as

25. Rebecca Styler, *Literary Theology by Women Writers of the Nineteenth Century* (Farnham, UK: Ashgate, 2010), 72. For other examples of evidence of transatlantic exchange, see Taylor and Weir, *Let Her Speak*, 10.

26. On reconsidering these divisions, see for example Sue Morgan, "Introduction," in *Women, Religion and Feminism in Britain, 1750–1900* (Basingstoke, UK: Palgrave Macmillan, 2002), 1–19.

"The Angel of the House" or the Cult of Domesticity, have been understood by scholars.[27] Hearing a variety of women's voices on what it meant to be a woman at different times in the nineteenth century illuminates the debate about the nature and role of women—the infamous Woman Question.[28]

Negotiating Changes: Gendered Exegesis

At a number of critical points, debates about the Bible in the nineteenth century intersected with debates about gender. Historically, the academic study of Scripture and of theology had excluded women. Only exceptional women throughout history had the kind of education and resources necessary to participate in the academic study of Scripture and theology. Although barriers to women's education in general, and to theological education in particular, were very slowly breaking down, the academic study of Scripture, especially historical criticism, was unavailable to women and often described in masculine terms. As Oxford notable Benjamin Jowett argued in "On the Interpretation of Scripture," the historical critical approach to interpreting the Scriptures "like any other book" was a "manly" activity reserved for the highly educated and cultivated chosen ones.[29] The task of a critically-attuned interpreter was to clear away the dogmatic, systematic, controversial, and fanciful interpretations of past interpreters, who, Jowett suggests, were blind to the original meaning of the text by their rootedness in their present context.[30] While legitimate interpretation was for the few, Jowett believed that the application of Scripture could be done by philosopher or poor woman alike as long as the resulting interpretations were "not

27. "The Angel of the House" is a poem written by Coventry Patmore. For a complete version, see *The Angel of the House* (London: Macmillan, 1866). The Cult of Domesticity or the Cult of True Womanhood is discussed in Barbara Welter, "The Cult of True Womanhood: 1820–1860," *American Quarterly* 18 (1966): 151–74.

28. Further discussions of the nineteenth-century cultural contexts for these writings can be found in the introductions to Taylor and Weir, *Let Her Speak,* and de Groot and Taylor, *Recovering Women Interpreters of the Bible.* See also Rebecca Styler, *Literary Theology,* and Timothy Larsen, *A People of One Book: The Bible and the Victorians* (Oxford: Oxford University Press, 2011).

29. Benjamin Jowett, *The Interpretation of Scripture and Other Essays* (London: George Routledge and Sons, Ltd., 1907), 34, 36, 55. His groundbreaking essay "On the Interpretation of Scripture" was first published in *Essays and Reviews* in 1860.

30. Jowett, *The Interpretation of Scripture,* 7.

the vehicles of [the interpreter's] own opinions, but expressions of justice, truth and love."[31]

Against a highly rational "manly" approach to the interpretation of the Bible was an approach that a number of nineteenth-century women identified as a particularly "womanly" way of reading Scripture. This womanly approach was tied into commonplace assumptions about women's nature, as noted above. In her 1835 publication, *Woman's Mission*, Sarah Lewis set in binary opposition a male intellectual and a female heart approach to interpreting Scripture. She expressed the sentiment of many when she associated the male intellectual and rational critical approach with unbelief and doubt:

> Man have been scanning [Scripture] with the intellect, and not with the heart! what wonder is it then, that a system addressed to the heart, and intended to operate upon the heart, has eluded their researches! How have they repaid for these researches! By unbelief, which makes them objects of compassion, not of blame.[32]

In this way, Lewis and a number of other women authors criticized academic approaches that seemed to incite unbelief.

Josephine Butler, who lived in Oxford following her marriage to an Oxford scholar, challenged what she thought were Jowett's erroneous assumptions about women's hearts, as well as his concomitant conviction that "truth can only be arrived at by a life spent on academic research."[33] Jowett's academic work gives no evidence that he changed his views as a result of his correspondence with Butler, who continued to be critical of a strictly academic approach to interpreting Scripture and any traditionally male-focused interpretations that discounted the interpretive voices of women. In her interpretations of Scripture, Butler modeled a woman-sensitive alternative to rational biblical criticism.[34]

31. Jowett, *The Interpretation of Scripture*, 55.

32. Sarah Lewis, *Woman's Mission*, 4th edition (London: John W. Parker, 1839), 138.

33. In the one letter that remains of her correspondence with Jowett on this subject, Butler accuses Jowett of thinking "that women generally accept Christianity without a thought or a difficulty; that they are in a measure instinctively pious, and that religion is rather an indulgence of the feelings with them than anything else." Butler argued that academic research could not prove the existence of God, but God's existence could be known in the same way a mother knows that she loves her children, but also that they love her. JB to B. Jowett, nd (c 1865–68) as cited in Helen Mathers, *Patron Saint of Prostitutes: Josephine Butler and a Victorian Scandal* (Gloucester: The History Press, 2014), 35.

34. Marion Ann Taylor, "'Cold Hands Upon Our Threshold': Josephine Butler's Reading of the Story of the Levite's Concubine, Judges 19–21," in *The Bible as a Human Witness to Divine*

Many of the women excerpted in this book felt authorized to interpret Scripture because their heart approach was not only different from either traditional ecclesially-blessed approaches or modern manly rationalistic approaches, but was also more appropriate and life-giving.[35] However, not all women used a womanly approach to interpretation. In preparing their publications, many women read the commentaries and sermons of scholars and clergy who interpreted and applied Scripture for the needs of the church, and their interpretive work was influenced by what they read. Some blended the interpretive approaches associated with men and women. In fact, as the century proceeded, women such as Harriet Beecher Stowe, Elizabeth Rundle Charles, and Josephine Butler recognized that they could use some of the insights of biblical critics as well as changing perceptions about the nature of Scripture to advance the cause of women. They were more aware of the gender bias of biblical interpreters and even the shapers of the canon. These women called for a variety of changes, including new readings and new approaches to interpretation.[36]

Changing Perspectives:
Nineteenth-Century Women Writing on the Gospels

This book features the stories of women found in the gospels as read through the eyes of nineteenth-century American and British women. These interpretations provide windows into the lives of the nineteenth-century authors. In selecting the forty-two excerpts presented in this

---

Revelation: Hearing the Word of God Through Historically Dissimilar Tradition, ed. Randall Heskett and Brian Irwin (New York and London: T & T Clark, 2010), 259–73.

35. In a letter to her scholar/husband, Harriet Beecher Stowe mocked the value of biblical scholarship: "If you studied Christ with half the energy that you have studied Luther—. . . If you were drawn toward him & loved him as much as you loved your study & your books then would he be formed in you, the hope of glory—But you fancy that you have other things to do . . . you must write courses of lectures— . . . you must keep up with the current literature—& read new German books—all these things you must do & then if there is any time, any odds & ends of strength & mental capability left, why they are to be given occasionally to brushing up matters within, & keeping a kind of a Christian character." Letter to Calvin E. Stowe, cited in Gail Smith "Reading the Word: Harriet Beecher Stowe and Interpretation," dissertation, University of Virginia, 1993, 58.

36. See Bulter's discussion of the exclusion of the longer version of the book of Esther and the book of Judith from the Protestant canon in Sarah A. Tooley, "The Sex Bias of the Commentators: An Interview with Mrs. Josephine Butler," 417–18.

book, our goal was a representative not an exhaustive collection. As noted above, a decade and a half of retrieval work has clearly demonstrated that hundreds of nineteenth-century women published on subjects related to the Bible, including women in the gospels. This book moves beyond recovery work, and begins the work of analysis. By making these excerpts by women on women in the gospels available in a collection like this, we hope to encourage the integration of women's writings into teaching and preaching on the gospels, and invite further analysis of these and similar works.

A book's purpose

The thirty-one women whose work is excerpted in this collection came from diverse backgrounds. Among the writers are famous authors, social justice advocates, and preachers such as Harriet Beecher Stowe, Elizabeth Cady Stanton, Josephine Butler, and Phoebe Palmer. Also included are women about whom we know very little, such as M. G., Mrs. Donaldson, and Margaret Black, who also put pen to paper to comment on the lives of women in the gospels. Although we attempted to include diverse literary genres, theological perspectives, and authors from various church affiliations and countries in this collection, most of the authors were British, and were a part of the Church of England. None of the women excerpted in this book received a university education; most studied privately, by reading material that they found themselves or that was recommended by fathers, husbands, family friends, and clergy. These women overcame their lack of formal education, and developed competence and confidence to teach, preach, and publish on the Bible.

These women wrote on the women in the gospels for a variety of reasons. Some, who recognized the absence of women's voices from history, including the history of the interpretation of the Bible, wrote at least in part to right the wrongs of such omissions. They sensed the need to connect to their foremothers. Sarah Hale's encyclopedic work, *Woman's Record, or, Sketches of All Distinguished Women from the Creation to A.D. 1854*, included the biographies of women in Scripture as well as distinguished women throughout history in order to prove "that WOMAN is God's appointed agent of *morality*, the teacher and inspirer of those feelings and sentiments which are termed the virtues of humanity."[37] This early feminist agenda was just one of the many ideological causes that motivated women to write about the Bible. Women also used the stories of gospel women to promote religious, social,

---

37. Sarah Hale, *Woman's Record, or, Sketches of All Distinguished Women from the Creation to A.D. 1854* (New York: Harper & Brothers, 1855), xxxv.

or political agendas, including specific issues such as the evils of dancing and drink, the dangers of Catholicism, women's right to preach, and the importance of conversion. These ideological readings remind us of the importance of knowing our biases as interpreters.

Most nineteenth-century women wrote to educate; educational work, even writing for publication, was an acceptable avenue for women to pursue if they needed to support themselves. Whether they needed the income or not, many women described their published work as educational. Many studied Scripture devotionally and then shared what they learned with their own children, the children in their churches and local schools, then more widely with both children and other teachers through print. Similarly, women taught or preached the Bible to older teenagers and various groups in church or in the community and then published their work for others to use. The money earned in publishing endeavors was used to support themselves and their families, or given to a charitable cause.

Three particular themes recurred in our analysis of the nineteenth-century women's writings on women in the gospels: Christian piety or spirituality, women's public preaching and teaching in the church, and women as interpreters of the biblical texts. The topics of spirituality, preaching, and hermeneutics (or interpretation) are the broad categories we used to divide the book into three sections.

The first section of this book, "Heart and Hands: Women's Spirituality," features fourteen excerpts on three important women in Jesus' life—his mother Mary, and his close friends, Mary and Martha of Bethany. Women's writings on Jesus' mother elicited discussion about Mary's character and life, as well her ongoing significance. The figures of Mary and Martha drew out very different responses from women living in a culture that honored women's Mary-like piety on the one hand, yet also expected women to serve as Martha did.

The second section, "Unsealed Lips: Women Preaching," features the writings of thirteen women on four women: Anna, the Samaritan woman at the well, Herodias, and her daughter, Salome. The stories of these women prompted discussion on the controversial subject of women's public roles in society and church. Anna and the Samaritan woman provided role models for women challenging traditions or dogma that restricted women from preaching. Herodias and Salome were subjects of women's sermons on the appropriate use of power. This section includes not only discussions of biblical precedents for women's preaching and evangelism, but also examples of women's sermons preached with the pen or in public.

The third section, "Unveiled Eyes: Women Interpreting the Biblical

Text," includes fifteen selections written by twelve women on two unnamed women, the Canaanite woman and the adulterous woman, and Mary Magdalene, whose identity has long been debated. These excerpts demonstrate the scope and breadth of women's engagement with biblical texts, highlighting women's distinctive reading strategies, and challenging assumptions about the nature of nineteenth-century women's interpretations of the Bible. The story of the Canaanite woman prompted women's experiential reflections as they taught and traveled. The story of the adulterous woman from John 8, always a troublesome text for women, became more controversial later in the century after the Revised Version of the New Testament (1881) was published with the passage in brackets. Women writing on Mary Magdalene drew on a long and rich written and visual interpretive tradition of this intriguing woman to discuss her relevance for themselves and their contemporaries.

Each of the three sections of the book contains an introduction providing the context specific to the topic covered in that section. With the exception of the chapters on Mary and Martha of Bethany and Herodias and her daughter, each chapter within a section features a particular gospel woman. The chapter introductions provide a synopsis of the relevant gospel stories and highlight common interpretive questions. The introduction to each excerpt gives the context for that particular piece of writing. This context includes information about the author and about the larger work from which the selection is excerpted.

this is helpful.

Within each chapter, the excerpts on particular gospel women are ordered by genre, then chronologically within the genres. This arrangement highlights the fact that the nineteenth-century women wrote about the gospel women using a variety of genres. The genres represented in this volume include commentary, scripture biography, essays, travel diaries, children's lessons, and sermons.

While commentaries were considered a male genre, women wrote commentaries throughout the nineteenth century. The commentaries featured in this volume begin chronologically with Sarah Trimmer's one-volume commentary on the whole Bible, published in 1805, and end with Elizabeth Baxter's commentary on the gospel of John, published in 1887. Women's commentaries tended not to be technically detailed; rather, they interpreted the biblical text, verse by verse or paragraph by paragraph, for those who wanted to understand and apply the Bible in their own lives. Both Sarah Trimmer and Mary Cornwallis, for example, wrote commentaries on the whole Bible. Trimmer wrote for people she called "unlearned" in the title of her work, *A Help to the Unlearned in the Study of the Holy Scriptures* (1805);

the unlearned were people who didn't have access to technical commentaries produced by scholars. Trimmer may have had her former Sunday School students in mind: literate adults of the lower classes. Cornwallis wrote her commentary, *Observations, Critical, Explanatory, and Practical, on the Canonical Scriptures* (1817), based on her own study notes, which she used to teach her daughters and her grandson. Her commentary was probably directed toward her peers: women and men studying the Bible and teaching it to their families. Both Trimmer and Cornwallis wrote for literate adults: Trimmer for those without extensive resources studying for their own benefit, and Cornwallis for parents, particularly mothers, who studied in order to teach.

Scripture biographies were a genre that women found particularly attractive and useful. In Scripture biography, a single character is described in some detail. In commentaries, both male and female authors are constrained by the text itself; good commentaries emphasize what the biblical text emphasizes. Often women were background characters in the gospel stories. Scripture biography allowed nineteenth-century women to focus on these background characters. Using clues in the gospels, other biblical passages, and their sanctified imaginations, nineteenth-century women brought first-century women to life. The stories of the gospel women's lives were usually collected with stories of other women into a larger volume. The collective biographies were authored with different intentions. Some, such as Clara Lucas Balfour's *Women of Scripture* (1847), were inspirational; others, such as Harriet Beecher Stowe's *Women in Sacred History* (1873), were ideological. Scripture biography allowed women to say more about background characters in the gospels, women like them, who provided examples and inspiration for their lives.[38]

Because the nineteenth-century authors wrote for their own time and place, twenty-first century readers in a different time and place can find them difficult to understand. With that in mind, the excerpts in this book are best understood when carefully read and re-read with sympathy and humility. Why did this author say this? Appreciating the context of each writer is the key to understanding their work. How does she illuminate the biblical narrative in asking her particular interpretive questions? Though they speak in

---

38. For further reflections on nineteenth-century women's use of collected biography, see Rebecca Styler, *Literary Theology*, particularly chapter 4. Styler underestimates the breadth of women's biblical interpretation at the time, but does some helpful work with collective biography as a feminist move.

a different accent, women's voices from the nineteenth century still speak clearly, and can be understood by sensitive listeners.

Every time we read the selections in this volume we found that there was more to say. We do not pretend to have exhausted the ways these selections are connected, nor their implications for better understanding how women's Christian faith influenced every aspect of their lives. These excerpts, together with the bibliography of the nineteenth-century works by women we consulted in putting this book together (see the Appendix), show that there is still work to be done mapping the landscape of the reception of the Bible. We hope that this volume serves to interest others in taking up this important task.

PART 1

Heart and Hands:
Women's Spirituality

Introduction

The terms "devotion," "piety," and "heart religion" were the nineteenth-century words for what we call spirituality.[1] It is not surprising that women living in the nineteenth century, who were considered naturally more pious and religious than men, embraced devotional practices and purchased devotional books published by clerics, academics, and devout laymen. Nineteenth-century women, however, did not only purchase these books; they published their own books on spirituality. While some women wrote books specifically about devotional practices, others discussed spirituality in books of other genres, such as commentary or Scripture biography. This section contains fourteen excerpts from nineteenth-century women's writings on the Virgin Mary, and Mary and Martha of Bethany. These readings reveal glimpses of a robust, complex, and mature spirituality, encompassing both the private and public spheres of women's lives. Particularly, this section reveals women's thoughts on virtues associated with Christian piety, their understanding of such devotional practices as prayer, their commitments to the importance of participating in communal worship, and their thoughts on the practical challenges of Christian discipleship.

The spiritual practices of nineteenth-century Christians in Britain and North America varied according to tradition, experience, knowledge, and personal preference. Many common devotional practices were church-based and varied according to denomination. While the Eucharist, for example, was

---

1. See, for example, Hannah More, *Practical Piety; or, the Influence of the Religion of the Heart on the Conduct of Life* (London: T. Cadell, 1811; printing cited here, Baltimore: J. Kingston, 1812), passim. See particularly 18–19 for a discussion of what she means by these terms.

central to Catholic church–based devotion, the Salvation Army did not celebrate this sacrament. Anglican or Episcopalian spirituality centered around the creed and the liturgy in the Book of Common Prayer. Less liturgically-based deonominations encouraged regular meetings for worship, prayer, and Bible study. Women and men gathered together for public worship in most church services. Mothers' Meetings and Sunday Schools afforded women places to teach and lead services.

Private devotional practices were more diverse and are difficult to quantify and document. Some written records of private devotional practices are extant, however, including published devotionals on various subjects, as well as materials not intended for publication such as journals, letters, and notes and in the case of Florence Nightingale, an interleaved Bible, complete with prayers and study notes in a variety of languages.[2] Many devout Roman Catholics and Anglo-Catholics used aids to private devotion, including rosaries, medals, icons, and manuals of prayer.[3]

Christian spirituality was not simply associated with church services and private devotional practices. Anglican writer Hannah More described Christian piety as not an "abstraction of the mind," but rather a practice that animated action.[4] Many devout Christians in the nineteenth century similarly believed that in addition to public and private devotional practices, the public expression of faith as love to one's neighbor was a vital expression of Christian faith. Most women writers excerpted in this section included hospitality toward others and actions of social justice in their understandings of spirituality. Their faith was not simply an interior, private matter, it also included outward, public acts of service; both attitudes and actions, being and doing, needed to be integrated into the life of the Christian woman. Spiritual practices bridged women's private and public worlds.

The key virtue that nineteenth-century women associated with Chris-

2. Nightingale's interleaved Bible attests to her practice of journaling, her prayers, thoughts, and comments inspired by commentaries and academic works on Scripture she read over a number of years. On the blank pages opposite the published text of Psalm 42:4–8, for example, Nightingale wrote: "All thy waves and thy billows are gone over me; *les eaux d'une violente mortification* [the waters of a violent mortification] 27 October 1861, 15 October 1867, 3 January 1873, 22 February 1874." *Florence Nightingale's Spiritual Journey: Biblical Annotations, Sermons and Journal Notes*, ed. Lynn Mcdonald, Collected Works of Florence Nightingale, vol. 2 (Waterloo: Wilfred Laurier University Press, 2001), 144.

3. For more information on Catholic piety in Victorian England see Mary Heimann, *Catholic Devotion in Victorian England* (Oxford: Oxford University Press, 1995).

4. More, *Practical Piety*, 18.

tian piety was humility. This virtue, along with others such as gentleness, temperance, discretion, and love, was exemplified by the biblical women examined in this section. The Virgin Mary was the premier example of humility, though the sisters of Bethany also learned this virtue. Martha served joyfully; Mary of Bethany loved Jesus and showed her loyal love in all her actions. Virtues were fruit of a spiritual life, of spiritual practices, and of the presence of God in a person's life. The nineteenth-century authors featured in this section saw the virtues as characteristics for themselves and their readers to strive after. Their inward spiritual lives should be shown outwardly in Christian virtues.

In the case of some nineteenth-century women, their spiritual practices led them to produce published devotional materials. These materials included a variety of genres, such as books for Sabbath reading, manuals on prayer and preparation for Holy Communion, children's Bibles, hymns and inspirational poetry, as well as aids to the reading and studying of Scripture. The intended readers of these works included children, teens, women, and a general Christian audience. Especially relevant to this section on spirituality are topical studies, Scripture biographies, and commentaries authored by women.

While very few women had the privilege of a formal theological education in the nineteenth century, many were conversant with the theological and spiritual issues of their time. The tract *Cottage Controversy*, attributed to Catherine McAuley, the Irish Catholic founder of the Congregation of the Sisters of Mercy, presents a series of conversations between Margaret Lewis, a Catholic cottager, and Lady P., the Protestant Lady of the manor, that show how women from different classes and denominations participated in theological debate and Scripture interpretation.[5] This tract and many other works of nineteenth-century fiction featured theological discussions, which showed women engaged with theological and spiritual issues such as conversion or denominational differences.[6] Without opportunities for formal theological education, women pursued knowledge by reading and attending classes or lectures. They then taught others what they had learned. The works excerpted in this section were primarily written with that teaching intent.

5. See the discussion of this tract in Elizabeth M. Davis, "Wisdom and Mercy Meet: Catharine McAuley's Interpretation of Scripture," in *Recovering Nineteenth-Century Women Interpreters of the Bible*, ed. Christiana de Groot and Marion Ann Taylor (Atlanta: Society of Biblical Literature, 2007), 67–68.

6. Susan M. Griffin, *Anti-Catholicism and Nineteenth-Century Fiction* (Cambridge; New York: Cambridge University Press, 2004).

Three named women of the gospels are discussed in the two chapters of this section: Mary, the mother of Jesus, Mary of Bethany, and her sister, Martha. The nineteenth-century women featured in this section used an exemplary hermeneutic when discussing the Virgin Mary and the Bethany sisters: the characters in the gospels provided examples of piety to be followed. A straightforward application of this kind of hermeneutic can be seen in Elizabeth Wordsworth's address to the women of Lady Margaret Hall in which she called them to follow the Virgin Mary's example in being good, saying prayers, and being obedient and loving. One example of a more nuanced approach to this kind of hermeneutic can be found in the writings on Martha of Bethany. Nineteenth-century women preferred Martha's example of hosting and preparing meals, and so had to find out what Jesus found objectionable in her actions so that they would not fall into the same mistake. The authors in this section held up the Virgin Mary and the Bethany sisters as important models for nineteenth-century women. Much about the lives of these gospel wormen remained veiled or hidden. To fill in the blanks of their lives, ninteenth-century women used their own life experiences, tradition, and their sanctified imaginations.

The two women called Mary featured in this section modeled the spiritual practices of contemplation and prayer. The silence of the Blessed Virgin Mary, both her own silence as she pondered things in her heart and the silence of the gospels on aspects of her life, spoke to the need for contemplation as an important habit of mind. Women were encouraged to take time in their busy lives to be silent and still. Mary of Bethany was held up as an example of a contemplative devotional style endorsed by Jesus.

These two women were also exemplary students of Scripture. Mary knew Scripture well and modeled keeping "all these things, and ponder[ing] *them* in her heart" (Luke 2:19); Mary of Bethany "sat at Jesus' feet, and heard his word" (Luke 10:39). Many nineteenth-century Christian women regarded reading, studying, and meditating on Scripture as essential to the life of a Christian disciple. The collect for the second Sunday of Advent in the Anglican *Book of Common Prayer* called Anglicans to study Scripture: "Blessed Lord, who has caused all Holy Scriptures to be written for our learning, grant that we may in such wise hear them, read, mark, learn, and inwardly digest them."[7] The two Marys provided examples of women who loved to read and study Scripture.

A number of women studied the Scripture in the original languages.

7. This prayer is the collect for the second Sunday of Advent in the *Book of Common Prayer*.

Mary Ann SchimmelPenninck, Elizabeth Wordsworth, and Elizabeth Rundle Charles, who are excerpted in this section, were themselves students of Greek and/or Hebrew. Those who did not know the original languages drew on the writings of scholars who did. Women appropriated a variety of classical approaches to interpreting Scripture, including careful attention to the literal sense of texts and an exploration of the fuller sense of Scripture when the literal sense warranted it. SchimmelPenninck, for example, expounded the literal sense of the meaning of Jesus addressing his mother as "Woman," before turning to the spiritual sense of the text, claiming Mary was a type of the church.

Not all women felt that the tools used by academics and clerics to open up the meaning of the Scriptures were adequate. Phelps, for example, made it clear that women did not have to study the Scriptures in the same way men did; in fact, she argued that women alone properly understood the parts of Scripture about women. She believed that women's perspectival readings often introduced new insights and issues missed in more traditional readings and prompted fresh ideas and reflection. Behind many of these writings is the early feminist conviction that women were authorized by a sense of call, vocation, and experience to teach others about the inward and outward expressions of Christian spirituality. The women excerpted in this section discipled their readers, acting as mentors from a distance. They wrote to transform their readers' lives. This mentoring at a distance was a two-step process. The women were first inspired and discipled through their reading and studying of Scripture—specifically the stories of Jesus' early female disciples, Mary, the mother of Jesus, and the sisters Mary and Martha of Bethany. Then they wrote about the spiritual life for others to learn and be transformed.

1

Mary: The Exemplary Disciple

Introduction

The Virgin Mary has been the most important female religious figure for Christians throughout church history.[1] During the nineteenth century, Mary had a powerful influence on the spiritual and devotional lives of women, both Protestant and Roman Catholic. While Mary's impact on Catholic devotion and spirituality is well known and documented,[2] her effect on Protestant spiritual thought and practice is not. The selections found in this chapter were written by Protestant and Anglo-Catholic women who regarded Mary as a guide for their spiritual lives. Mary's profound interior life, her unique relationship with Jesus, her knowledge of the Scriptures, and her extraordinary experiences provided them with an example of a blessed life. In good Protestant tradition, most women excerpted here structured their reflections about Mary around the gospel stories.[3] Christina Rossetti was a notable

---

1. For a defense of the importance of the Virgin Mary throughout Christian history, see Sarah Jane Boss, ed., *Mary: The Complete Resource* (London: Continuum, 2007), 1. This entire volume is a helpful and detailed resource for issues around the Virgin in Christianity, with one chapter on Mary and Islam.

2. Evidence of the veneration of Mary by Roman Catholics is embedded in the catechism compiled by Irish-Canadian author Mary Anne Sadlier:

Q. "What great prophecy is contained in the Magnificat?"

A. "Behold, from henceforth all generations shall call me blessed." These sublime words, put in the mouth of the Blessed Virgin by the Holy Ghost himself, clearly foretell the great honor and devotion which the faithful in all ages have paid, and ever shall pay, to the virgin mother of God."

Mrs. J. Sadlier, *A New Catechism of Sacred History: Compiled from Authentic Sources for Catholic Schools* (Montreal: D. & J. Sadlier, 1875), 120.

3. A number of Protestant women, however, expressed considerable intererst in the tradi-

exception: her reflections on Mary are structured around the feast-days of the church year. Within this structure, Rossetti used the Bible, weaving a variety of Scripture passages into her reflections. These women all found in the gospels a portrait of Mary that encouraged them in their spiritual journeys, which they shared with their readers.

Mary the mother of Jesus is mentioned in all four gospels, at the beginning of Acts, and in the epistle to the Galatians.[4] The infancy narratives, found in Matthew and Luke, provide the most information about Mary. Luke provides the most detailed account of Mary's involvement in the birth of Jesus, beginning with the annunciation and culminating in the presentation of Jesus in the temple. Matthew focuses on Joseph's point of view in telling the story of Jesus' birth. Matthew also records the visit of the Magi from the east, and the holy family's flight to Egypt to escape Herod. The excerpts found in this chapter draw primarily from Luke's infancy narrative with its focus on Mary's story. Elizabeth Rundle Charles, for example, meditated at length on Gabriel's visit to Mary. Clara Lucas Balfour harmonized the two infancy narratives, placing Joseph's doubts about the wisdom of marriage to Mary (Matt. 1:18–25) after Mary's return from visiting Elizabeth (Luke 1:39–56).

Mary appears at the wedding in Cana, at the beginning of Jesus' public ministry. Many commentators discussed Jesus' apparent rudeness to Mary when he called her "Woman." Mary Ann SchimmelPenninck wrote an extensive theological meditation on Jesus calling Mary "Woman" both during the wedding (John 2), and from the cross (John 19). There are a few very brief references to Mary during the time of Jesus' ministry. In Luke 8 and Luke 11, Jesus responded to the presence of his family and statements about his family by stating that it is better to hear the word of God and do it than to be a member of his biological family. Matthew and Mark record parallel incidents.[5] The phrase "Blessed rather" (Luke 11:27–28) was often repeated

---

tions that grew up around Mary through church history. Harriet Beecher Stowe, for example, included two chapters on Mary in her book *Woman in Sacred History* (New York: J. B. Ford and Company, 1873): "Mary the Mythical Madonna" and "Mary the Mother of Jesus," the former based primarily on tradition, and the latter on the gospels. Anna Jameson wrote *Legends of the Madonna: as represented in the fine arts, forming the third series of Sacred and legendary art* (London: Longman, Brown, Green, and Longmans, 1852).

4. Matthew 1:16, 18–25; 2:10–11, 13–14, 20–21; 12:46–50; 13:53–58; Mark 3:31–35; 6:1–6; Luke 1:26–56; 2:1–51; 4:16–30; 8:19–21; 11:27–28; John 2:1–12; 6:42; 19:25–27; Acts 1:14; Galatians 4:4. Note that Mary is not named in the gospel of John, nor in Galatians, but is referred to as the mother of Jesus.

5. Luke 8:19–21 is paralleled in Matthew 12:46–50 and Mark 3:31–35. Luke 11:27–28 has no

by the women interpreters; they imbued this phrase with significance for themselves and their readers, though what exactly it signified varied from writer to writer.

As nineteenth-century women pondered the gospel portrayal of Mary, they found a model of the perfect "Christian" woman. They presented Mary as the first exemplar of humility as well as an example of devotion, purity, faith, obedience, piety, submission, contemplation, thoughtfulness, love, prayer, and other positive characteristics. These characteristics, they thought, must have been found in the woman chosen to give birth to the Messiah.

When interpreters encountered silences and gaps in Mary's story, they filled these using a variety of methods. They used scriptural intertexts, including verses from the Song of Songs, to illuminate Mary's life. The writers excerpted in this chapter also drew upon their own experiences as women and mothers as resources for understanding Mary, at times claiming they could understand her when men could not.

Questions of exegesis and language translation also concerned the women writing on Mary. They used their knowledge of languages, as well as scholarly commentaries, histories, and travel books to shed light on the difficulties they encountered in the text. For example, SchimmelPenninck discussed the etymology of Hebrew names in her essay. Her knowledge of biblical languages informed her theological reflections and spiritual applications. Other women used the resources of their faith communities to help them understand Mary. Anglican women writing on Mary read her through the lens of the church's tradition including the historical creeds, the liturgy, and various holy days. Sarah Trimmer, for example, drew a lesson on believing the creed from Mary's belief in the angel's words at the Annunciation.

The eight authors chosen for this chapter are representative of nineteenth-century women writers who found Mary an exemplary Christian disciple. Writers explored this theme using a variety of literary genres. Balfour and Phelps wrote creative retellings of the life of Mary. Sarah Trimmer and Gracilla Boddington wrote more traditional commentaries. SchimmelPenninck and Elizabeth Wordsworth wrote thoughtful essays. The selections by Christina Rossetti and Elizabeth Charles provide clear examples of devotional writing based on the life of Mary. They pondered the things written in the gospels about Mary, just as Mary pondered her experiences as the mother of Jesus.

---

parallel in the other gospels, though the teaching on Beelzebub which preceeds this is paralleled in Matthew 12 and Mark 3.

CLARA LUCAS BALFOUR (1808–1878)

Humility: The Noblest Virtue

Clara Lucas Balfour was a prominent author, lecturer, and temperance champion.[6] The daughter of John and Sarah Lucas of Gosport, England, she married James Balfour at 15. Clara Balfour educated herself by reading extensively. She used this education to support her husband and six children by giving lectures to women's groups and writing novels, journal articles, and books over a forty-year period. She was raised an Anglican, but became a Baptist when she joined the temperance movement at thirty-two.

Balfour's essay on Mary was originally published in *Women of Scripture* (1847), and was entitled "Humility: The Virgin Mary." Balfour's essays on women were intended to provide examples of the virtues found in biblical characters. Her stated purpose was "to bring prominently forward those peculiar principles of piety, feminine excellence, moral conduct, and mental power, which the sacred heroines individually exhibited."[7] Balfour encouraged her readers to study these women to learn from their spiritual lives. She desired to transform her readers' lives.

Balfour's work on Mary is quite lengthy as she attempted to harmonize every gospel reference to Mary into a single reflection on her life. A shorter version of her essay, published in an American collection of Scripture biography, is extracted here. Balfour drew on her experiences as a woman and her worldview as she retold Mary's story. She added emotion to every scene, focusing on Mary's feelings as a woman and a mother. Balfour particularly emphasized Mary's virtue of humility, claiming that Mary displayed humility in a new way. At the same time, she allowed Scripture to challenge her own and society's values. Mary's courage and faithfulness together with that of the other women at the foot of the cross challenged the world's theories about women's nature. Balfour believed Mary's exemplary spiritual characteristics made her the ultimate example of a Christian disciple.

6. Kirstin G. Doern, "Balfour, Clara Lucas," in *The Oxford Dictionary of National Biography* (Oxford: Oxford University Press, 2004), 3: 514–15.

7. Balfour, *Women of Scripture* (London: Houlston and Stoneman, 1847), v.

The Virgin Mary

The character of the highest importance, and most spiritual significance, in the New Testament, is the Virgin mother of our Lord:—"the *Mater Dolorosa* of eternal sympathies;"[8] the lowly maiden of the house of David, of whom all generations, taking up the salutation of the angel, exclaim, "Blessed art thou among women." If by woman sin first entered our world, and death by sin, it is a blessed contemplation that woman was honoured as the means of giving life to the human nature of our Divine Redeemer.[9] Womanhood itself was for ever elevated and dignified by the sublime mystery of the birth of Him who was "made of a woman," "made under the law" [Gal. 4:4], who "was God manifest in the flesh" [1 Tim. 3:16].

We learn that the Blessed Virgin dwelt in the city of Nazareth, and her personal history commences with the salutation of the angel, "Hail! thou that art highly favoured, the Lord is with thee; blessed art thou among women." No words could convey a higher idea of the Divine approbation than these. Mary was highly favoured; the Lord was with her. The highest aim of spiritualized human nature is to obtain the favour and realize the presence of God. This, in her opening womanhood, was the blissful portion of the holy Virgin. In contemplating her life, therefore, it becomes us to observe her peculiarities, and learn from thence to deduce what qualities of mind and conduct are likely to secure the favour of God and to evidence His presence in our hearts. There is one primary characteristic of the mother of our Lord that does not appear in anything like an equal degree in any of the Old Testament heroines: this was HUMILITY. Many of the illustrious women of the former dispensation were gentle in word and deed, but gentleness and humility are not synonymous terms. Gentleness is an outward manifestation of a calm and equable spirit, subdued and regulated by reason, and it is sometimes merely the result of a kindly and genial temperament. Humility is a far nobler virtue; it involves both self-examination and self-knowledge; it fixes its adoring gaze on the perfections of Deity, and the moral requirements of a

8. Sydney Owenson, Lady Morgan, *Woman and Her Master* (London: Henry Colburn, 1840), vol. 1, 151. It is interesting that Balfour's reading included this work, which is a history of women that attempted to show that women were the victims of men, and of laws written and enacted by men without women's consent.

9. Here Balfour adjusted the language of Romans 5:12, which says "Wherefore, as by one man sin entered into the world, and death by sin; and so death passed upon all men, for that all have sinned." Balfour's twist on this verse acknowledged that Eve's sin was first. Balfour connected Eve and Mary as Adam and Jesus were often connected in the Pauline epistles.

pure and holy faith, and is the result of a just comparison of human faults and frailties with abstract principles of Christian virtue. There may be gentleness without humility, but there cannot be true humility without gentleness. It was meet that the Virgin mother of our Lord should be the first to exemplify the primary principle of her Divine Son's hallowed system.[10] The heathen world, with all its moral theories and philosophical precepts, knew of no such quality as humility; and the religion of the Jews but feebly embodied this great virtue. Hence, though Miriam and Deborah were gifted and noble women; Hannah and the Shunamite, gentle, tender, and benevolent; Esther, grateful and patriotic; and each spiritual and energetic; we should not say of all or any of them that they were humble. The Virgin's character was essentially so. When the heavenly visitor appeared before her, and the glorious salutation fell on her wondering ear, we find her "troubled at his saying." That serene spirit which had humbly performed the various duties of life in "cheerful godliness,"[11] had never thought of any other reward than the testimony of a good conscience; and we can feebly imagine how her perplexed thoughts caused her "to cast in her mind what manner of salutation this might be." . . . The angel speedily reassures her perturbed spirit, exclaiming, "Fear not, Mary, for thou hast found favour with God;" and then came the glorious announcement of the advent of Him of whom all the ceremonials of the law and all the predictions of the prophets had testified. Never had benign ministering spirits such a message to communicate before. Mary, evidently acquainted with the writings and predictions of the holy seers, was overwhelmed with natural astonishment, not at the announcement of the greatness of Him who should, as the angel declared, "be called the Son of the Highest: and the Lord God shall give unto him the throne of his father David: and he shall reign over the house of Jacob for ever, and of his kingdom there shall be no end." Mary knew that the Messiah—the consolation of Israel—when he appeared should be called "Wonderful, the mighty God, the everlasting Father, the Prince of Peace" [Isa. 9:6]; but her humility reverted to herself. Should she, a lowly virgin, become the mother of the Saviour? Had not numberless devout and distinguished women of Israel hoped for that honour? And amazed she hesitatingly exclaims, "How shall this be?"—an ejaculation of wonder, or an inquiry of surprise, by no means to be deemed

10. Balfour may have read Frances Elizabeth King who shares this view. See King, *Female Scripture Characters: Exemplifying Female Virtues* (London, 1813).

11. Phrase in William Wordsworth, "London, 1802," in *Poems in Two Volumes*, vol. 1, (London: Longman, Hurst, et al., 1807), 140. Wordsworth's phrase described John Milton (1608–1674).

an evidence of incredulity. The angel then informs her of the miraculous conception of the Son of God by the influence of the Holy Spirit; and also that her pious aged cousin, Elizabeth, would speedily become a mother, concluding his important annunciation with the solemn truth, "For with God nothing shall be impossible." With a sublime faith Mary replied, "Behold the handmaid of the Lord, be it unto me according to thy word."

This reply contains matter for extended reflection. Mary, with humble boldness, speaks of herself as a servant of the Lord, and acknowledges that the first condition of that service is perfect subordination to the will of her Divine Master. It was fit that such a sentiment should proceed from the lip of one destined to be the mother of Him who fulfilled "all righteousness," and who, in the mysterious agony of his human nature, exclaimed in his hour of trial, "Not my will, but thine be done" [Luke 22:42]. Religion has not completed its perfect work in us until it has subordinated our wills. The very first operation of faith in the soul is to raise our confidence from our frail selves, and fix it on Him "who is too wise to err,"[12] with unquestioning and perfect reliance. The pious ejaculation of the Virgin shows not only complete submission, but an absence of all human weakness—in reference to fear of man, or selfish considerations. As a betrothed maiden, the law required of her the undeviating chastity of an espoused wife. Her life, according to Jewish institutions, would pay the penalty of any substantiated charge against her conjugal fidelity.[13] And yet no such thought shades the brightness of her faith. Let human malice or legal severity say or do what they will, "Be it unto me according to thy word," is the serene reply of the holy maiden.

It is a beautiful instance of the yearning of her youthful heart for human sympathy, and pious communion in her extraordinary circumstances, that "Mary arose," and "went into the hill country with haste," to that aged relative of whom the angel had testified. The contemplative character which subsequent events prove her to have possessed, was not the result of a cold, unsocial temperament; in her complete dedication of herself to God, she yet found the comfort, nay, the necessity, of communion and fellowship with the excellent of the earth, and thus "with haste" she sought the presence of that pious relative, whose virtuous age demanded honour, and whose simi-

---

12. The statement "God is too wise to err" appears as a statement which has "the power of incontrovertible axiom among religious people," in Adam Clarke's sermon "The Plan of Human Redemption," in *The Miscellaneous Works of Adam Clarke*, vol. 5 (London: T. Tegg, 1836), 57.

13. See Deuteronomy 22:20–21.

larity of circumstances invited sympathy. To give and to receive counsel and comfort was the object of the Virgin's prompt visit.

How beautifully are the characters of Mary and the priest Zacharias, the husband of Elizabeth, contrasted! The good old priest had "walked in all the commandments and ordinances of the Lord blameless" during a long life; still when the angel of the Lord appeared to him in the temple, and announced the birth of a son, Zacharias doubted the testimony of the holy visitant. Yet the event was not unprecedented; every pious Jew remembered that Sarah in her old age became a mother [Gen. 21:2], and that Abraham's faith was counted to him for righteousness [Rom. 4:9]. Yet Zacharias doubts, and dumbness for a time was permitted to afflict him. Mary, to whom a far more miraculous event was announced, who might in vain call upon memory to tell of any parallel case, yet in all humility believes; and, as the first evidence of her full belief, departs on a long journey of nearly a hundred miles, to commune with her cousin, Elizabeth, on the event.

The salutation of these two holy women is unequalled in the Divine records for beauty and sublimity. . . . This hallowed welcome, so sympathetic and soul-refreshing to the humble and devout Mary, called up all the deep emotions of her spirit, unfolded all the energies of her mind. Previously to this, though we might infer that the blessed Virgin possessed all lovely gifts and graces in a supereminent degree, her being "highly favoured of God" sufficiently attesting her varied excellencies, yet we have no personal manifestation of unusual mental powers: now, we find her pouring forth her thoughts in strains equal to the loftiest utterances of the Sweet Singer of Israel,[14] and rendered more deeply interesting from the event to which they refer, and from the tender, lowly, feminine grace that pervades them.

There is a similarity, in some of the thoughts expressed, to the song of Hannah[15]—a similarity by no means involving a servile imitation of that sacred ode, uttered by maternal piety, but sufficient to mark the fact, that Mary was well read in the sacred writings, and fully conversant with the prophecies relating to Him who was to be born of her, and with the poetic treasures of inspired antiquity.

The visit of the Virgin to Elizabeth continued three months; at the expiration of that time a severe trial awaited Mary on her return to Nazareth. She became the subject of the suspicions of her betrothed husband, who, reasoning from apparent evidences, naturally came to conclusions unfavourable to

14. That is, David, who is called the "sweet psalmist of Israel" in 2 Samuel 23:1.
15. See 1 Samuel 2:1–10.

the chastity of Mary. There is no trial that humanity is subjected to, equal in bitterness to that of being suspected and misunderstood by near and dear friends. . . . We cannot suppose so womanly a character as the Blessed Virgin was indifferent to the sentiments she excited in the mind of one with whom her future destiny was to be united; yet we perceive in her conduct on this trying occasion a serenity of holy innocence, a sweet maidenly reserve, that enhances our admiration. She never communicated to Joseph the Divine annunciation of the angel. It became not her humility to proclaim the honour conferred on her, still less to vindicate her innocence, by speaking of the sacred mystery of which she was the depository. He who had "remembered" her "low estate" would not suffer her purity to be questioned, but would Himself bring forth her "righteousness as the light" [Ps. 37:6]. Even on her speedy visit to her aged cousin, and when evidently yearning for sympathy, Mary had not been the first to speak of the celestial visitant, or his tidings. Elizabeth was supernaturally endowed with a knowledge of the event, and was permitted by her first salutation to do away with the necessity for that reserve, which, like a graceful veil, was thrown over Mary's bright perfections. What the Virgin was not the first to speak of, even to a beloved relative of her own sex, she was far less likely to name to Joseph. Yet, doubtless, many perplexed thoughts must have visited her, when she found that "Joseph, her husband, being a just man, and not willing to make her a public example, was minded to put her away privily" [Matt. 1:19]. As an act of mercy, due to his own benevolent character and former love, he would interpose between her and the public executioner; but an obscure retirement to hide her degradation from the world was to be her portion. . . . Well may erring mortals endure patiently reviling and misconstruction, when the spotless innocence of the immaculate Virgin was not unsuspected.[16] The angel, whose glorious mission it was to proclaim to Mary the incarnation of the Redeemer, visited Joseph in a dream, and related the miraculous event, removing the perplexities of that just man, as the light of the sun removes the morning mist. And he forthwith fulfils the Divine injunction, "to take unto him Mary his wife" [Matt. 1:24].

The next important circumstance in the history of the Virgin was caused by a great political event, by which an important prophecy in reference to our

16. This language around the innocence of Mary is surprising from a Baptist writer. Note that the papal encyclical declaring the Immaculate Conception of Mary to be official doctrine was issued by Pius IX on Dec. 8, 1854 (*Ineffabilis Deus*), seven years after Balfour wrote the original essay on Mary. The language, conversation, and debate around the sinlessness of Mary were current when Balfour wrote.

Lord's birth-place was accurately fulfilled. The prophet Micah, several hundred years before, had expressly said, "Thou, Bethlehem Ephratah, though thou be little among the thousands of Judah, yet out of thee shall He come forth to me, that is to be Ruler in Israel; whose goings forth have been from of old, from everlasting" [Mic. 5:2]. . . .

The whole empire being included in this decree, it affected every family; "and all went to be taxed, everyone to his own city." Joseph and Mary, being of the house of David, had to go up from Nazareth to Bethlehem, the city of David. Four days' weary journeying was accomplished by the mother of our Lord; and when arrived at their destination, the travelers found there "was no room for them in the inn;" and they were fain to seek shelter in the stable. . . . In that lowly stable, an outcast from the dwellings of man, the holy Child was born. . . .

Mary is not long left to lonely yet blessed contemplations of her holy Child. That birth, unnoted on earth, is being proclaimed from heaven. A serene midnight sky spread over the plains of Bethlehem as the shepherds watched their flocks; the solemn stillness of the hour was felt in all its deep tranquillity, the silent stars watching with loving eyes the sleeping earth, and "quietly shining to the quiet moon,"[17]—when the heavens were suddenly opened, streams of light from the glory of the Lord spread over the horizon, and a sun-bright angel appeared before the wondering and trembling shepherds. . . .

With grateful homage they told the wondrous story of the angelic vision, and, full of joyful faith, communicated the glad tidings, to the astonishment of many. Mary, the contemplative Mary, "kept all these things, and pondered them in her heart." Nothing was mentioned, nothing forgotten, that related to the mission of her Divine Son; too sacred for words, it was food for holy contemplation and devout thought. A distinguished modern poet has beautifully described the visit of the shepherds to the Babe of Bethlehem and his Virgin mother. [Here Balfour quoted in full Samuel Taylor Coleridge, "A Christmas Carol or The Shepherds went their hasty way" (1799).]

We next find Mary, in accordance with the law, going up to Jerusalem to present her first-born in the temple, and to offer sacrifice. . . . [Balfour put the dedication of the firstborn into context (see Exod. 13:2, 12–15). Mary did not attempt to avoid these obligations. Balfour called her readers to also "walk in all the ordinances of the Lord blameless." Balfour then described the encounter in the temple with Simeon, concluding with a reflection on Sim-

17. Samuel Taylor Coleridge (1772–1834), "Frost at Midnight" (1798).

34

eon's prophecy.] From the venerable lips of devout old age, and surrounded by the sanctities of the temple, she had to learn that though he [Jesus] was "a light to lighten the gentiles, and the glory of my people Israel," he was also to cause many commotions, and to be a sign spoken against; and her maternal sorrow was to be so great that it would penetrate the inmost recesses of her spirit. From that time the Virgin mother must have had a dim prescience of a destiny sorrowful in proportion to its sublimity, and her character would take a deeper tone from the trials and solemnities awaiting her. We can suppose her dedicating herself afresh in the temple to perfect unquestioning obedience—taking up her discipleship to her Divine son, and consecrating her whole life entirely to him.

This principle of unquestioning obedience was soon to be put to a severe trial. Herod, impatient of hearing no more of the wise men, suspecting that they wilfully disobeyed him, with all the cruelty that invariably accompanies guilty fear, determined on that slaughter of the innocents in Bethlehem which covers his name with deserved infamy. Before this murderous edict went forth, Joseph received an angelic warning, commanding him to take the young child and his mother and flee into Egypt alleging as a reason that Herod would seek the young child to destroy him. Again, we find the Virgin mother on a toilsome journey with her sacred infant. How full of vicissitudes had been her maternal career! From the time of her journey to her cousin Elizabeth, she appears to have had a multiplicity of sorrow. First, her innocence doubted; then a toilsome journey, when her wearied frame most required rest; then the exposure of her holy babe to the rude accommodations shared equally by the beasts of the field; then the journey to Jerusalem; and now, when, with all her sex's love of home and quietude, she might hope to be permitted the discharge of her maternal duties in peace and safety, the sudden mandate comes, and in the dead of night, in silence and secresy [sic], she departs for a strange land. When we think of all these trials, and the harsh grasp of poverty, constantly making every trouble more bitter we may understand a small portion of the Virgin mother's early sufferings.

After the flight into Egypt, . . . the holy family turned aside into the region of Galilee, to their former residence, the city of Nazareth, where they were known.

And now commenced the first interval of rest and security, of any continuance, that Mary enjoyed. In her lowly Nazarene home she beheld the gradual unfolding of that holy mind, which combined angelic innocence and seraphic wisdom with human affections and sympathies. "And the child grew, and waxed strong in spirit, filled with wisdom: and the grace of God was upon him."

[At this point, Balfour gave an account of Jesus going to the temple with his parents when he was twelve, and staying behind after the Passover.]

In the mean time, it is recorded that "his mother kept all these sayings in her heart." They were dimly apprehended by her understanding, but faith and feeling fully appreciated them, and they were treasured in her heart. Oh! for a religion that dwells in the heart: that abides there—kept safe alike from all intrusion and all wandering! It was fit that the pious Mary, as Christ's first disciple, should keep his sayings in her heart, and "ponder them" there; her soul being nurtured by holy contemplation, while her human affection was daily gratified as her Sacred Son "increased in wisdom and stature, and in favour with God and man."

An interval of eighteen years elapsed from the time that Jesus stood in the midst of the doctors in the temple until the period of his baptism and the commencement of his ministry. As Joseph is never mentioned after that commencement, the inference is plain that Mary, who is often brought before us, was a widow when our Lord's sacred work began. We hear of the Virgin as a guest at a marriage-feast at Cana of Galilee, and Jesus, with his recently called disciples, was bidden also to the nuptial festival.[18] It appearing that either the number of guests exceeded expectation, or that the circumstances of the parties making the feast were straitened, so that they could not provide adequately for the company. Mary, with ready perception of the deficiency, and a kind desire to spare the feelings of the entertainers, and also conscious of the marvellous power that dwelt in Jesus, ventured to tell him privately, "They have no wine." Our Lord's reply to this remark of Mary's at first sounds harsh, "Woman, what have I to do with thee? mine hour is not yet come." It is the misfortune, rather than the merit, of modern refinement, that terms noble in their plain simplicity have sunk into contempt. The word "woman" is, in reality, a superior appellation to Lady or Madam, or any other conventionalism or title. The general name of the half of the human race can never sound either harsh or coarse, unless the ear has become vulgarized with tawdry phrases of fleeting fashion. At the time our Lord spoke, the name "woman" was honourable, and conveyed no disrespect. His reply was addressed privately to Mary, in answer to a private suggestion; and, from the tenour [sic] of the whole of it, it may be gathered that our Lord's ministry having commenced, he mildly asserted his authority,

18. See John 2:1–12.

and gently remonstrated against any prompting as to what he should do, the relationship subsisting between the Virgin and himself rendering such a course in the outset necessary. Mary replied not to his words, but, full of sacred confidence, with characteristic piety, she addressed the attendants at the feast, saying, "Whatsoever he saith unto you, do it." How important is the injunction of that short sentence! It contains the essence of all practical divinity and vital christianity. We have seen that a woman was favoured to be among the earliest prophesiers of our Lord's coming, and the first to apply the term Saviour to him. A woman also was undoubtedly his first disciple, for when the Virgin mother ministered to him in infancy, and kept all his sayings in her heart, she was fulfilling the office of a disciple: and now we find her the first to proclaim his divine mission by counselling obedience to him.[19] Many volumes of sermons could not exhaust the richness of the sentence Mary uttered on this memorable occasion. The wondrous miracle was wrought;—"The conscious water saw its God and blushed;"[20] and the assembled guests beheld the commencement of that series of miracles which attested that "the day-spring from on high" [Luke 1:78] had visited our world.

The mother of our Lord, after this manifestation, accompanied Jesus and his disciples to Capernaum. She seems during his ministration to have kept with or near him, except at short intervals. The babe of Bethlehem—the child of Nazareth—the youthful querist of the temple—the being "full of grace and truth" [John 1:14] whom she had tended through years of helplessness, and shielded in many dangers, was wound too closely round her heart in his human nature for her to quit him more than circumstances or his will directed; while his utterances as her teacher, his miracles as her Saviour, must have had a sublime significance to one who from her early youth "had found favour with God" [Luke 1:30]. . . .

We hasten to the last solemn scene, when the prediction of good old Simeon was fulfilled in the holy Virgin's history, when the "sword pierced through her soul" [Luke 2:35]. The "hour" of which her sacred son had so often spoken "was come." He had frequently adverted to his death, and always with dignified composure—occasionally with benevolent complacency,—"I have a baptism to be baptized with, and how am I straitened till it be accomplished" [Luke 12:50]; but we cannot suppose that the maternal

---

19. Nineteenth-century women authors commonly produced a list highlighting the importance of women in Jesus' life. They often used such lists to argue that women should be allowed public or official roles in the church.

20. From a poem "Epigrammata Sacra" by Richard Crashaw (c. 1613–1649). For the full poem, see Crashaw's *Complete Works*, vol. 2, ed. Alexander Ballochgrosart (London, 1862), 97.

heart ever contemplated such an awful termination of that pure, gentle, divine life, which had scattered blessings in such rich profusion, and embodied wisdom in such bright perfection. How with each successive event in that stupendous tragedy her spirit must have agonized! . . . We perceive the immense power of her love in the effort she made at the last crisis; being present at a scene so agonizing, when human nature would shrink appalled; yet when strong men had fled, panic-stricken, and deserted their Divine Master,—the weak, worn, tender, affectionate mother made her way through the brutal crowd; unheeding their ribald scoffs, fearless she stood among the rude soldiery, and gazing up to the fearful cross, saw that holy brow convulsed with the awful pangs of a lingering and dreadful death. Yes; she who had wept glad tears of pious joy over the babe of Bethlehem, now stood in the rigid, tearless extremity of grief beside the cross of the "man of sorrows" [Isa. 53:3]. But she stood not there alone; her sorrows were shared by devout women, who, like herself, braved every peril, and were faithful unto death. And there also was the youthful disciple whom Jesus loved. Womanhood and youth met and mourned at that cross! The world has theories which say these are weak and changeable, and little to be trusted; yet in this, the most solemn event our earth ever witnessed, they proved brave and true, and all else faint-hearted and false.[21]

While the faithful few sympathized with Mary's sorrow, a divine manifestation of sympathy was given to her. Her son beheld that anguish-stricken face; how changed from the serene brow that his infant eyes had gazed on with delight! He understood—he only could understand—the amount of her sorrow; the last throb of human affection thrilled in his sacred heart, and he exclaimed, looking on his mother and the youthful disciple "whom he loved." "Woman, behold thy son; son, behold thy mother." How tender the bequest—how exquisite the consolation conveyed in those hallowed words! The most faithful, gentle, heavenly-minded of the disciples was selected for the performance of filial duty to the sorrowing mother. "From that hour that disciple took her unto his own home;" her age found shelter, and her sorrows sympathy, in that friendly dwelling: the Redeemer's dying charge binding each to the other with a love "strong as death" [Song of Songs 8:6].

It seems as though the scene at Calvary was such a climax to the Virgin's anguish, that she was present only till her son and Saviour cried with a loud voice, and gave up the ghost. "From that very hour" she was taken to the

---

21. Mary is listed among those at the cross in John 19:25. Jesus committed her to the care of John (whom Balfour called "the youthful disciple") in John 19:26–27.

house of John. We hear nothing of her at the glorious event of the resurrection. Worn out with sorrow, she was not a watcher at the grave; though, doubtless, the good tidings soon reached her of the risen Lord, and her mourning was turned into joy, thankfulness, and adoration.

The last record of Mary delightfully harmonizes with her whole character. In the Acts of the Apostles it is recorded that in an upper room at Jerusalem "abode Peter, and James, and John, and Andrew, Philip, and Thomas, Bartholomew, and Matthew, James the son of Alpheus, and Simon Zelotes, and Judas the brother of James; these all continued with one accord in prayer and supplication, with the women, *and Mary the mother of Jesus*" [Acts 1:13–14]. Her history commenced with heavenly annunciations, and ends, appropriately, with prayer. Her parentage and birthplace, her death and burial, are not recorded. The event and personage that reflect sublime honour on her name are fully made known; before and after the holy advent, are equally left in obscurity. Her youth was distinguished by the favour of God; her maturity by active piety and faithful discipleship—her age by fervent devotion, and hallowed communion with the first church. Happy the life that is rich in deeds of piety, rather than chronological detail,—whose records are not those of birth and death, and dwelling-place, but of holy acts and heroic fidelity! When the Sun of Righteousness arose [Malachi 4:2], Mary was like a graceful shadow tracking His glorious path, and called up by His brightness; when He departed, she vanished.

Source: Clara Lucas Balfour, "The Virgin Mary," in *Women of the Old and New Testaments*, ed. Rev. H. Hastings Weld (Philadelphia: Lindsay & Blakiston, 1848), 176–98.

ELIZABETH STUART PHELPS (1844–1911)

Receiving the Divine

Elizabeth Stuart Phelps was a prolific American author of 47 books, 17 works of children's fiction, 142 short stories and 95 essays as well as some poetry.[22]

22. For a fuller discussion of Phelps, see Erin Vearncombe, "Phelps, Elizabeth Stuart (1844–1911)," in *Handbook of Women Biblical Interpreters*, ed. Marion Ann Taylor and Agnes Choi (Grand Rapids: Baker Academic, 2012), 407–9.

Phelps was born in Boston, to Austin Phelps, a professor of sacred rhetoric and homiletics at Andover Seminary, and author Elizabeth Stuart Phelps. Phelps's maternal grandfather was Moses Stuart (1780–1852), a biblical scholar who also taught at Andover Seminary. Phelps was named Mary at her birth, but she assumed her mother's name sometime after her mother died in 1852. She married Howard Ward in 1888.

Phelps retold the story of the gospels in *The Story of Jesus Christ* (1897). In her introduction, she called the work a narrative, noting that it was not theology, criticism, history, or geography, but a story. She claimed to follow the gospel accounts with some probable details added to fill in some gaps.[23] Her book could be called a work of historical fiction which includes theological, critical, and geographical elements. It is clearly a work of biblical interpretation, though Phelps did not claim that this was what she was attempting to do. Her fiction addressed many of the interpretive issues that others dealt with in commentaries or theological essays. This work had an intended audience of women; Jesus was portrayed as the ideal friend of women.[24]

In the "Presage," which tells the story of the incarnation, Phelps recreated the story of Mary from Mary's perspective. She was interested in Mary's interior world as well as in her outer world and physical appearance. Curiously, Phelps's Mary was blonde, with fair skin and hazel eyes, a nineteenth-century northern-European woman. Like Balfour, Phelps emphasized Mary's exemplary spirituality. She did not make explicit connections to her readers' lives as Balfour often did, but more subtly, through the way she told the story, held Mary up as an example of a woman of prayer, a student of Scripture, and a contemplative. Phelps also addressed theological issues such as the reality of the virgin birth of Jesus, and the nature of angels. The final paragraph of the excerpt shows Phelps's feminist reasons for writing. Only women could

---

23. "No important departure from the outlines of his [Jesus'] only authorized biography has beguiled the pen which has here sought to portray the Great Story with loving docility. The few, unfamiliar strokes by which these outlines have been sometimes filled in have been reverently and studiously adjusted to the composition of the picture,—it is hoped without offense to probabilities. It is believed that these probabilities are so reasonable that they may serve to deepen, not to dissipate, our respect for such knowledge as we possess concerning the life of Jesus Christ." Elizabeth Stuart Phelps, *The Story of Jesus Christ* (Boston and New York: Houghton, Mifflin, 1897), vii-viii.

24. Erin Vearncombe, "Elizabeth Stuart Phelps and the 'Laws of Narrative Expression' in *The Story of Jesus Christ*: An Interpretation," paper presented at the Annual Meeting of the Canadian Society of Biblical Studies, June 2007.

understand Mary; the gospels had been preserved by men and interpreted by men, but parts of them could only be understood by women.

Presage

There was a fountain; the only one in the village. The women went with their urns on their shoulders to get water for the family supply; they stood, graceful, slow of motion, lazy and lovely, taking each her turn. It was approaching the cool of the day. The women chattered like birds; they raised their eyes to the mountains indifferently. The sky was taking on a great preparation of color; but the women preferred to hear what was to be said.

A girl put down her urn, and looked at the sky. She did not talk. She moved away a little from the other women, and leaned against a high, white rock. Her chin was lifted, her eyes upraised; her mouth had a sweet expression; her thoughts were high. She had the manner of one who preferred to be alone without knowing why.

The other women rustled, gossiping, away. The girl followed slowly, with obvious reluctance; she walked alone. The urn stood steadily upon her head; her carriage was straight and noble. She was of middle height, or possibly a little above it. She had a fair complexion, blonde hair, and bright, hazel eyes. Her eyebrows were arched and dark; her lips ruddy, and full of kindness when she spoke. Her face was long rather than round; her hands and fingers were finely shaped. "She had no weakness of manner, but was far from forwardness. She had no pride, but was simple, and free from deceit. She showed respect and honor to all. She was very gentle, in all things serious and earnest; she spoke little; and only to the purpose."*...

Now the maiden was a poor girl, born of working people, reared by them, and living among them. Yet she came of the lineage of a powerful and popular king. This country maid, this laborer's child, was born, not to the purple, but of it. She might be called a royal peasant. Her veins ran with the richest blood of the nation; her hands knew its commonest toil. A patrician ancestry and a plebeian training make, for certain ends, the most desirable inheritance that can befall one. She had it.

To call her devout, is to say that she was something more than a good churchwoman. In a girlish way she was a sweet student of the Law and the Prophets, but she was more than that. She was one of the rare natures in

*Tradition.

41

which faith is like breath. We see its gentle pulsations, and respect them unconsciously as we would a law of physiology. Many phrases have been invented to describe the soul that seeks the divine because it is the perfectly natural and inevitable thing for it to do; but none of them are satisfactory to us; perhaps because most of us are too far from that type of being ourselves to understand it. We can honestly revere dedication when we believe in it, however, and hers it is impossible to question.

She was one of those exquisite spirits that are able to rely on truth which they cannot comprehend, without any waste of the nature in doubt or evasion. She believed so utterly in the God of her people that He was more real to her than any other fact of life. . . .

The Galilean girl felt the holiness of beauty, for she was capable of feeling everything pure and exquisite; and she kept herself alone, to dwell upon the gentle thoughts developed in her by the divinity of the day elected for the marvel which glorifies the name of one little mountain town forever.

The hour of evening prayer among her people fell at the setting of the sun and the coming of the stars. But hers was no ordinary, mechanical nature, such as prays because it is ecclesiastical and civil law to do so at an ordered time. Prayer with her was the luxury of the soul.

She trod the village street abstractedly. Her feet, from modest habit, led her home. Without speaking, she emptied her urn into the water-jar that stood near the door, and quietly freshened the herbs that floated on the top of the water. She wished to be alone. The commoner minds about her were still dissipated in their distractions; hers had already entered into that revery which is neither wholly thought nor wholly prayer, but partakes of the reality of both.

In the space between the sunset and the twilight the girl stole up, unnoticed, to the roof of the house,—the flat roof, in all hot countries the place of family meeting, of relief from the scorching weather, of indulgence in private grief or of prayer; in fact, among the poor, it was the only possible place of retirement at home. Her poverty was not of the squalid, but only of the strenuous kind; and the usual conveniences or the usual comforts of a respectable home were hers. But these, in the East, were always few enough. . . .

In the village, roof-gardens sometimes added flowers to the gentle joys of home. One of these sky-gardens belonged to the poor home of which we think,—a little, cubic dwelling looking like a block—and tall, white flowers stood above the vines, leaning against the evening sky.

The girl crept among them. Her eyes were on the heavens. There was an aureola in her heart. Her prayer had passed the phase of words. She had ceased to address God, she had come so near Him. . . .

Then, did she see the Angel? Did he break a stalk of one of the white flowers, as he stirred, and so hold it in his hand, smiling to reassure her by the ease and cordiality of the act?

Whence came he? Had he swept from the heights of distant Lebanon, whose white head, turning gray in the twilight, was darkening as if the mountain drew a mantle over it? Had he floated on the departing cloud that rode like a chariot of fire past the sun whose own face was hidden from the marvel? Or had he formed from the ether, where he stood, against the faint sky, quietly and naturally, as inspiration forms in the soul, and faith in the heart that is fit for it? Whatever of the strange was in the manner of his coming, the angel came.

II

There have been in all ages three kinds of persons: those who never see mystical appearances, those who think they do, and those who do; and the three types may be confounded. It is also to be suggested that visitors from an invisible life, if such there are, and whoever such there are, may be responsive to the absence or the presence of welcome, like any other superior or sensitive being. Angels, like people, might come where they are wanted, trusted, or expected.

In fact, there are laws of spiritual hospitality, breach of which may, for aught we know to the contrary, deprive a human creature of the mystical privileges. The soul of this Hebrew girl was hostess to all that was pure and perfect, delicate, ethereal, devout. As the flower receives the sun at dawn, as the earth the rain at drought, she instinctively received the divine.

The angel stood quietly. He seemed to wish not to alarm the girl. She thought him a spirit of high rank. He spoke with the tenderness natural to strength and to superiority alone. Was he used to stand in the presence of God? Yet he said, "Fear not, Mary."

How astonishing the conversation which followed! The scene moved on steadily to its solemn climax. Question and answer succeeded with increasing courage on the part of the Galilean girl, and with growing definiteness on that of her celestial guest. Clearly but gently she was given to understand that she had not been made the subject of an inconsequent apparition, such as were frequent enough in Oriental experience or imagination; but that she was the medium of the most tremendous revelation which this planet has ever known.

Chosen out of all the world, the Hebrew maiden whose qualifications for her solemn mission were the simple, womanly ones of a pure heart and a devout life received the angel's message as she who could be chosen by it would be sure to do. The fiat of Deity was in the magnificent attitude of the angel; he stood tall, erect, majestic. Awed, the woman fell upon her knees before the messenger of God, and veiled her face from sight of him. "Be it unto me," she said, "according to thy word."

Now, when he perceived that Mary understood the import of his embassy, the angel left her. . . .

The woman was left, in a world like ours, to her unique experience.

She had received from the vision a prediction whose nature so utterly transcends all mortal laws and all mortal experience that he would profane the very courts of mystery who should descend to offer for it any human explanation.

There is no quibbling possible with the marvel. It must be rejected or accepted on its own great grounds. No compromise between fact and fancy has dignity in the isolation of the case.

Shall we be less high-minded than the instinct of the race and the faith of the ages?

Take the wonder as it is told.[25] . . .

Gabriel seems to have been something of a philosopher (as well as altogether an angel) when he reminded the astonished woman, at the close of his announcement of the incredible facts, that with God nothing is impossible. These were astute words under the circumstances, and worthy of a superior intelligence. The argument admitted of no reply.

Mary listened to it gently. Her soul was a lily. All motherhood has been dignified forever by the spotless mystery. All humanity is nobler for the delicacy of the womanly nature from which the Son Highest should be born into a low world.

III

The story of the Gospels was written by men. Men have studied and expounded it for two thousand years. Men have been its commentators, its

---

25. In these few paragraphs, Phelps dropped the subtlety of story-telling, turning to theological reflection to exhort her readers to be open to the mystery of revelation.

translators, its preachers. All the feminine element in it has come to us passed through the medium of masculine minds. Of the exquisite movements in the thought and feeling of Mary at this crisis of her history, what man could speak? Only the hearts of women can approach her, when, quite without angelic endorsement or even human protection, she is left to meet the consequences of the will of God upon her life.

Source: Elizabeth Stuart Phelps, *The Story of Jesus Christ* (Boston and New York: Houghton, Mifflin, 1897), 2–11.

SARAH TRIMMER (1741–1810)

Blessed Humility

Anglican Sarah Trimmer was a prolific author of some forty educational works, including Scripture interpretation. Daughter of John Joshua Kirby and Sarah Bull Kirby, Trimmer was well educated and well connected in English society; her father held a court appointment in the palace at Kew. She married James Trimmer of Brentford in 1762. They had twelve children. Trimmer gained experience in education by teaching her own twelve children at home. Friends encouraged her to publish educational works, and after the birth of her last daughter, she began her writing career. Trimmer published more than a volume a year between 1781 and her death in 1810. She also actively promoted early Sunday Schools.[26]

The work excerpted here, *A Help to the Unlearned in the Study of the Holy Scriptures* (1805), is a guide to reading and understanding the Bible, intended for lay people who could not access more scholarly commentaries. It was highly unusual for a woman to write a commentary on the whole Bible in the early nineteenth century. Like other popular commentators, Trimmer remarked on almost every chapter and sometimes on paragraphs within the chapters.[27]

---

26. For a fuller biography of Trimmer, see Heather E. Weir, "Trimmer, Sarah (1741–1810)," in Taylor and Choi, *Handbook*, 505–9.

27. Sometimes Trimmer grouped chapters together for comment. In her very terse comments on the Song of Songs, she directed readers to pass over the book, "as all which it is

In this excerpt on Luke 1, Trimmer commented on sections within that long chapter. Because of the genre and purpose of her work, she was much more explicit about the theological and interpretive issues raised by Luke 1 than some popular interpreters. Her choice of genre also allowed her to write with authority, and to speak directly to her readers about ways their lives could be transformed. Trimmer's interpretation was influenced by the rule of faith, and the liturgy of the Anglican Church. She connected the gospels to the Old Testament and the Apostles' Creed.[28] Like Balfour and Phelps, she speculated about Mary's feelings, though in a more restrained way.

Trimmer held up Mary as a spiritual example to all Christians, both men and women, calling Mary an example of belief, because she believed the words of the angel. Trimmer's notion of spirituality, however, involved more than belief; it included action. To this end, she encouraged emulation of Mary's character. Specifically, she challenged readers to follow Mary's example of humility as a Protestant alternative to Roman Catholic veneration of Mary.

Luke 1

Ver. 26 *to* 29. The Virgin Mary was a young woman in mean circumstances, but she was notwithstanding of the family of king David, as was also Joseph, to whom she was under a promise of marriage. Joseph was by trade a carpenter. It must have been a great surprise to Mary to be addressed by an angel from heaven as one *who was highly favoured and blessed among women.* This extraordinary occurrence happened about six months after the appearance of the angel to Zacharias.

The Angel's words to Mary concerning the son she was to have, together with what was revealed to Joseph in a dream, *Matthew* 1:23, explain an ancient prophecy written above 700 years before; *see Isaiah* 7:14. We find, from the Angel's message, that JESUS was to be both the SON OF GOD, and the *Son of David.* That he was really and truly GOD is revealed by *St. John, chap.* 1 and the genealogies in St. Matthew and St. Luke show that he was the Son of David. *The throne of his father David, ver.* 32, signifies the kingdom of

designed to teach us is taught in plainer words in other parts of Scripture." Sarah Trimmer, *A Help to the Unlearned* (London: F. C. & J. Rivington, 1805), 387.

28. For a more detailed discussion of the influence of the liturgy on Trimmer's interpretation, see Heather E. Weir, "Helping the Unlearned: Sarah Trimmer's Commentary on the Bible," in de Groot and Taylor, *Recovering Nineteenth-Century Women*, 19–30.

God; that kingdom which Daniel foretold, (*chap.* 2) under the figure of *a stone hewn out of a mountain without hands*, and (*chap.* 7) *that everlasting dominion which should never pass away*.

Upon this portion of Scripture the first two articles of the apostle's creed [sic], which relate to JESUS CHRIST, are founded, namely, that he was the SON of GOD, and that *he was conceived by the Holy Ghost*; and we are taught by Mary's example to believe them because they were revealed from heaven. Observe, that when the angel first told Mary that she should be the mother of a child who would be at the same time the SON OF GOD, and the *Son of David*, she said, *How can these things be?* But as soon as the angel informed her that they would be brought about by the miraculous power of GOD, she no longer desired to be acquainted with the *manner* of them, but was satisfied that they would be as the angel had said, because GOD had revealed them, and with GOD nothing is impossible. In this manner all Christians are required to receive the Truths of Divine Revelation. We cannot indeed comprehend the manner in which GOD performs his wonderful works, but we may believe in them notwithstanding, for if they are written in Scripture, we may be sure they are revealed from heaven. None but GOD could know that the Virgin Mary would have a son. . . .

Ver. 46 *to* 57. Observe, that Mary so far from being lifted up on account of her being assured that she was the blessed Virgin who was to be the mother of our Lord JESUS CHRIST gave all the glory to GOD. She also testified her faith, by declaring that she regarded what had been revealed to her by the angel, as the fulfilment of the ancient prophecies, made first to Abraham, and afterwards, to Isaac and Jacob, and other holy men.

Many ages had passed away from the time that GOD first gave the promise of a Saviour to Abraham, and many ages have passed since the angel was sent to the Virgin Mary, in all of which GOD has showed mercy upon his faithful people from *generation to generation*; there is no doubt but that GOD will continue to do so till the end of the world; our care, therefore should be to testify our faith by believing the promises of the Gospel, and living as the Scriptures direct us; then will everyone have cause to say with Mary, *My spirit hath rejoiced in* GOD *my Saviour*, for it is impossible to believe in a Saviour without rejoicing.

Mary spake a prophecy by divine inspiration when she said *All generations shall call me blessed*; for she is to this day called the *blessed Virgin*, and most probably she will have that appellation to the end of the world. But some Christians, namely, the Roman Catholics, pay too great honour to the Virgin Mary, calling her the *mother of God*, and *the queen of heaven*, and worshipping her as if she were equal with God, which is making an idol of her. Instead of doing so, we should imitate that humility and lowliness of mind which distinguished her character, and gained her the particular favour of God.

Source: Sarah Trimmer, *A Help to the Unlearned* (London: F. C. & J. Rivington, 1805), 583–85.

GRACILLA BODDINGTON (1801–1887)

Worshipping with Mary

Gracilla Boddington was a prolific biblical commentator who published under her initials, G. B.[29] The daughter of Benjamin and Grace Boddington of Titely, Herefordshire, Boddington lived first with her parents, then alone, in a cottage on the family estate where she researched and wrote full-time. Her published work includes commentaries on every book of the New Testament.[30] Her commentaries were written to help ordinary Christians understand the Bible and grow in their spiritual lives. They contain practical reflections on the Bible, including, at times, prayers related to Boddington's exposition of a text. She also wrote devotional works on prayer and the Lord's Supper. Boddington was an evangelical Anglican whose writings stressed conversion, the evidences of true faith in life and work, the importance of studying Scripture, and prayer.

Boddington wrote her commentary on the gospel of Luke late in her career as a commentator. She followed the convention of remarking on sections of a chapter under subheadings. After explaining each passage, Boddington drew sermon-like applications to enhance her readers' spiritual lives. Boddington's confidence as an experienced interpreter of Scripture is evident in the authority and tone of her applications.

29. For a fuller discussion of Boddington, see Agnes Choi, "Boddington, Gracilla (1801–87)," in, Taylor and Choi, *Handbook*, 82–85.

30. Boddington's commentary project began with the epistles, which she treated in canonical sequence from Romans (1837) to James, Peter, John, and Jude (1852). She then published a volume on each of the gospels (1861, 1863, 1869, 1870), Acts (1876), ending her life work with Revelation (1881).

Boddington's comments on Luke 1 focused only on material not found in other gospel accounts. She made a strong exegetical argument against her perception of the Roman Catholic view of Mary by comparing Mary to Jael (Judges 5). Like Trimmer, Boddington connected Scripture to Anglican liturgy. She commented upon the use of the Magnificat in Anglican services, calling her readers to apply the words to themselves and not just recite them without thought. Boddington's commentary reveals her theology of Scripture as she believed that when Scripture was properly read and applied, lives would be transformed.

Luke 1

VER. 26–38.

The Virgin a pattern of obedience, faith and trust.

To have been chosen of God to be the mother of Jesus was indeed a great honour but it is worthy of remark that the Virgin Mary is spoken of by the angel as blessed *among* women, while in the Old Testament we find Jael the wife of Heber spoken of as blessed *above* women [Judges 5:24]. Had that expression "above women" been used in reference to the Virgin Mary, it might have given some grounds for the Roman Catholic idea that she was more than human; but as it is, there is none and we can only regard her as a pattern to us of humble faith. The announcement made to her by the angel, wonderful as it was, she received in the spirit of faith and obedience. "Behold the handmaid of the Lord, be it unto me according to thy word." She must have felt that her position as an unmarried woman having a child would expose her to blame by those who would be ready to judge her without knowing the truth; but, she trusted in God and left her honour in His hands; and we see how He had provided for her protection, by her having been previously betrothed to Joseph, who, like herself, was a descendant of David. Oh! if we would but be ready in all things to obey God, what need we fear? "The Lord will provide" [Gen. 22:14], should answer every anxiety. It matters little what the world thinks of us if only we have found favour with God and all those in whose heart Christ dwelleth by faith are highly favoured. Let us then pray earnestly for the teaching, guiding, and comforting of God the Holy Ghost, that as by Him Christ was born into the world and became partaker of our nature, so by Him we, being born again, may be partakers of the Divine nature. Let us pray that the image of Christ may be deeply impressed upon our souls, and that it may be seen by our life and conduct that we, through the Spirit, have been born again, and are become the sons and daughters of God Almighty.[31]

VER. 46–56.

The answer of Mary teaches us how praise ought to be received.

Not one word of self-exaltation is to be found in this beautiful hymn of the holy Mary. On the contrary, she acknowledges, with the deepest humility, her unworthiness, and her dependence wholly upon the mercy of God through the merits of the coming Saviour; but she fully declares her sense of the wonderful favour conferred upon her; and though she might then have to bear the scorn and contempt of the ignorant and unfeeling, she expresses a just conviction that throughout all generations she would be called blessed. Thus have we in the behaviour of Mary not only a lesson how to receive the language of praise—namely, by ascribing all to the undeserved mercy of God; but her very words may be applied to ourselves with the greatest propriety, and, therefore those who framed the services of our church, most wisely appointed this hymn of praise to be in constant use by us. If we are true believers in Christ we have through Him received such unutterable mercy in the hope of salvation, that it may well be the language of every individual worshipper—"My soul doth magnify the Lord, and my spirit hath rejoiced in God my Saviour." But, alas! how many, it is to be feared, use these words with their lips without any just notion of their meaning. They consider not their low estate as lost and ruined sinners, and, therefore they do not with sincere joy and thankfulness acknowledge what great things the Almighty has done for them. Oh! what need there is for everyone who, Sunday after Sunday, uses this hymn, to consider with what feelings the words are uttered![32] . . . But let us come now as humble suppliants to the throne of grace, taking the place of lowest degree, and then God will surely remember His mercy and not send us empty away. If we truly hunger and thirst after righteousness, we shall be filled [Matt. 5:6].

Source: G. B. [Gracilla Boddington], *A Practical Commentary on the Gospel of St. Luke, in Simple and Familiar Language* (London: James Nisbet and Co., 1869), 7–11.

---

31. Notice here that Boddington used inclusive language for the children of God.

32. The Magnificat, or Song of Mary, was sung or recited in a variety of services in the Christian Tradition. It was used in Evening Prayer in Anglican services, and this may be the Sunday after Sunday use that Boddington has in mind here.

MARY ANNE SCHIMMELPENNINCK (1778–1856)

Hail Her as the Woman

Mary Anne SchimmelPenninck, author, intellectual, and activist, was influenced by a variety of Christian traditions.[33] Born to Quaker parents, Samuel Galton and Lucy Barclay, SchimmelPenninck was educated at home through her reading and conversation with her parents' guests, who included Joseph Priestley, Benjamin Franklin, and Erasmus Darwin.[34] Following her marriage to Lambert SchimmelPenninck in 1806, she resided in Bristol, England. After associating with different churches, SchimmelPenninck joined the Moravian church in 1818.

SchimmelPenninck was encouraged to follow her literary pursuits by her husband. Her most studied work is *Theory on the Classification of Beauty and Deformity* (1815). Her works of biblical interpretation include *Psalms according to the Authorized Version; With Prefatory Titles, and Tabular Index of Scriptural References from the Port Royal Authors* (1825), and *Sacred Musings: on Manifestations of God to the Souls of Men* (1860). *Biblical Fragments* (1821) is a collection of essays and notes originally written as part of her own Bible study. She published them to encourage women to take up serious study of the Bible and biblical languages, particularly Hebrew, so that they could give their daughters a thorough religious education. Though *Biblical Fragments* was ostensibly written for mothers, the audience actually addressed in her essay includes "sons and daughters" and "sons" of the church.

SchimmelPenninck wrote an extended exposition on the two passages in the gospel of John where Jesus calls his mother "Woman." In the first section of this essay, she examined the term "Woman," which she argued is full of theological meaning. SchimmelPenninck proposed that Jesus used this word to comfort his mother in two difficult situations when Mary needed to "hope

33. For a fuller discussion of SchimmelPenninck, see Lissa M. Wray Beal, "Schimmelpenninck, Mary Anne (1778–1856)," in Taylor and Choi, *Handbook*, 436–40; see also Lissa M. Wray Beal, "Mary Anne SchimmelPenninck: A Nineteenth-Century Woman as Psalm-Reader," in de Groot and Taylor, *Recovering Nineteenth-Century Women*, 81–98.

34. Joseph Priestley (1733–1804), best remembered for his discovery of oxygen, a dissenter from the Church of England, who became a Unitarian, contributed significantly to the fields of education, moral philosophy, theology, metaphysics, political economy, history, and physical science. Benjamin Franklin (1705–1790), American founding father, was an author, printer, politician, diplomat, inventor, and scientist. Erasmus Darwin (1731–1802), grandfather of the biologist Charles Darwin, was a learned philosopher, poet, scientist, and physician.

against hope." This is what she called the literal sense of "Woman" in John 2 and John 19. SchimmelPenninck then shifted to a spiritual reading of these texts, arguing that Mary is a type of the church. Here, SchimmelPenninck differed from Balfour, Phelps, Trimmer, and Boddington, all of whom derived spiritual significance from the example of Mary found in the literal sense of the text. Instead, SchimmelPenninck sought the spiritual significance in the deeper or hidden meaning of the text, following a tradition of interpretation that found multiple layers of meaning in the biblical text.[35]

Mary, the Mother of Jesus

"Jesus saith unto her, WOMAN, *what have I to do with thee? mine hour is not yet come."*—JOHN 2:4.
"When Jesus therefore saw his mother and the disciple standing by whom he loved, he saith unto his mother, WOMAN, *behold thy son."*—JOHN 19:26.

The above concise sentences are the addresses of our Lord to his mother. They were uttered on the two most important occasions of his mortal life: viz. on the first exercise of his miraculous powers at Cana of Galilee; and at that stupendous hour which brought his mission on earth to its full accomplishment.

. . . [SchimmelPenninck wrote at length about Jesus calling Mary "Woman." She was concerned that this might be misunderstood. She described the relationship between Jesus and Mary in biblical terms; she called Jesus "holiness itself," "God, whose *eyes search the very inmost heart*" [Jer. 17:10], "Sovereign Judge," and "Him *whose delight is in His saints*" [Ps. 16:3]. She called Mary *"blessed among women,"* "this most eminent saint, this most favoured and devoted person." She described the relationship of Jesus and Mary both in human terms, son and mother, and in cosmic terms, God incarnate and the fulfillment of prophecy. The apparent rudeness of Jesus calling his mother "woman" prompted SchimmelPennninck's extended explanation of Jesus' use of the term "woman" through harmonization. She asked: "are these the words of that same gracious Lord who wept tears of sympathy over Lazarus, whom he was yet just about to raise?" She reasoned

35. In the Middle Ages, a four-fold method of interpreting Scripture was commonly used. The four layers of meaning were the historical, allegorical, moral, and anagogical.

that if these two addresses do not make sense, they must be interpreted so that they do make sense in light of the relationship between Jesus and Mary.]

Let us, then, once more view these two short addresses; addresses, whose very discrepancy from the style ever used by a child to a parent, must fully convince the believer that they convey some hidden meaning, to which these apparently harsh terms are the emphatic expression. Let us look to Him for their interpretation, well assured that *in his light we shall see light* [Ps. 36:9]; well assured that when we behold them in a just point of view, we shall see that this perfect Son fulfilled the law to his earthly parent, just as perfectly as to that heavenly Father, *whose will it was his meat to do* [John 4:34].

And we shall, upon mature and prayerful investigation, discover that these two short addresses, when properly comprehended, include and combine, under one forcible epithet, selected by GOD himself, all that could be honourable to the blessed Virgin, as a most eminently favoured saint; all that was most reverential from the most perfect and dutiful of sons; and all that the most tender and sympathizing pity could offer as the most heart-cheering cordial, and the most strong and powerful consolation.

Let us, then, under this full assurance, weigh these words in a spirit of prayer, and beseech the aid of that Holy Spirit, who is the author of Scripture, likewise to become its interpreter; and to fulfil the gracious promise of revealing to our hearts the things concerning Jesus. In his light may our spirits deeply attend to these momentous words of our Lord, in connection with the occasions on which they were offered!

. . . [Here SchimmelPenninck expanded on the literal sense of the address "Woman" on the two recorded occasions Jesus spoke to his mother in this way. She first noted that the two occasions were "the most heart-searching and trying occasions to the heart of a mother." The first was at the beginning of Jesus' public ministry at the wedding in Cana, and the second was at the close of Jesus' ministry, when he was on the cross. Schimmel-Penninck set up the scene in Cana by noting that despite the miracles attending his birth, Jesus, "at the end of thirty long years, still remained an unnoticed peasant in the despised town of Nazareth." In the second case, "every gleam of hope which had since arisen, and so brightly gleamed, was apparently fully and finally extinguished." In both instances, Mary needed to "hope against hope." SchimmelPenninck argued that to encourage his mother in both of these discouraging situations, Jesus addressed her as Woman. SchimmelPenninck called this "the comprehensive scriptural epithet WOMAN!" She claimed that this word would comfort Mary.]

He at once poured the strong cordial of comfort into her heart, as a mother and as a Christian, by addressing her, at once, by the comprehensive scriptural epithet WOMAN!

That one emphatic word, which at once pointed her to the remembrance of the promise, and designated her as being emphatically THE *woman*, THE *virgin*, ה עלמאה, HA NGALMAH, *whose seed*; whatever appearances might be to the contrary, *should* yet, assuredly, *break the serpent's head*; and which tenderly consoled her, by suggesting the remembrance, that it was a part of that very promise, that *the serpent should* also *bruise* him; but that it should only be *his heel!* [Gen. 3:15].

By this one emphatic and potent word, did our Lord, as her son, as her friend, as her Redeemer, and as her GOD, at once address her, by that, which was HER appropriate and distinguishing title; a title of the highest and most super-eminent dignity ever bestowed upon any mere creature; and at the same time, did he revive her heart, by presenting to her faith the strongest and richest cordial of consolation.

By this one word, all the promises of Scripture, all the types of the law, all the prefigurations of prophecy, all the stupendous expectations of the promised glory of Messiah, were at once recalled; and at once centred IN HER.

By this single expression, all the force of the magnificent salutations of the angel, of Elizabeth, and of the Magi,—all the hopes of all the saints and prophets,—all the strength of the august tide of divine promises, which had rolled on its broadening flood of light from century to century,—were at once, as it were, concentrated, and presented to this blessed saint and most afflicted mother, in the very hour of need, in the very moment of extremity.

And this one word, HER DISTINGUISHING APPELLATION OF HONOUR, was presented, a heart-cheering and faith-enlivening cordial, by Him, who was at once the tender Son, the strong Redeemer, the mighty GOD, the ever-lasting Father; and who, in the very depth of affliction, is yet experienced by his saints to be the Prince of Peace! And, in the very gulf of the fiery furnace, she remained unhurt, because HER *Son, the Son of* GOD, *was with her!* He was the restorer, as well as the first author of her faith.

. . . [SchimmelPenninck stated that Mary was blessed, but Jesus was the source of blessing. After expounding the literal sense of the text—the word Woman as a comfort to Mary—SchimmelPenninck turned to the spiritual sense of the text.]

But all that Jesus did, in his human nature, was done not only for the expiation of our sins, but to set us an example, that we might walk, as he also walked. Nor is any Scripture of merely private interpretation. These Scriptures, then, in the same manner as all others, must contain a spiritual, and universally practical, as well as a literal sense, confined to the particular occasion on which they were uttered. And that spiritual or universal sense must be one containing a practical application to every heart and conscience; for *all Scripture is given by inspiration, is profitable for doctrine, for reproof, for correction, for instruction in righteousness* [2 Tim. 3:16]. Consequently, all Scripture must be capable of such an exposition as will fulfil these ends.

Let us then meditate, for a few moments, upon the spiritual sense of those Scriptures, whose literal interpretation we have just been considering.

The MOTHER OF JESUS, whilst she is literally that blessed and highly favoured woman, whose seed should bruise the serpent's head, is likewise, in a spiritual sense, the especial type of that still more favoured virgin, the spiritual woman, the church, the spouse of Christ; to whom that prophecy applies, in a still more exalted, and distinguished sense.

The Church of Christ is really, in truth, not only that spiritual *Eve*, הוה, CHAVAH, *the mother of all living* [Gen. 3:20], who was formed from the opened side of the spiritual Adam, the Lord from heaven, and *builded* up, whilst he slept the sleep of death. She is, also, the spiritual Mary. She is truly *מרים, MIRIAM; and that in both its senses. She was *in bitterness*; in Egyptian bondage and servitude; but the Lord hath *taken her from the dunghill, to set her amongst princes* [1 Sam. 2:8].

She is the daughter of Anna,†חנה, CHANNAH, the offspring *of grace*; and she is, therefore, now *the exalted*.

She is that woman, in her first estate loathsome, polluted, and uncleansed; whose birth and nativity was, indeed, in the land of Canaan; but whose father was an Amorite (a rebel), and her mother an Hittite, (or destroyed) [Ezek. 16:3]. She is that wretched infant, vile and polluted, to whom the Lord said, in the midst of her pollution, LIVE! that abandoned child, on whom his eye yearned with compassion; with whom he entered into an everlasting covenant; whom he betrothed unto himself; whom he washed and cleansed in his own blood; and whose loathsome rags he exchanged for spotless white raiment, the robe of his own righteousness; and whom he decked and adorned for himself, with gold and with silver [Ezek. 16:3–13].

She is that same woman whom Solomon beheld by faith, *coming up out of the wilderness; leaning upon the arm of her beloved* [Song of Songs 8:5].

---

*The Hebrew מרים, *Mereeam* or *Mary*, may be derived from two roots. If derived from מר, *Moor*, with the plural termination ים, it then means *bitternesses or afflictions*. If derived from רם, *Ram*, with a formative מ, it then means *the instrument of causing or bringing exaltation*.

†St. Anna is said to have been the mother of the blessed Virgin.

She is that *king's daughter, whose raiment is of wrought gold, and who* is *all glorious within* [Ps. 45:13].

She is the faithful and the virtuous wife of the book of Proverbs [Prov. 31:10]. All the saints of old heard of her by the hearing of the ear [Job 42:5], and spake of her glory, as of the reflected glory of her bridegroom.[36] The whole record of the word of GOD which bears witness to him, speaks of her, in him likewise. *For the man is not without the woman; nor the woman without the man, in the Lord* [1 Cor. 11:11]. And what GOD *hath joined,* even Christ and the Church, *let no man ever put,* in his view of divine truth, *asunder* [Matt. 19:6, Mark 10:9].

She is that faithful wife, *whose price,* even the blood of the Son of GOD, *is above rubies* [Prov. 31:10]. She is that fruitful mother, who is as a luxuriant vine and whose abundant offspring [Ps. 128:3], from the east and from the west, from the north and from the south, shall come and sit at the king's table [Luke 13:29]; shall break of that bread of life which strengthens man's heart; and drink of that new wine which maketh his heart glad [Ps. 104:15]; and shall show like springing olive trees, abundant oil and fatness.

She is that glorious woman who is clothed upon with the sun; who has the mutable moon under her feet; and in whose crown the just from each various tribe of Israel shall shine as stars [Rev. 12:1].

She is that woman, the true mother of all living [Gen. 3:20], promised when the typical Eve fell; and was spoken of throughout the whole of Scripture, as opposed to the unfaithful woman of mystical Babylon [Rev. 17:5]. And this faithful woman is, in a very especial manner, typified by MARY, THE MOTHER OF JESUS.

To that glorious Church, at once the mother, and yet the bride of the Lamb [Rev. 21:9], it may, indeed, be truly said, even by those holy angels who have never left their first estate; who have the favour ever to stand in the presence of GOD, but who yet earnestly desire to look into the mysteries of redemption; and who, like the sons of Adam, find the true manna from heaven, angels' food: *Hail, thou that art highly, favoured, the Lord is with thee, blessed art thou amongst women.*

Fear not, Mary, once in bitterness, now *the exalted;* base as was thy original condition, *thou hast found favour with* GOD!

The saints of GOD, who, like Zachariah* and Elizabeth,† have ever *remem-*

---

36. This may be a reference to Psalm 45.

*זכריה, *He remembered Jehovah, or Jehovah He remembered*
†אלישבת, *God is my rest,* or, אלישבע *God is my fulness of satisfaction*

bered the Lord [Jonah 2:7], and found in *the Redeemer their rest* [Jer. 50:34]; and who have, therefore, *walked in all the commandments and ordinances of the Lord blameless* [Luke 1:6]; may well address the mystical woman, in the language; *Blessed art thou amongst women, and blessed is the fruit of thy womb; and whence is this* (unspeakable favour) *to me, that the mother of my Lord should visit me!* [Luke 1:42–43]. And, with respect to the Church herself; well, indeed, may she take into her own mouth the anthem of Mary, and from her very inmost heart and spirit sing aloud:

My soul doth magnify the Lord, and my spirit hath (even from the beginning*) *rejoiced in* GOD *my Saviour;* for in him alone has been from the beginning her hope.

For he hath regarded the lowliness of his handmaiden; when she had destroyed herself; *for behold, from henceforth all generations shall call me blessed.*

For He that is mighty hath done to me *great things, and holy is his name.*

And his mercy is on them that fear him, from generation to generation.

He hath showed strength with his arm, he hath scattered the proud, in the imagination of their hearts! The force of the arch-enemy he hath broken, and the devices of Satan brought to nought.

He hath put down the mighty from their seats, and hath exalted them of low degree. The angels who sinned, have finally quitted their high estate; whilst *his delights are with the* frail *children of men.*

He hath filled the hungry with good things and the rich hath he sent empty away.

He hath holpen his servant Israel in remembrance of his mercy.

As he spake to our father Abraham and his seed for ever.[37]

If the Church, the redeemed spouse of Christ, may take this glorious and triumphant language into her own mouth;[38] what then shall be the reverential language, which it best becomes all her sons and daughters to use towards her, who hath the promise of such glorious things, and who has the foretaste of the heavenly inheritance.

Jesus, in the days of his flesh, left us an example, that as he walked, so also should his disciples walk likewise.

37. The prayer of Mary, the Magnificat, is found in Luke 1:46–55.

38. The use of the Magnificat is common in the liturgy of the Christian Tradition, including Evening Prayer and other Anglican services.

*Since this was the original promise.

May we then ever remember, that the Church of Christ is that mother, that woman, in whom, through Christ, all the promises of GOD centre!

And that not only the glorious, but likewise the painful ones, equally belong to her.

As a sword pierced through the heart of her, who was, literally speaking, the woman, the Mother of Emmanuel; so, that the thoughts of many hearts may be revealed, shall a sword pierce through the heart of her, who is, antitypically speaking, the woman, the Church, the mother of the Son of GOD; even that sword of the Spirit [Eph. 6:17], keen, sharp, and two-edged, proceeding from the mouth of him, who is the Alpha and the Omega; the living word of GOD, whose countenance is as when the sun shineth in his strength; whose eyes are as a flame of fire [Rev. 1:11–16], and whose sword, the written word, applied by him, shall be quick and powerful, piercing even to the dividing asunder of soul and spirit, and of the joints and marrow, and is a discerner of the thoughts and intents of the heart [Heb. 4:12]. . . .

Let all her faithful children follow the example of our Lord to his mother in her hour of affliction. Wherever, then, a church is really founded upon Christ, and upon the word of his patience; whether the flame be sunk smouldering in the hearts of her children, under the ashes of Laodicean lukewarmness at home [Rev. 3:14–16], or scattered by the uncontrolled disobedience of barbarians amidst missions abroad; though numerous tares have been sown by an enemy in the field, whilst the servants, it is to be feared, instead of diligently watching, have slept [Matt. 13:25]; yet still never let her children abandon *the woman*. . . .

In her deepest perplexity then, in her lowest and her most weak estate, still may all her faithful children ever address the church, as *the* WOMAN; reminding her of her hope and consolation, and pointing her to the source of her strength; that she may wait on Him, who is at once the Child born, and the Son given to her, and yet who has the government on his shoulder; who is her Counsellor, her mighty Redeemer, her everlasting Father, and her Prince of Peace [Isa. 9:6]; then, though the hour of Jesus be perhaps not now yet come, she shall yet assuredly behold the miracle, and, at its appointed season, her first-born Son shall manifest His glory.

And as we hail her as *the woman*, may her faith be renewed, and may she turning aside from every other hope, say to all her servants and ministers, like Mary, *Whatsoever* HE *saith unto you, do*: and hearing, may all her ministers and servants like the faithful servants of the marriage of Cana, obey! . . .

Happy that church whose sons, with unfailing faith, but with inflexible truth, shall still in every state view her as the woman! the woman who shall inherit that promise, but inherit it only as she truly ponders the things of Jesus in her heart; and who shall receive the accomplishment of those immortal hopes, on which the church, even from the beginning, was built; and O how happy shall those favoured individuals be, of whom Jesus shall in the last great day say to that mother, WOMAN, *behold* THY SON!

Source: Mary Anne SchimmelPenninck, *Biblical Fragments*, vol. 2 (London: Ogle, Duncan, and Co., 1821), 253–80.

ELIZABETH WORDSWORTH (1840–1932)

Cleopatra or Mary?

Elizabeth Wordsworth was a distinguished writer, educator, and advocate for women's education at Oxford.[39] The eldest of seven children of Christopher Wordsworth and Suzanna Hatly Frere, Wordsworth was educated at home by her father, governesses, and through her own reading. She taught herself Greek from her younger brother's schoolbooks. She worked as research assistant and secretary to her father, the bishop of Lincoln, helping him write a multi-volume biblical commentary. Wordsworth became the head of an Oxford residence for women, and later was appointed as the first principal of Lady Margaret Hall, Oxford, where she served from 1878–1909. She lectured regularly to women students on biblical and theological topics.

Wordsworth published 27 books on diverse topics. *Illustrations of the Creed* consists of twenty-two addresses on the Apostles' creed, given to her students in Oxford in 1885–1886. The excerpt below is from her address on the creedal statement "Conceived by the Holy Ghost, born of the Virgin Mary." Like Phelps, Wordsworth thought women could draw "special lessons" from female figures in the Bible; thus, she noted that the words "born of the Virgin Mary" were of particular importance for her audience.

Wordsworth compared the Virgin Mary to Cleopatra, and encouraged

---

39. For more information on Wordsworth, see Rebecca G. S. Idestrom, "Wordsworth, Elizabeth (1840–1932)," in Taylor and Choi, *Handbook*, 540–42.

the members of her audience to use their particular gifts for good and not for evil. Wordsworth's broad education and her ability to use the tools of scholarship contributed to her argument for the authority of Scripture and for the importance of following the example of the Virgin Mary. Wordsworth used her sermon-like lectures both to challenge the worldly values of her privileged students at Lady Margaret Hall and to empower them to transform themselves and their world.

Born of the Virgin Mary

But we must pass on to our last point. The special lessons to us, as women, from those words, "Born of the Virgin Mary."

It is a truism to say that woman's position has been entirely changed and unspeakably elevated by Christianity. But do we always remember that if it is a great honour, as it undoubtedly is, to belong to the same sex as that of the mother of our Blessed Lord, yet that such a benefit cannot be conferred on us without a great enhancement of our own responsibilities? Perhaps this will be better understood by an historical illustration.

Contemporaneously with Augustus, in whose reign, as you know, our Lord was born, there flourished a most remarkable woman—a queen, beautiful in person, fascinating in manners, witty in speech, but who seemed to have come into the world to show how woman may pervert herself and all her gifts to the degradation, instead of the elevation, of man. You will guess that I mean Cleopatra. Her presence in Rome during the last years of the life of Julius Caesar has left a blot on that great man's memory. Unscrupulous as beautiful, she thought nothing of sacrificing her own nearest relations to what she considered her interests. Of her unbounded luxury as Queen of Egypt, her fatal influence over Mark Antony, whom she deserted at the most critical moment of his life, her attempts to win Augustus, and her cowardly suicide at the age of thirty-eight, you will not need to be reminded.

Could any figure have been invented by a poet's imagination better calculated to show what womanhood, even when most brilliant, most gifted, and most intelligent, had sunk to before the birth of our Lord?

Now, it is not a little remarkable, when we come to the Blessed Virgin Mary, that we are never told she was beautiful, witty, fascinating, highly educated. Purity, obedience, piety, thoughtfulness, and love of her own kindred, seem to have been the chief characteristics of the maiden to whom

Gabriel came. And may we not say, in passing, that if anything were needed to convince us of the far higher level on which the Gospels stand than that of other literature of a late period, which usually has a tendency to redundancy of detail and word-painting, it would be this severe and dignified silence, which bestows not one epithet of personal loveliness, one touch of physical description,* on her whom painters of all succeeding ages have delighted to make their ideal of womanly beauty, and to surround with every accessory of graceful art?

How much did the world know of Cleopatra, how little of the Blessed Virgin!

Now, there may be people here who feel that they have some gifts, beauty, talent, wealth, attractiveness, and the like. Surely the lesson to them is, not to despise such gifts, but to consecrate them, and to remember that, as they may be perverted to do a great deal of harm, so, with God's blessing, they may, when rightly used, be very powerful for good.

But there may be some one here who feels, "I have not a single gift. I know I am not beautiful. I have no talent, no accomplishment, no charm, very little money. No one has ever made much of me."

And yet you may be like the Blessed Virgin. We are not aware that she had any of those gifts. But we can all try to be good, as she was; to say our prayers, as she did; to be obedient and loving, as she was.

The greatest blessing ever given to mortal was given to a woman whom the world would have passed over as insignificant, and some of the greatest mischief ever done in the world has been done by women of high rank, great talents, great beauty, and great powers of influence. If we have gifts, let us remember that they are worse than nothing without goodness; if we have none, we may be sure God can bless us without them, if we only say as Mary did, "Behold the handmaid of the Lord."

And now let us sing—"Once in royal David's city."[40]

Source: Elizabeth Wordsworth, *Illustrations of the Creed* (London: Rivington's, 1889), 133–36.

---

40. This hymn was written by C. F. Alexander to help children remember the credal phrase "Was conceived of the Holy Ghost, born of the Virgin Mary." Cecil Frances Alexander, *Hymns for Little Children* (London, 1848; 66th ed. London: Master's, 1887), 30–31.

*Contrast, *e.g.*, such a *chef d'oeuvre* of literary skill as the almost contemporary description of Venus (Virgil, "Æneid," i. 406).

CHRISTINA GEORGINA ROSSETTI (1830–1894)

The Veiled Virgin

Christina Georgina Rossetti was an important Victorian poet, lay theologian, exegete, and author of devotional prose.[41] The daughter of Gabriele Rossetti and Frances Polidari Rossetti, Christina was educated and lived in London with her artistic family. Rossetti, her mother, and her sister Maria were all drawn to the Anglo-Catholic Oxford Movement in the 1840s. Renowned pre-Raphaelite painter and poet, Dante Gabriel Rossetti, used his sister, Christina, and his mother, Frances, as models of the Virgin Mary and St. Anne in his painting, "The Girlhood of the Virgin Mary" (1849). Gabriel Rossetti wrote two sonnets on the symbolism used in this painting. The Virgin was undoubtedly part of the Rossetti family's ongoing dialogues about religion, art, and poetry.

In a five-hundred-page work, *Called to Be Saints*, Rossetti wrote reflections for the holidays and saints days found in the Anglican *Book of Common Prayer*. Rossetti's reflections on the saints included Scripture texts, the biography of the saint under discussion, a prayer to receive the characteristic virtue of the saint, a memorial, a flower to illustrate the saint's life, and a poem. The Virgin Mary is particularly remembered at the Feast of the Presentation and the Feast of the Annunciation.

Rossetti was a brilliant poet, and used her ability to play with language and images in writing about Mary. She filled in details about the Virgin Mary, not simply by using sympathetic imagination, as Balfour and Phelps did, but by drawing upon tradition and other Scriptures, such as the Song of Songs. Like SchimmelPenninck, Rossetti acknowledges the multiple senses of Scripture. By including prayers, Rossetti goes further than the other authors in this section in providing spiritual direction for readers. Rossetti recognized that she could be wrong in her portrayal of Mary, yet she pursued her attempt to unveil Mary, providing resources for meditating on her life, and learning from her life and character.

---

41. For a fuller discussion of Rossetti, see Diane D'Amico, "Rossetti, Christina Georgina (1830–94)," in *Handbook*, ed. Taylor & Choi, 425–29. See also Amanda W. Benkhuysen, "The Prophetic Voice of Christina Rossetti," in *Recovering Nineteenth-Century Women*, ed. de Groot and Taylor, 165–80.

The Presentation of Christ in the Temple, and Purification of St. Mary the Virgin.

2 February

[Rossetti began with a section called "The Sacred Text" which quoted the following passages in the AV: Exod. 13:2; Exod. 22:29; Num. 18:15, 16; Lev. 12:2–8; Luke 2:22–39.][42]

Glories of the Presentation

On this day the mother of the great King brought the burnt offering of the poor, the virgin mother of the Sinless Firstborn submitted to ceremonial purification. On this day, for a few shekels, He was redeemed Whose life-blood paid our costlier ransom; and embraced in aged arms, Who made the round world and them that dwell therein; and recognised by Simeon whom He would shortly comfort in the valley of the shadow of death; and hailed by Anna, whose fastings and prayers He that instant paid and overpaid. On this day the Second Adam did homage, the better Abel cried from the ground on behalf of His brother, the true Isaac was pledged to be sacrificed and not spared, the Avenger of Blood gained on him who was a murderer from the beginning, the swifter David hasted and ran to meet the Philistine, the Greater Solomon chose for His portion the good of His people, the Lamb of God drew nigh to the altar. On this day in Christ we were presented, in Christ accepted:—

He hath made us accepted in the Beloved. Ephesians 1:6.

The Sacred Text (Resumed.)

AFTER the inspired record of to-day's events the Blessed Virgin mother is named or clearly designated not many times in Holy Scripture, and never except in closest connection with her Divine Son. Only the following passages in the Gospels and the Acts bring her distinctly before us, and help towards completing her history. [Rossetti cited in full Luke 2:41–51; John 2:1–5; Luke 8:19; Mark 3:31; Matthew 12:46; John 19:25–27; Acts 1:14.]

---

42. Note that Rossetti alluded to many biblical passages in her meditations. We have not attempted to cite all allusions. All the Scripture references provided are hers. Nineteenth-century readers would have heard the scriptural echoes in these meditations much more readily than do twenty-first-century readers.

Biographical Additions.

THUS briefly do the sacred historians note some few points in the life of her who was full of grace, but of whose birth and death they tell us nothing. Yet students of the inspired record have elicited from it that this modest and unassuming Virgin, however inconspicuous may have been her actual condition, was, like her husband, a scion of the royal stock of David; and was moreover in her own person possessed of property, the latter point transpiring from her liability to taxation. We know that from the day of our Saviour's crucifixion St. John stood to her in the place of a son; a generally accepted tradition asserts that she attained a ripe old age, and a sepulchre excavated in the rock of Gethsemane is even pointed out as purporting to be hers: yet surely the good providence of God has veiled her from our curiosity, even while holding her up to our admiration. We catch sight of her, but hidden as in the clefts of the rock; we discern her, but dimly as withdrawn within the secret places of the stairs: wherefore ascribing unto God alone the glory of all her glories, known to Him Who conferred them, not fully known by us, we turn from the creature to the Creator, we cast ourselves down at His feet Who was dead and is alive for evermore, and with our stammering lips we take up the hymn of the thousand times ten thousand and thousands of thousands of angels, saying after them:—

Worthy is the Lamb that was slain to receive power, and riches, and wisdom, and strength, and honour, and glory, and blessing. *Revelation* 5:12.

Thou hast ravished my heart with one of thine eyes, with one chain of thy neck. *Song of Solomon* 4:9.

It might not be safe for pilgrim souls saluting only from afar the heavenly Sion and its choirs, it might not be safe for us to see as yet except through a glass darkly. For if retaining fleshly eyes and fallible hearts we were at once to behold that which eye hath not seen neither hath entered into the heart of man, it might even be that the consummated splendour of created loveliness would blind us to the peerless loveliness of the Creator. And (if I err not) it may perhaps be, at least in part, for a kindred reason, that we as yet know so little of what our Lord's Virgin Mother appeared in the days of her flesh: for truly, even as it is, one of her eyes and one chain of her neck have sufficed as it were to ravish the world. The hour comes when (please God) knowing as we are known we shall also know all things: meanwhile let her be to us as violets not pried after but sweetly and surely proclaimed by the fragrance of their odour, as a leaf-hidden dove revealed by the melody of its cooings, as a moon not yet mounted above our horizon yet foreshown by the outskirts of its proper halo. If it was well for ancient Israel that the sepulchre of Moses was concealed from man's veneration, well may it be for us no less that the Blessed Virgin remains as it were veiled until we be strengthened.

[Rossetti cited Deut. 34:5–6 in full.]

Worship God. *Revelation* 19:10.

A Prayer for Acceptance in Christ.

O God our Father, by Whose cherishing grace Thy choice Virgin Mary grew up as a fair stem to bear Thy Lily, as a cup of moss to encircle Thy Rose, as a planet to wait upon Thy Sun, as a censer to offer unto Thee fragrance of acceptable Incense; O God, by the bounty of Whose grace St. Mary Thy Blessed pure Virgin, as a king giving unto the King, gave back to Thee Thy Son Whom Thou hadst given unto her to be her Son; Grant us no less, I beseech Thee, to yield ourselves up to Christ, and thus to offer Christ in our hearts back to Thee: Whom we plead as our Innocence and our Purity, our Robe and our Righteousness, our Lamb and our Lily, our Lord and our God, our Beloved and our Spouse. Amen.

Source: Christina G. Rossetti, *Called to Be Saints: The Minor Festivals Devotionally Studied* (London: SPCK, 1881), 130, 133, 134, 136–38.

The Annunciation of the Blessed Virgin Mary

25 March

[Rossetti again began with a section called "The Sacred Text" and quoted Isaiah 7:13–14, and Luke 1:26–38. She continued with the Glories of the Annunciation, focusing on the prophecies about Jesus fulfilled on this day.]

The Sacred Text (Resumed.)

A CURTAIN of silence hides from us the Blessed Virgin for the most part of her life; only in the early days of her blessedness do we learn much of her exaltation, her acts and words. The following verses from two Gospels complete such portions of her history as in the order of the Church Calendar are commended to our reverent thoughts before the Feast of her ceremonial Purification.

[Rossetti here inserted Luke 1:39–56; Matthew 1:18–25; Luke 2:3–7; Luke

2:15–19; Matthew 2:1, 11, 13–15a, 19–20a, 21, 23a. Rossetti omitted parts of the story in Matthew 2 without noting that she did so.]

We know not how appeared that aspect of feminine loveliness which the Archangel Gabriel beheld when he saluted blessed St. Mary: yet can we discern in her soul, if not in her face, much of the dove, to us the sweet symbol of tenderness; whereof the voice, though not a song, is music, and the rosy feet seem too delicate for earth's dusty paths, and the plumage is whiteness, and the eye beauty, and the manner endearment.

By the operation of the adorable dove-like Spirit was that adorable One born of her, Who infinitely excelling her, yet in her showed forth a measure of His own likeness: He above all others being meek and pure and single of aim; and His eyes being as the eyes of doves by the rivers of waters.

When St. Mary sought the hill country to visit her cousin Elisabeth, she went with haste, as fly the doves to their windows: and thenceforward, however her feet might journey to and fro in accordance with the Divine behest, her heart abode in the haven of the Divine Presence; as of old the dove took refuge in the Ark of Salvation, earth affording no rest for the sole of her foot. And at length, when upon the Virgin Mother came that night which darkness seized, even that day which was stained by darkness and the shadow of death, then how must her heart have sunk like a trembling dove: mourning as doves, as valley doves which mourn on mountains, she stood on Calvary. Whence also amid a sound of love and lamentation, "a voice of doves," St. John led her.

From which winningness and beauty of doves let us draw out a prayer that our compassionate Saviour would make us also harmless as doves, holy as doves of sacrifice: that we be not "like a silly dove without heart" [Hos. 7:11], but may glow with hearts so pure and loving that the dovelike Divine Spirit may of His infinite condescension delight Himself in us, and may in each of us set up His rest for ever.

Afterward he brought me to the gate, even the gate that looketh toward the east: and, behold, the Glory of the God of Israel came from the way of the east. And the Glory of the Lord came into the house by the way of the gate whose prospect is toward the east. *Ezekiel* 43:1–2a.

Then he brought me back the way of the gate of the outward sanctuary which looketh toward the east; and it was shut. Then said the Lord unto me, This gate shall be shut, it shall not be opened, and no man shall enter in by it; because the Lord, the God of Israel, hath entered in by it, therefore it shall be shut. It is for the Prince. *Ezekiel* 44:1–3a.

Blessed St. Mary seems to shine forth very luminously as that hallowed

Eastern Gate of the mystical Temple, which Ezekiel in a rapture beheld first open and then shut for ever. Instructed by such a symbol piety has adored the Will of God, and has cherished with great devotion a belief in the perpetual virginity of the Virgin Mother; contemplating in her a glowing rose of motherhood grafted on a lily of intact purity.

As the lily among thorns, so is My love among the daughters. *Song of Solomon* 2:2.

In another sense, moreover, and to ourselves she is a shut gate, not a gate of access: Christ is our open door. She is Christ's gate through which He once came to seek and save us: He is to us that only door, by which, He helping us, we may with boldness enter into the Holiest; here into communion with our God, hereafter into the revealed presence of the most sacred Trinity in Unity. Amen.

Then said Jesus unto them again, Verily, verily, I say unto you, I am the door of the sheep.—*St. John* 10:7.

Behold, I have set before thee an open door, and no man can shut it. *Revelation* 3:8.

If she be a door, we will inclose her with boards of cedar. *Song of Solomon* 8:9.

Of all festivals this Feast of the Annunciation alone can fall on Good Friday: thus bringing together the beginning and the end of Him Who, having neither beginning nor end, did for our sakes take unto Himself beginning of days and end of life; that so sharing with us our death, He might no less share with us His own immortality. Thus also appear as in a symbol two other mysteries of love: for as our Lord's birth first gave Him to His dearest Mother, though His subsequent labours may for awhile have withdrawn Him from her society; so His Cross, being the stepping-stone to His Resurrection and Ascension, gave Him back to her from whom thenceforward for ever neither life nor death nor any other creature should part Him.

A Prayer for Self-Devotion.

O GOD beneath the shadow of Whose wing Thy beloved Daughter and Handmaid St. Mary abode in peace; blessed among women, blessed in believing the sure word of promise, blessed (yet with prophecy of a sword) by the mouth of faithful Simeon, blessed in bearing Christ, blessed in giving suck to Christ; yea, rather, blessed in hearing the word of God and keeping it, and called blessed by all generations;—O God, Who didst so fill her with grace that in will she obeyed Thee, in heart entertained Thee, in word conformed herself to Thy behest, with body and spirit worshipped Thee, and in her life was lovely and pleasant unto Thee: keep us, Lord, keep us also obedient, humble, retired, holy, pure; full of service, of submission, of adoration, of love. Cleanse what we have defiled, replace what we have lost, renew what we have destroyed: bring us all, keep us all, within the pale of obedience, the bands of love, the cords of a Man. Of that Man Who being God once died for us, the Man Christ Jesus: Whom we plead, in Whom we take refuge, Who changeth not, Who doth earnestly remember us still. Amen.

Herself a rose, who bore the Rose,
    She bore the Rose and felt its thorn.
    All Loveliness new-born
Took on her bosom its repose,
    And slept and woke there night and morn.
Lily herself, she bore the one
    Fair Lily; sweeter, whiter, far
    Than she or others are:
The Sun of Righteousness her Son,
    She was His morning star.
She gracious, He essential Grace,
    He was the Fountain, she the rill:
    Her goodness to fulfil
And gladness, with proportioned pace
    He led her steps through good and ill
Christ's mirror she of grace and love,
    Of beauty and of life and death:
    By hope and love and faith
Transfigured to His Likeness, "Dove,
Spouse, Sister, Mother," Jesus saith.

Source: Christina G. Rossetti, *Called to Be Saints: The Minor Festivals Devotionally Studied* (London: SPCK, 1881), 172, 173–74, 176–83, 193.

Elizabeth Rundle Charles (1828–1896)

....

Communion and Sacrifice

Elizabeth Rundle Charles was a prolific author of more than fifty books, best known for her historical fiction, particularly *The Chronicles of the Schönberg-Cotta Family* (1862).[43] She also wrote poetry, spiritual and devotional reflections, commentaries, and translated German prose and poetry into English. Charles was the only child of John and Barbara (Gill) Rundle. She was well educated at home in Devon, England, where her parents encouraged her gifts for languages and writing. After her marriage, she lived in London with her husband, Andrew Paton Charles. Charles was raised in the Church of England, and was influenced by both the Anglo-Catholic and the evangelical stream of Anglicanism. She was well connected with leading men in the church and academy including Benjamin Jowett, Edward Pusey, Archbishop Archibald Tait, and William Booth.[44]

Charles was particularly fascinated by the Virgin Mary, writing two books and several poems about her. *Ecce Ancilla Domini* (Behold the handmaid of the Lord) was the culmination of Charles's lifetime of study and meditation on Mary. It contains reflective and devotional studies inspired by what the gospels reveal about Mary, the Mother of the Lord.

Like Rossetti, Charles used typology, tradition, sanctified imagination, and art to fill in the gaps in the story of Mary. Like Balfour, Charles connected Eve and Mary; in similar ways, these women saw Mary providing redemption where Eve provoked the Fall. Charles's work as a translator sensitized her to problems associated with translation. She wondered what language the angels spoke, and how Mary could understand Gabriel, as well as how to best render the angel's greeting in English. Charles advocated imitation as a form of spiritual discipline. For Charles, Mary was the Christian ideal of womanhood.

---

43. For a fuller discussion of Charles, see Krista M. Dowdeswell, "Charles, Elizabeth Rundle, Elizabeth Stuart (1828–96)," in Taylor and Choi, *Handbook*, 120–23; see also Marion Ann Taylor, "Elizabeth Rundle Charles: Translating the Letter of Scripture into Life," in de Groot and Taylor, *Recovering Nineteenth-Century Women*, 149–63.

44. Arthur Stanley (1815–1881) was Dean of Westminster Abbey; Benjamin Jowett (1817–1893) was a theologian and Master of Balliol College, Oxford; Edward Pusey (1800–1882) was a theologian and Regius Professor of Hebrew at Christ Church, Oxford; Archibald Tait (1811–1882) was Archbishop of Canterbury; William Booth (1829–1912) was the founder of the Salvation Army.

I.

THE SILENCES.

So closely is the veil of reverent silence folded around the Mother of our Lord, the silence as to her outward life, the silence which characterizes her inward life—"keeping these things and pondering them in her heart," that many among us have a shrinking from approaching the subject as in any way apart or detached. Three reasons especially seem consciously or unconsciously to lead not a few of us to this: the silence folded, it would seem purposely, around her; the tendency of everything she said or did, of her few words, of her one Song, as of her silence, to direct our hearts upward away from herself; and the predominance, as it seems to many, of the passive elements in her character.

And yet when we look further into the subject, each one of these reasons seems a reason not to repel us from the subject, but to draw us towards it.

The life of Mary seems to gather us into a stillness like her own, into a peace and quiet which is what many of us, in these restless days sorely need. In these days of "much coming and going," there often seems indeed "scarcely leisure so much as to eat," [Mark 6:31] and we need inward leisure so to eat and drink of the great realities that they may nourish our life. There can be no growth in a whirlpool; there can be no progress in a whirlwind; and to "come apart and rest awhile" [Mark 6:31] in the shadow of that steadfast life may help some of us to comprehend and approach nearer the ideal of womanhood which it enshrines.

If we are to learn from the life of any of the saints, surely none might help us more than hers whose canonization was visibly and audibly direct from Heaven, to whom the angel Gabriel was sent with the crown of supreme benediction. "Full of grace," "highly favoured," in whatever direction we interpret the fullness of that angelical salutation, it must surely mean that the Divine wisdom and love which elected her to be the mother of our Lord, divinely fitted her for that transcendent election. For in that kingdom of God, which is the world of truth, the distinctions and the ranks are all real, from within outward. The names are definitions, the outer glory grows out of the inner; and if there is but one supreme type for all humanity, the likeness of the Son of Man Himself,—but One whom to follow wholly is not mechanically to copy but livingly to grow,—yet surely it is worth while to study closely and reverently the blessed Mother who was nearest Him at the manger, in the home, and at the Cross. . . .

And as to that most undeniable tendency of all she said and sang and did, or did not say and do, to lead away from herself to her Lord and ours, what stronger attraction can there be to the study of her life than this? She, indeed, has solved the problem of escaping from her own shadow, by the perpetual turning of her whole being towards the light.

The longer we look at her, the more our eyes will follow the guidance of hers. As in one of Raphael's pictures, whilst the angel is holding the crown above her head, she, entirely unconscious of the crown, sees only the child Jesus springing into her arms; or as in one of Correggio's, as she gazes on the infant on her knee, she makes us feel how the light beams from Him.[45] It is the very hush of silence around her and within her, which is the essence of the lesson of her life, the *being* which is at the heart of all the *doing*. The silence is not the silence of emptiness or stagnation, but the hush of a tide "too full for sound or foam."[46] The quietness is the quietness of a strong will resolutely offered up, rather than of a weak will easily yielded. The passiveness is the passiveness of strength enduring; not of helplessness submitting, not of the lifeless victim, but of the willing sacrifice. The retirement is the self-effacement of one who could face for hours a ferocious mob, standing by the cross of her Son. The silence is the silence of the voice capable of the Magnificat.

There is indeed another reason for not approaching the subject in words at all; the deep sense of inadequacy in the writer; and the example of the silence of the heart closest to the mystery. It is so certain that all we say must be imperfect; it is so possible that it may be mistaken! But this is a reason which might silence us on any high spiritual or moral theme. We can only reverently study and humbly say what we have learned, through the searching of sacred Scriptures enforced on us by the lips of the Master, and trust that the truth we learn, and try to utter, may help those who need it, and not hinder those who have learned more.

45. The Holy Family, by Raphael, in the Louvre, and by Correggio in the Dresden Gallery. The Italian painter and architect, Raphael, lived from 1483–1520. The Italian painter, Correggio, lived from 1489–1534.

46. This quote is from the second verse of Lord Alfred Tennyson's 1889 poem, "Crossing the Bar."

II.

THE ANGELICAL SALUTATION AND THE RESPONSE

In the story of the Holy Child Jesus, we seem to touch again the childhood of the world.* The story is taken up, not from the last chapter of the earlier history, but from the first. It is not a mere reformation or restoration, but a new creation which is dawning on the world. Yet this new creation is not the superseding but the fulfilment of the old; no mere destroying it as a failure, but the breathing into it of a new life.

The ancient world of the Sons of the Morning opens again to us—that ancient world to which our human world was so new; yet is itself ever young with immortal youth, while our world is growing old.

Heaven and earth are blended again. The angels come and go naturally, as if the intercourse had never been broken. They are heard singing in the sky; one alone, and then a multitude; singing in words the shepherds understand. They are indeed "afraid," stricken with the awe which always characterizes a real manifestation of the supernatural. But they understand. The voices once heard, there is no perplexity about the language. "The tongues of Angels" do not share the confusion of Babel. We have traveled back beyond Babel into Paradise; the Angels are there, coming and going among men; only the flaming swords are gone.

And so with Gabriel and that first "Ave." He is "sent from God to Nazareth, the little town of Galilee, to a virgin espoused to a man named Joseph, of the house and lineage of David;" the royal house, from which in its deepest humiliation had never died out the expectation that from it was to arise one day a King, greater than Solomon. "And the virgin's name was Mary."

The Angel came in beside her where she was, and he spoke to her in quiet words and tones that she alone was to hear.

"Una voce modesta
Forse qual che fu dal Angelo a Maria."[47]

---

47. Dante, *Purgatorio*, xiv.

*"The Feast of the Annunciation may well be called the Feast of the Incarnation. Then our redemption began. . . . We cannot enough praise Mary, that high and noble creature."— MARTIN LUTHER. [To cope with her grief following the death of her husband in 1868, Charles translated Luther's work *Watchwords for the Warfare of Life* (New York: Dodd, 1869).]

"Hail!" he said, "rejoice," "welcome." Heaven was open again, welcoming and pouring its joy into earth. It tasks any of our languages to render the fullness of the two words of this Salutation, the χαιρε κεχαριτωμενη.

The two words are so allied, they seem, like a double star, to radiate into infinite and intertwining vistas of light and joy.

Joy, grace, love, the grace of all beautiful creatures, the graciousness and charity and light of Heaven are in them. "Highly favoured" seems too external and courtly; "full of grace" perhaps scarcely expresses the freshness of the new tide of joy and life poured in, however full of grace that soul had been before. Probably, however, the words were not Greek words at all, but some ancient provincial popular Aramaic speech, such as is not extinct even now, it is said, among the secluded valleys of the Lebanon; perhaps the heavenly "Hail" was akin to the usual Oriental greeting of "Peace be with thee." But, whatever the words were, being, necessarily in the first form they reached human ears, a translation of the original in "the tongues of angels," they doubtless meant more than can be compacted into the "tongues of men." "*Hail! rejoice!*" thou that hast reason above all to rejoice, "*the Lord is with thee.*" An echo of the promise of "Emmanuel" which must have been so well known in her own house and lineage of David.[48] "*Blessed art thou among women,*" Christian art has lavished its richest treasures in picturing that greeting. The majesty and radiant beauty of the Heavenly Messenger, glowing from the presence of God; the purity, grace, and simplicity of the maiden. It was a message of infinite joy; Heaven pouring into earth the deepest fountain of its own eternal bliss. But to Mary this first impact of the Infinite brought trouble and agitation—as a sea agitated by winds, as an army thrown into disorder, as a people in tumult. It is the word used to express the agitation from which our Lord would guard His disciples when He was leaving them. "Let not your heart be troubled," and it is a more emphatic form of the word. She was "greatly troubled;" and it is in this tumult of her thoughts that we get the first glimpse of the strength and self-control of her character, the power of silence, the dialogues that could go on unspoken in the inner world of that lowly, lofty soul until the right moment came for words. She "reasoned within herself" what this Salutation might be. She needed the quieting "Fear not" as much as the shepherds.

The Annunciation was to bring transcendent joy to her, new life to the world. Her name was to be blessed by countless lips throughout the ages.

---

48. The much-debated question of the harmonizing of the two genealogies is not one to be entered on here.

But the first steps of that path of blessing were steps into such isolation with God as can scarcely have been known by any other human spirit. The benedictions, the felicitations, of the ages rest on Mary, the mother of Jesus, but she stands before us ever as the Blessed Virgin as well as the Blessed Mother, the type of lowly, lofty, pure, self-possessed maidenhood as well as of gracious motherhood.

Absorbing as were the joys and sorrows, the duty and the devotion to her Son, and linked as she is through Him to all the generations, she learned first to stand alone, to be *herself*, the one unique creature God meant her to be. God does not indeed ever create souls in batches. Each personality is unique, and so essentially itself, called by its own individual name, that its loss would make a gap in the harmony of the worlds, clearly perceptible to Him who listens to all. It is significant that our Lord in addressing Mary, twice calls her not mother but "woman," as if recognizing and honouring not only the immortal relationship, but the distinct womanly personality and character.

The great prophets have, indeed, again and again learned or begun their mission in the wildernesses. Moses, St. John the Baptist, and St. Paul had their Horeb, their desert, their Arabia, until "the day of their showing forth;" but with Mary the solitude was the deeper solitude in the midst of the home. Walking along the common paths, doing the common duties, yet with the soul alone, isolated in the solitude of an unutterable mystery—a mystery which was to be the redemption of the world, but was for the time known to her alone. To comprehend the beauty of her soul, to realize the possibilities involved in her life for all maidenhood and motherhood, for all women, we must first recognize her isolation, her election, her setting apart for the fulfilment of this great mystery of love and sacrifice, designed before the world began, revealed immediately the race had fallen.

"The Lord is with thee," "the Holy Ghost shall come upon thee, and the power of the Highest shall overshadow thee," had indeed for Mary a depth of mystery none else can comprehend. Her response involved a grace and a surrender none else can fathom. But the moral and spiritual side of that grace and that surrender, all that made her not an exception, but an example and type of perfected womanhood, is involved in those two sentences: the Salutation from heaven to earth: the response from earth to heaven.

Gabriel's "*The Lord is with thee*" turns aside the fiery swords which barred the gates of paradise, and begins to rend all the separating veils and walls of partition.

Mary's "*Behold the Handmaid of the Lord*" breaks the echo of Eve's distrust, whilst it fulfils her highest aspirations.* The "Practise of the Presence of God"[49] is the starting-point and the goal, the original and continual beginning, the high and perpetual end, the root and fruit of Mary's religion. Doubtless this did not begin for her with the angelical salutation. The spirit was prepared for the gift. The greeting and the grace were given to one already well known in the Presence where Gabriel stood.

Yet every fresh step upward in spiritual life must begin in a fresh direct communion with the Source of life: as every new widening of the path of blessing begins with the new entering in at that strait gate of lowly obedience. And every fresh revelation of the presence of God—every fresh draught from the fountain of life—must issue in a fresh surrender of the whole being to God.

Isolation with God, with her as with each of us, must be the secret of all true service of man; subjection to God the secret of all true freedom of soul. Gabriel's *"The Lord is with thee,"* and Mary's *"Behold the handmaid of the Lord"*—between these two poles of Divine communion and complete self-sacrifice all the highest spiritual life must vibrate.

Source: Elizabeth Rundle Charles, *Ecce Ancella Domini* (London: Society for Promoting Christian Knowledge, 1894), 17–31.

STUDY QUESTIONS

1. How do these commentators fill in the gaps or silences in Mary's story? Are these attempts effective? Creative? Helpful? Why or why not?
2. How do the nineteenth-century writers use the story of Eve (Gen. 1–3) in their interpretation of the Virgin Mary? What theological points are made in the use of Eve in discussions of Mary?

49. *Practice of the Presence of God* was written by Brother Lawrence (Nicolas Herman, c. 1605–1691), a lay brother in a Carmelite monastery in Paris. He stressed the importance of being aware of God's presence in even the most mundane tasks of life. This book is often republished. One nineteenth-century edition was published in London by J. Masters in 1855.

*One of the most significant and lovely of all the living pictures in the *Divina Commedia* is that of Eve, restored and glorified, and beautiful with the beauty of heaven, at the feet of Mary:
"La piaga che Maria richiuse ed unse
Quella ch' è tanto bella da' suoi piedi
E colei che l' aperse e la punse."
Paradiso, xxxii. 6.

3. What is the highest goal of spiritual formation according to the women writing on Mary? How do their goals compare to current understandings of the goals of spiritual formation?

4. Read John 2:1–11 and John 19:16–30, where Jesus calls his mother "woman." How do the commentators explain these passages? What troubled them about the passages? Is this still a problem for current readers of the text? Why or why not?

5. Several writers use church liturgies, lectionaries, major feasts, and corporate prayers in their discussions of Mary. How does their church context influence their interpretations? What does this emphasis on worship say about their purpose in reading and studying these biblical texts?

2

Mary and Martha of Bethany:
Spirituality in the Workplace

Introduction

There are three scenes involving Mary and Martha of Bethany in the gospels of Luke and John. The first scene takes place in Martha's home, and is recorded in Luke 10:38–42. Martha busied herself preparing a meal for Jesus and his disciples, while Mary sat and listened to Jesus' teaching. Martha asked Jesus to intervene and have Mary help with the preparations. Jesus told Martha that she was troubled with many things while Mary had "chosen that good part which shall not be taken away from her."

In John 11:1–40 we find the sisters concerned over the grave illness of their brother, Lazarus. They sent for Jesus to come and heal Lazarus. Jesus stayed away until Lazarus was dead, arriving in Bethany four days after he was buried. Martha, and later Mary, told Jesus that if he had come sooner her brother would not have died. Martha made a clear statement of faith in Jesus as the Messiah that paralleled that of Peter found in the other gospels. Jesus accompanied Mary and Martha to Lazarus's tomb, where, after weeping with the sisters, he raised Lazarus from the dead.

In John 12:1–8 Jesus was the guest of honour at a supper in Bethany. Martha served, Lazarus was also at the table, and Mary anointed Jesus' feet with ointment. Jesus commended Mary's action in response to Judas's criticism that the expensive spikenard could have been sold to feed the poor. Jesus' defense of Mary hinted that his death was at hand.

The selections in this chapter highlight how the stories of Martha and Mary helped nineteenth-century women to reflect upon the nature of the spiritual life. Most nineteenth-century interpreters noted the obvious differences between the two sisters, yet emphasized that both Mary and Martha were loved by Jesus. Sarah Hale, though not included in this chapter, summarized this kind of reflection well in her biographical dictionary of women.

> The sisters were of one mind in the reverence and love they bore him [Jesus]; yet the characters of the two are in striking contrast—Martha was active, Mary contemplative. Martha seems to have been a creature of impulse; Mary was slower of apprehension, and, of course, less sudden in her resolves and movements. Martha had the most fervent faith; Mary the most humble piety. "Jesus loved Martha and her sister, and Lazarus." What a beautiful illustration is here! Showing that the sweet, pure affections of domestic life are sanctified by the best blessing of heaven.[1]

A different estimation of the two sisters' abilities and differences can be found in the writings of Irish Catholic Catherine McAuley. McAuley noted that the differences between Mary and Martha had traditionally been used to characterize the divisions between two kinds of sisters in monastic communities. The highly educated Mary-like choir sisters were often involved in education, medical care or administration, and chanting the liturgy. The less-educated Martha-like lay sisters were in the domestic realm and recited the rosary, litanies, and other prayers in the vernacular in common. McAuley herself valued the vocations of both the Marthas and Marys: "the functions of Martha should be done for Him as well as the choir duties of Mary . . . He requires that we should be shining lamps giving light to all around us. How are we to do this if not by the manner we discharge the duties of Martha?"[2]

Like Hale and McAuley, the authors excerpted below all recognized the contrast between the sisters. They did not all agree on the characteristics of the sisters, nor on which sister made the better example for their contemporaries. Luke 10 was an important passage for nineteenth-century women to think through carefully. Martha did what they did. Each author in some way worked to redeem Martha's active busyness since they closely identified with her hospitable concerns. They tried to understand what Jesus meant when he appeared to rebuke those very attitudes as faults.

Because these nineteenth-century women interpreters were so sympa-

---

1. Sarah Hale, *Woman's Record; or, Sketches of All Distinguished Women, from the Creation to A.D. 1854* (New York: Harper & Brothers, 1855), 130.

2. *Retreat Instructions of Mother Mary Catherine McAuley,* ed. Mary Bertrand Degan (Westminster, MD: Newman, 1952), 159. See also Elizabeth M. Davis, "McAuley, Catherine (1778–1841)," in *Handbook of Women Biblical Interpreters,* ed. Marion Ann Taylor and Agnes Choi (Grand Rapids: Baker Academic, 2012), 352–54.

thetic to Martha, it is important to ask whether the gospel story transformed them, or whether they transformed the gospel story to conform to their own ideas of what a spiritual woman should be. Some authors transformed Martha's practice of hospitality into a nineteenth-century affair with descriptions of her white table cloths and choicest foods. Yet they also applied Jesus' rebuke of Martha to these same practices. In her commentary on Luke 10 (not included in this chapter) Mary Cornwallis applied the passage in this way:

> Were this simple, but interesting narration properly studied and applied, it would set aside that profusion, and useless decoration of the table, which renders a dinner visit in high-life a sacrifice of some hours, and which, if it do not lead to surfeit and intemperance, at least consumes time which might be more profitably employed.[3]

Hospitality took on a particular cultural form in these writers' minds, and they saw and heard the gospel story in light of their cultural setting.

The women authors answered questions raised and filled gaps in the gospel stories using their experience, their understanding of other parts of Scripture, their theological knowledge, and their imaginations. Some commonly asked questions included why Martha was listed as the head of the house in Luke 10:38, and how Simon the leper (listed as the host of the banquet given in Jesus' honor in Matthew 26 and Mark 14) was related to Martha, Mary, and Lazarus. Because Simon is not named in John 12, and Martha, Mary, and Lazarus are not named in Matthew 26 or Mark 14, bringing Simon into the family at Bethany involves harmonizing the gospel accounts. This practice of harmonizing the gospel accounts was a key strategy used by the women authors to fill in gaps in stories.

The integration of interior spirituality and the active life was an important application of the studies of Martha and Mary for nineteenth-century women. The active life was necessary, but a deep interior life provided them with inner strength and resolve to actively do their daily household work. The gospel texts spoke into the reality of their own lives, and the lives of their readers. Their applications of these texts thus give us glimpses into their nineteenth-century lives and thought.

The excerpts on Martha and Mary of Bethany begin with three spiritual biographies by Copley, Balfour, and McFadyen. Each larger biographical

---

3. Mary Cornwallis, *Observations, Critical, Explanatory, and Practical, on the Canonical Scriptures*, 2nd ed., vol. 4 (London: Baldwin, Cradock, and Joy, 1820), 134.

work has a different focus, with Balfour's essay focusing on Mary and Martha in some detail. McFadyen fictionalized the life of Jesus, with the Bethany family appearing as other characters surrounding Jesus. Woosnam, M. G., and Smith wrote sermons for girls and women on Mary and Martha based on their work in Bible classes or Mothers' Meetings.

ESTHER HEWLETT COPLEY (1786–1851)

Consecrated Abilities

Esther Copley was the author of more than 40 books including popular cookbooks and household manuals, as well as books for youth and young adults on the Bible.[4] Copley was the youngest daughter of a wealthy silk manufacturer, Peter (Pierre) Beuzeville and his wife, Mary (Marie) Meredith, both of French Huguenot descent. In April 1809, she married James Hewlett, an Anglican curate in Oxford. They had three sons and two daughters. After the death of her husband, she married William Copley, a Baptist minister in Oxford, in 1827. He was an alcoholic, and to assist him with his congregation in Eythorne, Kent, Esther Copley wrote his sermons and managed the congregation. She also used the earnings from her writings to supplement the family income. William Copley left both his wife and the church at Eythorne in 1843. She stayed in the village until her death in 1851.

Copley's *A History of Slavery and Its Abolition* (1836), written for children, is presently considered her most significant work. *Scripture Biography* (1835), the work excerpted here, was written with the aim of aiding readers in their spiritual lives. The book presents all the named characters in the Bible arranged alphabetically with the view to "point[ing] out such hints of instructions as they appear calculated to suggest."[5] The entries for Martha and Mary of Bethany are separate; only the entry on Martha is included here.

Copley was interested in why Martha asked Jesus to have her sister help

---

4. For further information on Copley see Heather Weir, "Copley, Esther Beuzeville Hewlitt (1786–1851)," in Taylor and Choi, *Handbook*, 138–41.

5. Esther Copley, *Scripture Biography: Comprehending All the Names Mentioned in the Old and New Testaments* (London: Sunday School Union, 1835), iv.

her, and why Jesus rebuked Martha. Copley and other nineteenth-century women saw domestic duties as a part of their identities as women, so felt there must have been something other than the actual duties themselves that led to Martha's rebuke. Copley found Martha's faith and affectionate spirit to be her redemptive qualities. She commended both Martha and Mary for serving "according to their various abilities."

MARTHA—WHO BECOMES BITTER;
MISTRESS; or, THAT TEACHES.

Martha, the Sister of Mary and Lazarus, resided with them in the village of Bethany, about fifteen furlongs from Jerusalem. This family was honoured with the peculiar intimacy of our Lord, and often entertained him at their dwelling.

Martha is uniformly mentioned first; she was probably the eldest sister, and appears to have had the principal management of household affairs. Her active stirring disposition led her to take pleasure in that kind of employment. Her ardent love to her Saviour and her Friend induced her to consecrate it to his service in hospitably ministering to his comfort and that of his followers; but, like every worldly pursuit, however lawful, there was a danger of its being carried to excess—in unnecessary pomp and splendour—in irritation of temper—and in a decay of spirituality of mind. In these respects Martha was endangered: and on one occasion she received from the Lord a pointed, yet gentle, admonition. In one of his recesses from public labour, Jesus and his train visited the beloved family at Bethany, and, while provisions were being prepared for their entertainment, his "doctrine dropped as the rain and distilled as the dew" [Deut. 32:2] on the happy circle that surrounded him. Mary was one of them:—with great delight she sat at the feet, and listened to the instructions of the great Teacher sent from God. Martha, too, would gladly have been there, but domestic cares pressed hard upon her, she "was cumbered with much serving"—perhaps needlessly perplexed and distracted in her solicitude to provide a sumptuous entertainment, as an expression of her high and affectionate sense of the dignity and condescension of her guest. At length she found herself harassed and overwhelmed in accomplishing the details of her too hospitable outline, and even admitted a degree of envy of the tranquillity her sister was enjoying at the Saviour's feet. With a very unbecoming petulance, she addressed her expostulation to Him, as if he had encouraged Mary in inconsideration and neglect of domestic duties—"Lord, dost thou not care that my sister hath left me to serve alone? bid her, therefore, that she come and help me." And Jesus answered and said unto her, "Martha, Martha, thou art careful and troubled about many things, but one thing is needful, and Mary hath chosen that good part which shall not be taken away from her." Weighty and solemn admonition! may it ever be present to our minds, and influence us to live in habitual superiority over the multitude of trifles which engross the attention of worldly men; and so to regulate our necessary and lawful attention to temporal concerns, as to keep all in subserviency to true religion,—that "one thing" which is absolutely and indispensably "needful," in order to our enjoying or improving life, and being prepared for death, judgment, and eternity.

The ardent affectionate spirit of Martha was next called forth, and displayed in tender solicitude for her beloved brother. Lazarus was seized with dangerous sickness—his sisters immediately applied to their best friend, no doubt expecting that he would immediately come to their aid. But that friend treated them with apparent neglect. He abode two days still in the place where he was, and then moved towards Bethany with a pace little calculated to satisfy the impatient anxiety of Martha. While Jesus delayed, Lazarus died. Still, however, when Martha at length heard of her Saviour's approach, she hastened forth to meet him, and, with a strange mixture of unbelieving reproach and ardent faith, addressed him, "Lord, if thou hadst been here, my brother had not died. But I know that even now, whatsoever thou wilt ask of God, God will give it thee. Jesus saith unto her, Thy brother shall rise again." Martha replied, "I know that he shall rise again in the resurrection of the last day. Jesus saith unto her, I am the Resurrection and the Life. He that believeth on me, though he were dead, yet shall he live: and whosoever liveth and believeth on me, shall never die. Believest thou this? Martha said Yea, Lord, I believe that thou art the Christ, the Son of God, which should come into the world." After this noble confession of faith, Martha secretly summoned her sister, who came forth to meet the Master, and they went together to the tomb of Lazarus, where the glory of the incarnate God was strikingly manifested in calling forth the dead to life.

Martha is mentioned on one occasion more. When Jesus, six days before the last passover, dined in the house of Simon the leper, the family of Bethany was there, each displaying characteristic tokens of their love and gratitude. The re-animated Lazarus sat at meat near his benefactor, to listen to the gracious words that proceeded out of his mouth. The devout and contemplative Mary anointed him with costly ointment; and the cheerful busy Martha thought herself honoured in being among those that served her beloved Lord. Happy are they who thus, according to their various abilities, are found consecrating their all to Him who loved them, and gave himself for them. Luke 10:38–42. John 11, 12:1–3.

Source: Esther Copley, *Scripture Biography: Comprehending All the Names Mentioned in the Old and New Testaments* (London: Sunday School Union, 1835), 421–23.

CLARA LUCAS BALFOUR (1808–1878)

Action and Contemplation

Clara Lucas Balfour was a popular British speaker, writer, and social justice activist.[6] Balfour wrote four books specifically on women, one of which was *Women of Scripture* (1847). *Women of Scripture* examined various women of the Bible beginning with a chapter on Eve and others of the patriarchal period and ending with a chapter on Priscilla and Phoebe. Balfour highlighted the virtues of the biblical characters, holding them up as examples to her readers.

The title of Balfour's essay on the Bethany sisters, "Action and Contemplation," indicates the key characteristics Balfour thought the sisters displayed. Like Copley, she stressed the sisters' character differences, arguing that they served God differently. Balfour read Scripture carefully, filling in gaps in the gospel accounts with insights from life and careful attention to context. For example, she inferred from the earlier part of Luke 10 that many disciples were with Jesus in Bethany at that time, so that serving all of them dinner overwhelmed Martha's household. According to Balfour, Luke 10 displays Mary's strength and Martha's weakness, whereas John 11 displays Martha's strength and Mary's weakness. While Balfour accepted the differences in character seen in Mary and Martha, she argued that Lazarus's character, a combination of active and contemplative, represented the ideal of the spiritual life.

---

6. For more information on Balfour and *Women of Scripture* see the chapter on Mary, the Mother of Jesus.

Action And Contemplation.— The Sisters Of Bethany

AMONG the devout women of the Gospel times, who ministered to our Lord, we read of two sisters whom he condescended to honour with his gracious friendship; of whom it is specially said, "Jesus loved Martha, and her sister, and Lazarus, their brother." These three comprised a family who dwelt at Bethany, and whose dwelling was consecrated by the Divine presence of the Redeemer as their frequent guest. Oh! happy family that had such a friend! Oh! hallowed dwelling that had such a visitant!

It has reasonably been conjectured, that Martha was the eldest of this family, therefore, presided over the domestic arrangements; and also that Lazarus was youngest; and as he was evidently a believer in our Lord, honoured by his special tender love, and yet did not follow publicly as a disciple, it has been thought that he was afflicted with weak health, thus prevented joining in the sacred train who followed the Redeemer's footsteps.

The village of Bethany was situated near Jerusalem, in a lovely retired spot at the base of Mount Olivet. And the first introduction we have to these sisters is an account of our Lord's visiting them. "Now it came to pass, as they went, that they entered a certain village; and a certain woman named Martha, received them into her house."* The history of this visit has given rise to much misapprehension in reference to the character of Martha. Some have ventured to suppose that she was a narrow-minded woman, so absorbed in the petty details of her domestic duties, that she had no relish for the Redeemer's teaching, no soul to appreciate his words; no spirituality to rise superior to the earthly cares and troubles of the passing hour. This conclusion is as unjust as it is superficial. The fact that our Lord loved Martha is the highest evidence of her spiritual excellence; that her house was open to Him and his disciples, is a proof of her generous hospitality; that she cared for the wants of her guests herself, demonstrates her active benevolence; that she laboured to promote the comfort of others at the sacrifice of her own ease, shows she was completely free from the vice of selfishness.

Among the excellent of the earth, there is, however, great diversity of character. . . . As if to show us excellency of different kinds and to teach us to honour both, the fine contrast of these sisters of Bethany is presented to our contemplation. They illustrate the active and the meditative character,—are pure specimens of each, and as these two principles of action and contem-

*Luke 10:38

84

plation are here carried out by human beings, there is also shown for our instruction the failings incidental to their exercise.

It was consonant with the character of the Divine Redeemer, that he should employ every moment in instructing those around Him; and, therefore, when He sought the hospitality of Martha's house, He continued the sublime instructions He had been previously giving to his disciples. A new hearer was added to the throng who listened to his gracious words,—Mary, the younger sister of the generous, active Martha. She "sat at Jesus' feet, and heard his word." With what lowly reverence of humble prostration; with what rapt attention she sat at his feet, and hung upon his utterances!—her heart kindling with the consecrated fire of his sacred thoughts, her mind sublimed from all earthly contemplation, was soaring to celestial heights, and expanding in the atmosphere of his Divinity. What to her were surrounding circumstances? the crowded house, the gathering throng? her sister cumbered with much serving? These were all unnoted, unremembered. One face beamed before her gaze, and shut out all other objects; one voice filled her eager ear, and excluded all other sounds. It was the absorbing ecstasy of devout attention.

Meanwhile, Martha, the diligent, the hospitable, the careful, the active Martha, was ministering to the physical wants of the company gathered in her house. It is exceedingly probable, there was a very numerous assembly. Our Lord had very recently called and sent out a great number of disciples; these had, many of them, returned to Him again, after their labours in different places;* and it was immediately after delivering to them one of his divinest parables—the good Samaritan—that Jesus, attended by them, went to Bethany and entered Martha's house. The care of this generous woman was immediately exercised on behalf of the guests, and it is quite probable her active zeal for their wants shut out meditation from her mind. It is well worthy of remark, that the Saviour did not expostulate with Martha about her careful and laborious hospitality, until the anxiety of her spirit hurried her into error. While she was "cumbered with much serving," laudably desirous to promote the comfort of all, her anxious eyes alighted on the still, thoughtful face of the adoring Mary. She was instantly filled with the desire that Mary should be similarly engaged with herself; that she should manifest her love by the same course of action; and in the haste, which was a characteristic of her active temperament, she falls into the impropriety of appealing murmuringly to the Redeemer. "Lord, dost thou

*Luke 10

85

not care that my sister hath left me to serve alone? bid her, therefore, that she help me." There was certainly anger, as well as presumption, mingled in Martha's precipitate remark. She forgot for a moment to whom she spoke; and what was the cause of Mary's quitting for awhile all domestic cares. It is the peculiar failing of active practical people, that they sometimes do not give themselves time to think. Had Martha thought, she would have known that it was the best mode of dividing the attention of the family to their guests; that while one sister served the disciples, the other should devote her undivided attention to the Master of the assembly. The error of Martha, therefore, was not in her much serving, but in her hasty murmuring at her sister; reflecting by implication even on the Redeemer himself, "Dost thou not care?" This precipitate spirit called down our Lord's gentle rebuke, "Martha, Martha, thou art careful and troubled about many things;" there is tenderness as well as force in the repetition of the name,—it is the earnest remonstrance of love, regretting that so many minor things should have power to trouble her, and disturb the equanimity and benevolence of her spirit; and then our Lord continued, "But one thing is needful;" that is, care, trouble, anxiety; all should merge in one unquenchable desire for the "inheritance that fadeth not away" [1 Pet. 1:4]. An assured hope of that blissful inheritance once obtained, is sufficient to banish all trouble and anxiety on minor matters, and give the soul that "peace of God, which passeth all understanding" [Phil. 4:7]. Earthly things are then estimated at their true value, and are not permitted to disturb the calm repose of the spirit. Then followed our Lord's vindication of the younger sister: "Mary hath chosen that better part, that shall not be taken away from her." Earthly disappointments are as numerous as earthly occupations; every social duty, every human pursuit, every relative engagement, every personal employment, all are alike liable to failure, change, error, annoyance. But those who choose the better part, of fixing the supreme affections of the heart, and the aspirations of the mind, on heavenly themes, not only possess a treasure that no earthly power can take from them, but are shielded with a panoply divine from the corroding influence of petty cares and vexations. This better part, this spiritual frame of mind, does not exonerate or unfit for the due performance of earthly duties, and the discharge of human responsibilities, but it gives a calmness to the soul—a freedom from over-anxiety, which is only to be thus attained.

It is manifest that this lovely tranquility and sweetness were displayed by Mary on this occasion. Martha's complaint was public;—she appealed not to Mary, but to Jesus. It is quite likely this was not done out of unkindness.

Martha most probably saw that her sister was so absorbed, that all private communication would fail to rouse her,—that every faculty was locked up in adoring attention to one object; and, therefore, the common-sense way of recalling Mary to the ordinary pursuits of life was to appeal to Him who held her faculties spell-bound by his words. Still, this mode of complaining would have roused the anger of an undisciplined, earthly mind; but Mary, called from her holy contemplation of Jesus, shows the efficacy of his teaching, and manifests the "better part," by making no reply to her sister's complaint against herself. Angry temper has little power to disturb one who feels the serene influence of the Spirit of God spread abroad in her heart. That influence none can "take away:"—public complaints, though uttered by lips we love, and therefore hard indeed to bear, have no power to disturb the peaceful repose of that soul whose thoughts and desires are fixed on the Rock of Ages.

The next time these excellent sisters are presented to our attention is in connexion with one of the most stupendous miracles our Saviour wrought; and it is interesting to observe in that affecting narrative, from the pen of another Evangelist,* how the characteristic peculiarities of each are exhibited on the occasion. It is still the active Martha and the contemplative Mary. Lazarus, their brother, is sick, and the sisters, having probably tried every ordinary means for his recovery, sent to Jesus the pathetic message, "Lord, behold, he whom thou lovest is sick." The Redeemer knew that the event of this sickness would be to the glory of God, and therefore, somewhat to the surprise of his disciples, He remained two days in the place where He was after having received the message. At the conclusion of this time, our Lord said, "Let us go into Judea." To this the disciples, however, remonstrated by saying, "Master, the Jews of late sought to stone thee, and goest thou thither again?" The Redeemer answered their objection, and assigned as a principal reason for the journey, that Lazarus was dead, referring to some mighty work that should be effected in consequence. It shows the estimate in which the Saviour held Lazarus, that He should speak of him to the disciples by the dear, familiar term, "Our friend"; and it evidences the love generally felt by the disciples towards Lazarus, that Thomas, on hearing of his death, should exclaim, in the abandonment of grief, "Let us also go, that we may die with him!" [John 11:16]. It seemed as if the fine qualities of each sister must have met in the brother, and won all hearts.

We can imagine with what haste and silence the melancholy journey

*John 11

was performed. The hospitable house at Bethany was filled with sympathizing friends come to console the sisters. Yet, while they were not ungrateful for the condolence offered, there was ONE face they longed to see,—ONE voice they yearned to hear; and that ONE being absent, all consolation seemed to fall merely on the ear, and never reached the heart. Those only who have known what it is to meet a great affliction when the dearest of all friends is absent, can understand the sense of loneliness and helplessness in their sorrow, which the sisters of Bethany must have felt. But the tidings reached them that Jesus was coming; and no sooner does Martha hear that announcement, than with characteristic activity, "went and met him." But Mary, overwhelmed—dispirited,—her deep heart oppressed with its load of sorrow—she sat *still* in the house. It was the characteristic, and the failing also, of her thoughtful temperament to brood over sorrow. Meanwhile, Martha had met the compassionate Redeemer, and her first exclamation was, "Lord, had thou been here my brother had not died." This remark shows the firmness of this distinguished woman's faith in the divinity of the Saviour; but while it glows with the faith of the fervent disciple, it also contains the tender complaining remonstrance of an afflicted sister,—I know and own thy power; oh! why was it not put forth for me? Martha had heard of the many wondrous words of her Lord and Master, and probably seen many manifestations of his gracious power. Strangers, unbelievers, reprobates, had been benefited by his miraculous works; the sick and afflicted were constantly relieved, while Lazarus, his "friend" had died. Martha's faith, however, is not by any means weakened by her sorrow, for she continues in a lofty strain of piety to say, "But I know, that even now, whatsoever thou wilt ask of God, God will give it thee." Jesus replied to these remarks by an assurance that her brother should "rise again." Martha, ignorant of the Saviour's meaning, answered by stating her belief in the final resurrection of the body at the last day, when our Lord, with majestic dignity, made that glorious announcement so full of hallowed consolation,—"I am the resurrection and the life; he that believeth in me, though he were dead, yet shall he live: and whosoever liveth and believeth in me, shall never die. Believest thou this?" And she said unto him, "Yeah, Lord, I believe that thou art the Christ, the Son of God, which should come into the world." Throughout the whole Gospel history, there is not a conversation more rich and exquisite than this. It contains the condensed essence of the facts and purport of the Redeemer's mission, and of the faith required in reference to those facts. Those who love to attach a groveling idea to Martha's character, would do well to consider her declaration of faith, as given in this sublime conversation.

It seems as if our Lord, on the conclusion of it, had asked for Mary.

Doubtless, Martha derived sweet consolation from the glorious words just uttered by Jesus, and with all the warmth and swiftness of her generous nature, she wished to communicate comfort to her sorrowing sister, and therefore she immediately hastened back to the house, and secretly called Mary, saying, "The Master is come, and calleth for thee." It is worthy of remark, that contemplative as Mary's character was, it did not ever degenerate into listlessness. It has been very beautifully said by a living writer, "Reflection is a flower of the mind, giving out wholesome fragrance; but reverie is the same flower when rank and running to seed."[7] Mary's were lofty, not supine thoughts, and therefore, when she heard that the Master called for her, "she arose quickly," and leaving the house, went to the place where Martha met him. She went from her dwelling silently as well as hastily, so that the Jews thought she was going to weep at her brother's grave. When the tender, meditative Mary came into the presence of the Saviour, all the floodgates of her soul gave way, and she sank at His feet, uttering the same pathetic remark as her sister, "Lord, if thou hadst been here, my brother had not died." What perfect harmony of faith was felt by these sisters, though their characters were so different! How affecting to the gentle Saviour must this unity of opinion and utterance have been! He could not but perceive that his absence was the greatest grief—an aggravation of their sorrow—the cause and climax, in their estimation, of their calamity. An absent Saviour is indeed the test of all afflictions; every evil may indeed, with justice, be feared in that dwelling where Jesus is not an inmate. His presence either preserves his people from evil, or sustains them under it. His absence is the blackness of despair.

Mary says no more, tears impede her utterance, her grief smites on the hearts of all beholders; the Jews who followed her hasty footsteps from the house, weep at the sight of her affliction; and Jesus—the ever compassionate Jesus—when he saw her brow bowed to the earth, tears streaming over that face which he had recently beheld lifting up to him with adoring rapture, lighted by seraphic love and faith; when he saw her prostrate beneath the load of grief, "he groaned in spirit and was troubled." How graciously the Lord of life condescended to sympathize with human emotions! He rebukes not the ecstasy of sorrow—he shares it;—

7. Balfour may have been referring to the poet Martin Farquhar Tupper (1810–1889); the quote is also attributed to Desiderius Erasmus (1469–1536).

"In every pang that rends the heart,
The Man of Sorrows has a part."[8]

The hallowed narrative of the mighty events that followed at the grave of Lazarus is familiar as household words to all; while the brief statement—so comprehensive in its brevity, so noble in its simplicity, so tender in its pathos—"Jesus wept!" is a record that has thrilled all hearts, and every Christian mourner has felt an interest in those tears: they fill the heart with a warm gush of tenderness; they bring Jesus beside every believer's grave; they recognize him as sorrowing over every bereavement of his faithful followers. Some may say, "Why did he weep when he came to remedy their affliction, to turn their sorrow to joy?" He wept for the sorrowing that Lazarus must have passed through, he wept for the anguish that the sisters felt. And thus it is even now; he sees our tears, and knows that we often weep when a speedy deliverance is at hand; that events which are for the glory of God and the benefit of man, are received by us with affliction and anguish: we mourn at we know not what; yet, though he sees the end from the beginning, knows what is for our real good, and orders all things accordingly, he compassionates our immediate sufferings; he doth not willingly afflict, but "like as a father pitieth his children, so the Lord pitieth them that trust in him" [Ps. 103:13]. The tears of Jesus flow for even the temporary afflictions of his people. Oh, what a faith is ours! how encouraging and preserving in the time of happiness! how soothing and sublime in the hour of sorrow!

At the grave we find each sister acting in conformity with the leading peculiarities of her respective character. Martha speaks of the time her brother had been dead, of the awful change that must have taken place in the beloved remains; her practical mind dwells on matter-of-fact details, until Jesus recalls to her recollection his promise, "Said I not unto thee, if thou wouldest believe thou shouldest see the glory of God?" We do not hear that Mary uttered a word, we can imagine her looking on with profound awe and reverence, as that solemn voice resounded through space, and was answered from the mansion of the dead. We can feebly imagine both sisters prostrate with speechless wonder and gratitude, when "he that was dead came forth." It was no time for words, but a moment that concentrated the emotions of a lifetime, "an ocean in a tear," "a whirlwind in a sigh."[9] They must have felt what the poet has so beautifully indicated;—

8. From the hymn "Where High the Heavenly Temple Stands" by Michael Bruce (c. 1764).

9. Lines from "Of Love," in Martin Farquhar Tupper, *Proverbial Philosophy* (London: Hatchard, 1856), 160. First published in 1838.

"——I lose myself in Him,
In light ineffable; come then, expressive Silence,
Muse his praise."[10]

This is not the final mention of the favored household of Bethany. Time passes on, and Jesus again visits that secluded village; this time He and his disciples are the guests of Simon the leper. The reunited, happy family are there also. A supper is made, and Martha, the ever-careful, the ever-active Martha, served. Lazarus, he who of all the human race had dwelt longest in the region of the dead, sat at the table with our Lord. No wonder that many of the Jews were gathered there, that they might see one who had been released from the icy bondage of the king of terrors, and restored to life and life's enjoyments. No wonder that the prejudiced and malignant priests, hardened in unbelief, "consulted that they might put Lazarus to death," as well as his Lord. The minds that were not convinced by such a manifestation, must have been utterly reprobate—"earthly, sensual, devilish" [James 3:15]. Mary had her part in this great assembly, and her deportment was, as ever, conformable with her enthusiastic, meditative character. Jesus was her one object of contemplation and reverence; where he was, she saw him only. And on this occasion, obtaining a place near him, while he sat at meat,* and having "an alabaster box of very precious ointment," anointed her Lord with it, pouring it on his sacred head, and also on his feet—those feet that were so prompt to move in succouring the distressed, that "went about, doing good," that had stood at her brother's grave—and, in the enthusiasm of her womanly tenderness, heedless of the wonder, the sneers, or the misconstruction of those around, when she had anointed him, she wrapped her hair about those hallowed feet, twined it as close as her love and faith were bound around his person and offices. "And the house was filled with the odour of the ointment." It was a grateful, as well as a pious and generous offering; the purity of heart which dictated the deed made it come up with a sweet savour to the Lord; he received the homage of his tender worshipper with an infinite complacency. Very different was the feeling in some of those who stood around. One of the Evangelists[†] says, "When the disciples saw it, they had indignation, saying, To what purpose

---

10. From "A Hymn," by James Thomson (1730).

*See Matthew 26 and John 12.
[†]Matthew 26

is this?" But the beloved disciple,[11] more particularly, tells who was the murmurer on the occasion;—"Judas Iscariot, who should betray him," said, "Why was not this ointment sold for three hundred pence, and given the poor? This he said, not that he cared for the poor, but because he was a thief, and had the bag, and bare what was put therein."* This reproach caused our Lord again to become the vindicator of Mary. He knew her heart,—the deep love and gratitude that made her present this costly offering to him, with such personal manifestations of tenderness. "She hath wrought a good work upon me," was his gracious announcement; and then, alluding to his approaching death, He said, "Against the day of my burying hath she kept this;" and then follows the declaration, "Verily I say unto you, Wheresoever this gospel shall be preached in the whole world, there shall also this, that this woman hath done, be told for a memorial of her." Happy, honoured Mary! well hadst thou profited by the teaching of thy Lord; well didst thou exhibit the better part so wisely chosen! Thy memorial shall never pass away; all reverential minds, all loving hearts, shall delight to contemplate thy piety; thy name shall ever be as ointment poured forth.

These admirable sisters, so finely contrasted—alike in principle, yet differing in temperament and manner, furnish a peculiarly instructive lesson. They teach us that excellence is of varied kinds; that we have no right to expect uniformity of manifestation. They show us also that the great error of active temperaments is rashness and want of thought; of meditative characters, a brooding, sombre tone of mind; each evils to be specially avoided: and perhaps the highest perfection of character that human beings by divine grace can attain is, when the contemplative and the practical unite in one individual: a profound mind to think, a ready, active power to practice;—this is a model which, though few perfectly arrive at, all would do well to strive after.

Source: Clara Lucas Balfour, *Women of Scripture* (London: Houlston & Stoneman, 1847), 281–302.

---

11. "The beloved disciple" refers to John, here assumed to be the author of the Gospel of John.

*John 12:4–6

NINA L. MCFADYEN (1865–1941)

....

The Happy Home in Bethany

American author Nina L. McFadyen was born in Maine to Isaac Archibald and Sophia Collins. The Archibald family moved to California where McFadyen met and married Michael McFadyen, a clergyman. The McFadyens had two sons and lived in Oakland, California. The preface to her book, *Stories from the Life of the Wonderful*, written by W. Kellaway describes the author as "aimiable and talented," a woman whose purpose in writing has been "to do good."[12]

McFadyen's *The Life of the Wonderful* is a fictionalized life of Christ that harmonized and amplified the various gospel accounts. She embellished the gospels by using biblical intertexts and her sanctified imagination. She created connections between the lives of minor gospel characters. Mary of Bethany and Jairus's daughter, whom she named Miriam, became friends who reflected spiritually upon the significance of Jesus' teaching and life. McFadyen often used female figures to retell and interpret the significance of Jesus' life and ministry.

In contrast to Balfour who characterized Mary as thinking and Martha as not thinking, McFadyen portrayed Martha as a thinking woman and Mary as the deeply feeling and slightly flighty woman.[13] McFadyen's Martha is the ideal woman of Proverbs 31, the "queen of housewives," whose "whole deportment [was] caretaking and business-like." She resolved the tension between the sisters in Luke 10 by having Mary confess that she had been thoughtless in not helping Martha and offering to take her place, so that she too could sit at the feet of Jesus. McFadyen presented a complex portrait of these women's spiritual lives. She dignified their work in the home and in the ministry of Jesus. She also stressed their ability to think theologically and respond lovingly as disciples of Jesus.

The Happy Home in Bethany

We have already been introduced to that lovely home in Bethany where Jesus so delighted to be, and much of his unemployed time was spent in that refuge.

---

12. *Stories from the Life of the Wonderful* (Los Angeles, 1897), ix.
13. This difference in the way women read the character of the two sisters was illustrated in the chapter introduction by Hale, paralleling McFadyen, and McAuley, paralleling Balfour.

LAZARUS, the elder of the family trio, was about the age of Jesus, and a most ardent friend. It would have been hard to find in all that country a nobler youth than he; his mild blue eye, beaming with love and tenderness; his whole face aglow with intelligence, and lit up with smiles which scattered cheer around him; his dignified and manly bearing, all aided to prepossess one in his favor. But his sunny disposition and devout religious character impressed one most of all.

MARTHA, the elder sister, was such a one as SOLOMON thought of when he wrote the Thirty-first chapter of Proverbs.[14] Her eye was keener than her brother's; her love no less tender, perhaps, but more matter-of-fact; her whole deportment caretaking and business-like.

But MARY—the lovely, gentle MARY—who can describe her? Lacking the deep thought and dignity of her brother and sister, there was yet in her a warm, tender love, a trustful disposition, a nature submissive to goodness, and a piety so deep and fervent as to lend a charm which won for her an entrance to every heart.

But some one might say: "Had these, then, no faults? That is generally the way those we read about are represented. They are not like ourselves, constantly doing things we ought not to do, beside making many mistakes."

We admit authors are apt to picture their favorites as faultless; but in the Scriptures we have only one hero, GOD's beloved SON. . . .

But these three of our story, the happy family of Bethany, had their faults, although they were almost undiscernible amid their many virtues, as a glimpse of a little incident from their daily life will show.

MARTHA, as already said, was a queen of housewives. Always busy, and planning for the entertainment and comfort of her guests and family, she made social enjoyment of secondary importance; and it was not until the household cares were gone, her guests refreshed by an inviting repast— which was never wanting at her table—and their comfort well attended to, that she would indulge in the friendly chat, so enjoyable to most persons.

It might not have been thus had MARY not a special delight and aptitude for the social entertainment of company; so that the more laborious work of preparing for the refreshment of guests seemed unavoidably to fall upon her sister. Not that MARY was unwilling to do her share of the serving; for her sympathetic nature and loving heart could never rest while another was burdened. But MARTHA, anxious to shield this darling sister from every wearisome duty, left to her only the lighter tasks, imposing on herself the

14. See Proverbs 31:10–31 which describes the *isseth hayil*, the noble woman.

94

heavier. Thus it was that MARY was sometimes thoughtless, and neglectful of the many household duties; while MARTHA grew weary, and a little impatient, under their heavy strain.

Of all who came to their home, there was none whom MARTHA loved to do for as she did for Jesus. For him she made the most tempting viands; for him she spread the snowiest cloth, and brought out the costliest and best dishes; the choicest fruits and flowers graced their table, when he was there. All that her inventive brain could think of, and all that her skillful hands could do, was done for Jesus.

But MARY sat at his feet and listened to his gracious words. Eyes and ears wide open, she was eager to catch the meaning of every word as he discoursed upon the Scriptures, or uttered some instructive parable.

On this particular day, JESUS had been alone much of the time, engaged in prayer; and when he came out in the cool of the evening, and seated himself with his disciples, and LAZARUS and MARY, they took occasion to ask him to teach them to pray, as JOHN had taught his disciples.[15]

"When ye pray, say, 'Our FATHER'"; said he. Then he taught them the necessity of praying with desire that his kingdom come; this was to be their first petition. "Also, pray to be forgiven; as ye have already forgiven those who have sinned against you. And ask to be led away from all temptation and evil."

He then told them of a man who had a friend visit him at midnight. The visitor was weary and hungry with his long journey; and his host was minded to give him some refreshment before he retired; but when he went to fetch it, he discovered there was not so much as a piece of bread in the house.

"However, there is my neighbor," he thought; "whom I have befriended so many times; I will go and ask him for the loan of three small loaves." It was some time before his neighbor, who was in a deep sleep, could be aroused; but finally he awoke.

"I can not arise and give thee; for it is dark, and the door is latched. Beside, my children are all asleep, and I do not wish to disturb them. If any noise should awaken them, they might be frightened, imagining some thief was prowling around;" he said, in response to his friend's request, and to his great astonishment. Nevertheless he kept on knocking and pleading, for he must have the bread; so at last, being wearied with his begging, the unwilling and disobliging neighbor arose and gave him as much as he needed.

---

15. In the dialogue following, McFadyen summarized the teaching of Jesus found in Luke 11:1–13.

"I say unto you," said JESUS, "though he would not give him because he was a friend; yet, because of his importunity, he gave him. So, if ye knock it shall be opened unto you; if ye ask it shall be given you: your heavenly Father is more willing to give good things unto his children, than earthly parents are to give good gifts unto theirs; and he knoweth ye have need of all these things."

All this time MARTHA had been busy preparing the evening meal; and MARY, absorbed in the wonderful words she was hearing, had not noticed the look of exhaustion on her sister's flushed countenance, as she went in and out arranging the table. Finally, she stopped at the door, and addressing JESUS, said, in a discontented and injured, if not a slightly reproachful tone:

"Lord! dost thou not care that my sister hath left me to serve alone? bid her, therefore, that she help me."

MARY flew to her sister's side, as she heard this, saying:

"Forgive me, my Sister! I was thoughtless of thy cares; and JESUS' conversation so charmed me, I forgot everything else. Sit thou down here, by the Master, and listen, while I take thy place;" and in a moment she was gone.

JESUS well knew the pure love that prompted this unusual anxiety, and fully appreciated it; but desiring that his presence should be a rest and refreshment to them, rather than a care, he looked upon her, as she leaned back wearily, and said:

"MARTHA, MARTHA! thou art careful and troubled about many things; but one thing is more needful to the longing soul than all these; and MARY hath chosen that good part. Though all things else perish and decay, this shall never be taken away from her."

And O, how the words of JESUS soothed that tired, loving heart, as she afterwards recalled them:

"Come unto me, all ye that labor and are heavy laden, and I will give you rest. Take my yoke upon you, and learn of me; for I am meek and lowly in heart; and ye shall find rest unto your souls. For my yoke is easy, and my burden is light" [Matt. 11:28–30].

[McFadyen told the story of the resurrection of Lazarus from the point of view of Mary and Martha. The following excerpts are fictional conversations set after this event, putting the teaching and acts of Jesus into the mouths of women who heard and watched him.]

Never was home happier than that of Bethany on the night of LAZARUS' return from the sepulchre. Long sat the sisters and talked with their brother and JESUS. We do not know certainly; but it is highly probable they conversed of the time when all the graves will be opened [see Matt. 27:52–53;

John 5:28–29], and the shadows flee away [Song of Songs 2:17]; when the night will be as the day, and the sun shall increase her light seven-fold [Isa. 30:26].

"Who ever knew love like this?" said MARY to MARTHA, that evening, when, having parted for the night from their brother and JESUS, they were in their room alone. "The Master has risked his life to gladden our hearts."

"How could I ever have questioned his friendship?" spake MARTHA. "It maketh me so ashamed when I think of my lack of faith, that I long to hide my face in the folds of his garment, and weep away my guilt."

"Yet he had no words of reproof for thee, my Sister; had he?" said MARY, questioningly.

"Nay, nay; I could have borne that better; but he hath done so bountifully for us, and hath so filled our cup with blessing, until it runneth over, that my heart knoweth not how to express itself for his favors."

"Do not chide thyself so severely;" said MARY, soothingly, as she threw her arms about her sister, who was sitting with great tears in her eyes.

"The disciples say it is ever so: that he loveth to bless;" continued MARY; "and only grieves when the people refuse to receive him. JOHN told me this evening how he longed to come to us even before he did; but that the glory might be the greater, and that there might be no doubt of our brother's death, he stayed away; for thou knowest, Sister, that the unbelieving Jews might have said that LAZARUS was only in a trance, if the loathsome stench from the sepulchre had not convinced them that decomposition had already begun to feed upon him.

"I know it; I know it all. O, to think he hath taken this long journey just for us; and to-night he looked especially weary!"

"PETER says the hatred of the Jews is so bitter against him that he must depart on the morrow, and LAZARUS thinks of going with him;" said MARY. "Those who can be ever near him must be wonderfully blessed;" she continued. "Gladly would I follow him from city to city, over rough roads and burning sands, making the hard ground my couch by night, if I could be always with him; and sweet would be the coarsest bread if it but had his blessing."

Between MARY and JAIRUS' little daughter MIRIAM, there had sprung up a most intimate friendship.[16] The same love and hope had bound them together in mutual sympathy, and one was often the guest at the other's home.

It was on one of these occasions, when MARY was visiting the family of

16. For Jairus's daughter see Matthew 9:18–26; Mark 5:35–43; Luke 8:40–56.

JAIRUS, in Capernaum, that she and MIRIAM sat by the seaside talking of JESUS.

"It was just here," said the sweet young girl, "where he stood one day when he began to teach the people, and the throng became so eager that he stepped into a boat and asked PETER to push out a little from the land. Just about where thou seest yonder white speck on the wave, was where they drew in a multitude of fishes. Over there, around that curve, was where he fed the five thousand persons; and at that extreme point in the distance, the herd of swine ran violently into the sea and were drowned."[17]

"Lovely JESUS!" said MARY; "chiefest among the many thousands of ISRAEL! always going about doing good: carrying our sorrows, and loading us with blessings! The sweetest lesson I learned at his feet was, that in all his goodness he but reveals to us the love of GOD. 'My FATHER worketh hitherto; now, I work,' [John 5:17] he once said; and: 'As the FATHER hath taught me, so I speak' [John 12:50]. 'The words are not mine; but his who sent me' [John 7:16]. Is it not blessed to know that the great GOD, to whom belongs all power, really loves us; and that all these wonderful cures and blessings which come by JESUS, is but the carrying out of the divine plan of mercy." ...

SPRING-TIME had now returned, with her bright-eyed flowers and lengthening days, and JESUS turns his face toward Jerusalem. LAZARUS had been with him much of the time during the last few months; hence this home-coming was attended with special joy and expectation.

When LAZARUS had sent his sisters word that he, with his beloved Master and the disciples, would reach Bethany in just a week from the date of his writing, it had caused them great pleasure.

MARTHA, dignified as ever, and with her habitual forethought, set about re-arranging the rooms, for the accommodation of her prospective guests. Every thing was made as attractive as taste and love could suggest. Vases were replenished with flowers; furnishings and hangings were brightened anew; and all things seemed to speak welcome and cheer. MARY, sweet and lovely, kept her secret fast locked in her heart: she knew what she would do for JESUS when he came.

In the same little village where these friends of JESUS lived, there dwelt a man who had been a leper, and whom JESUS had healed. His name was SIMON; and he was distantly related to these sisters and their brother.

"SIMON! the Master and LAZARUS will come in four days, and with them

17. Stories referred to from Luke 5:3; Luke 5:4–11; Matthew 14:13–21, parallels Mark 6:31–44, Luke 9:10–17, and John 9:5–15; Matthew 8:28–34 with parallel Mark 5:11–20.

the disciples;" said MARY, one day, to her friend. The old man's eyes lighted up upon hearing the news; for there was ever in his heart great love for JESUS, for the benefit he had received from him.

"He shall be my guest;" he said.

"As thou sayest;" she replied, a little slowly; and then continued: "MARTHA was going to make a feast for them; but"—

"Let the feast be at my house. My rooms are more spacious than thine; and MARTHA can look after the guests, while my servants do her bidding;" he interrupted. "Will that please thee, my child?"

"Most certainly, SIMON;" she answered, in highest good nature and manifest satisfaction.

The party came as announced by letter, and the day of the feast arrived.

Among others who graced this social festival, was MIRIAM, JAIRUS' daughter and MARY'S companion. She had come to remain with MARY over Passover-week. The man whom JESUS had healed as he lay at the Pool, nearly three years before, was also there; as likewise the young man who was born blind, but whose eyes JESUS had opened.[18]

Nearly every guest who reclined at the table on this memorable occasion, could bear testimony for JESUS: he had done something for either themselves or their friends. But no one had greater cause for rejoicing than MARTHA and MARY, whose brother LAZARUS JESUS had raised from the dead. MARTHA had gladly undertaken the entertainment of the guests, as suggested by SIMON; and she thought not of the labor it entailed, in her delight to serve her friends, especially her best friend, JESUS. Fatigue was nothing; service of the Master was now as rest.

Before MARY had left her home to attend the feast, she had taken from her treasures a beautiful box of alabaster. It was of exquisite workmanship, and its snowy whiteness was made to appear even whiter by the streaks of yellow and of red that ran through it. It contained a pound of very precious ointment. She had bought it with the thought of anointing her brother LAZARUS for burial; but wealthy friends had sent such an abundance of perfumery and spices, that it was not needed; so she had kept it for some other use. As she took it in her hand at this time, she remembered the sadness of the event that necessitated its purchase. It was bought to anoint the dead; but now it should anoint the living LORD as her king.

"His name is as ointment poured forth" [Song of Songs 1:3], she had said to MIRIAM; "so sweet and delightful is his presence; and I will that he re-

---

18. For the man healed at the pool, see John 5:1–9. For the man born blind, see John 9:1–41.

ceive this honor at my hands who have tasted that sweetness and joy as few others have."

Drawing near to JESUS, as he reclined at the feast, she broke the box, and poured the contents on his head; and some she let fall on his feet. It ran down his beard, and fell on the folds of his garment, till his whole vesture was saturated with the perfume, and the house was filled with its fragrance. From his feet it dripped in pearly beads; and MARY, stooping down, took her long beautiful hair, which hung about her shoulders as a vail, and wiped it off. There was no kerchief near; beside, no linen was as soft as her hair: and so she pressed her hanging tresses into service of CHRIST. It gave her joy to do so; deep affection was in the act.

But there was some one to find fault, as there always is when some good work is done. JUDAS, who carried the community purse, containing the earthly means of JESUS and the disciples, desiring to have its weight increased, and thinking more of money than of the comfort of the Master, murmured at such "waste and extravagance"—as he termed it; and said, it would have been better to have sold it, and to have given the proceeds to the poor.

"The poor ye have always with you, and whensoever ye will ye may do them good; but me ye have not always;" said JESUS. "What this woman hath done is for the day of my burial: do not trouble her."

Source: Nina L. McFadyen, *Stories from the Life of the Wonderful* (Los Angeles, 1897), 124–29, 149–53.

ETTY WOOSNAM (1849–C. 1883)

Meddlesome Matty

Esther (Etty) Woosnam was an Anglican educator and author.[19] Woosnam was born in India to British parents, James Bowen Woosnam and Agnes Bell

19. Source of biographical information: Donna Kerfoot, "Etty Woosnam: A Woman of Wisdom and Conviction," in *Recovering Nineteenth-Century Women Interpreters of the Bible*, ed. Christiana de Groot and Marion Ann Taylor (Atlanta: Society of Biblical Literature, 2007), 217–31.

Woonsnam. In 1860, her family returned to England to reside in Somerset, where Woosnam taught a Bible class for privileged young women that became the basis for her two volumes on women of the Bible. She returned to India in 1881 and married John R. Theobalds, Surgeon-General in Madras in 1882. She died soon after.

In *Women of the Old Testament* (1881) and *Women of the New Testament* (1885) Woosnam emphasized one aspect of the spiritual life of each woman studied, and drew on a variety of sources and illustrations to make her point. She often quoted contemporary literature, and used illustrations from science or history to support her arguments. She called on her audience to use their imaginations and empathize with the biblical characters. *Women of the New Testament* included an essay on Mary, whom she lauds for her loving deeds, and another on Martha, excerpted here, whom she regards as a meddlesome woman.

Woosnam interpreted Scripture with great confidence. She felt free to challenge traditional and scholarly readings of texts. Like other interpreters, Woosnam asked why Jesus rebuked Martha. She criticized the way Martha was commonly portrayed in sermons and teaching. Spirituality for Woosnam centered around the teachings of Scripture. She drew spiritual lessons from the Bethany sisters and encouraged her hearers to find a balance between the characters of Mary and Martha: they were to pray and meditate like Mary and demonstrate works of love toward neighbour like Martha.

Meddlesome Matty

THERE have been many sermons preached and commentaries written on the Sisters of Bethany, in which usually the same line of thought is pursued. Their characters are regarded as types of two opposite phases of Christian life—the meditative and the practical; a comparison is drawn between them always unfavourable to Martha. This view has been clearly expressed and interestingly supported by so many writers, and you, my dear young friends, are so likely to hear it from the pulpit, that I have no need to enlarge on it. I avoid doing so more particularly because I am inclined to think that if we study merely the Bible description of them, unbiased by the comments usually made upon them, we may see that our Lord, in chiding Martha and defending Mary, did not intend us to learn the superiority of devotion over zeal, or of contemplation over activity in good works. To me it appears there was no such comparison established in His mind, for, indeed, all the other parts of the Bible lead us to suppose that no Christian life is of the right sort which does not combine both.

The general tenor of Scripture teaches that the soul must be fed; and if a life is spent in ceaseless work and activity without some quiet time for prayer, meditation, and the study of God's Word, the soul soon becomes impoverished, sickly, and starving. "Desire the sincere milk of the Word, that ye may grow thereby" [1 Pet. 2:2]. "In quietness and in confidence shall be your strength" [Isa. 30:15]. But, on the other hand, days passed in prayer and meditation without any works of love to our neighbour and the daily round of social duties, would be but barren of useful fruits. Saint Paul describes the Christian as "Not slothful in business, but fervent in spirit, serving the Lord" [Rom. 12:11]. And he says to his converts, "This we commanded you, that if any would not work, neither should he eat" [2 Thess. 3:10]. "That they do good, that they be rich in good works, ready to distribute, sociable, or ready to sympathise" (*margin*). While God's people are pictured as "praying always," [Eph. 6:18] as delighting in the law of God, and meditating therein day and night [Ps. 1:2]; they are also zealous of good works [Titus 2:14], labouring in season and out of season [2 Tim. 4:2]. Only by labour can life, physical, mental, or spiritual, be kept pure and happy. "Ich dien"[20] is the motto of every son of God and joint-heir with Christ. All "His servants shall serve Him" [Rev. 22:3]. The Marthas and Marys of the Christian world are well represented in these days. There are still some like Martha, very considerate of the wants of others, and zealous in serving the Lord; but their usefulness is impaired, perhaps, by a bustling self-righteousness. And others there are who are quite as devoted, but less active and energetic. While dwelling tenderly on the words of Jesus, they are apt to forget what is passing around, and so lose the opportunity of serving Him. When a Martha-like nature lives with a Mary, they are often a trial to each other. Martha finds Mary slow, absent, and unpractical; and Mary is disturbed by Martha's fussiness. But both dispositions are equally well understood and loved by their Lord, and He will take the part of whichever is blamed. I have an impression that He would never have instituted any comparison between them if Martha had not said, with self-righteous impetuosity: "Lord, dost Thou not care that my sister hath left me to serve alone; bid her, therefore, that she help me." It is very likely that when Mary was disturbed in the conversation in which she had been absorbed, she was all astir in a moment, and chiding herself for not assisting Martha in preparing a supper to do honour to their guest.

20. German for "I serve"; the motto of the Prince of Wales.

Our Lord, seeing that she blamed herself for indulging in the highest and holiest enjoyment, and that the exuberant love of both sisters made them fret because they could not show Him a hospitality more proportioned to their intense love for Him, assures them that but very little food is needful for Him, and that of the plainest sort.

"But few things are needful, or one" (*Revised Version*). He gently chides Martha for finding fault with Mary, and soothes Mary by a special word of encouragement and praise. Christ never made comparisons between His disciples, nor told St. Peter it was a pity he was not so loving and gentle as St. John, and St. John that he was not so bold as St. Peter. But nothing so quickly called forth a rebuke from Him as fault-finding. With the noblest tenderness He always defended the cause of the accused, or censured, as if it were His own cause. He answered the self-righteous indignation of the Scribes and Pharisees against one who had sadly sinned, with the verdict: "He that is without sin among you, let him first cast a stone at her" [John 8:7]. The expostulation of Simon the Pharisee is met with the very forcible story, beginning so pointedly, "Simon, I have somewhat to say unto thee;" and ending with: "Her sins, which are many, are forgiven, therefore she loved much: but to whom little is forgiven, the same loveth little. . . . Thou gavest me no kiss: . . . thou gavest me no water for my feet" [Luke 7:40–47]. The same afterwards, in defence of Mary's ointment. He corrected Martha for criticising her sister, because such meddling leads to evil-speaking, and its root is uncharitableness or jealousy. Faults are thick when love is thin. It was not Martha's officiousness or too great zeal that He blamed, for He was never unwilling to receive any attentions that were the marks of real love to Him. On a later occasion, when Mary seemed to outdo Martha and all others in lavish expenditure for the personal comfort of her adored Master, the Lord condemned, not her, but Judas, who would have deprived Him of the costly gift: this one touching symbol of a true friend's impassioned tenderness. Martha's appeal to Christ to reprove Mary has its parallel in the request of the man who said: "Master, speak to my brother that he divide the inheritance with me" [Luke 12:13]. The plaintiff, and not his brother, received our Lord's warning and implied rebuke: Why should I, an outsider, settle your family affairs? "Who made me a judge or a divider over you?" (St. Luke 12:14). Again, St. John forbade one casting out devils in Christ's name, and Christ reproved the reprover [see Mark 9:38–39 or Luke 9:49]. When the ten disciples were moved with indignation against the sons of Zebedee, because of Salome's request for them, He says nothing to the objects of the indignation, but enjoins humility on the fault finders [see Matt. 20:20–21].

So palpably does this appear to me to be the lesson of this passage that I draw from it a warning, not against a fussy religious activity or over-scrupulous attention to the social duties of life, but against that most unchristian act of comparing ourselves with others, criticising their conduct, and busying ourselves in other men's matters. The word "Meddlesome Matty" is an old proverbial expression for an interferer. Was this charactcristic of the excellent Martha of Bethany, handed down by the Christian Church, till it became a household word? I do not know; but I can find no other origin for the saying. Poor Martha! with all her unselfish consideration, her hospitality, her eagerness to minister to others, her warm-hearted love to her brother and to her Lord, her habit of interference is noticeable. After her brother's death, as soon as she heard that Jesus was coming, she went and met Him. A reproach was barely hidden in the words, "Lord, if Thou hadst been here"! Then (as we read in the 28th verse) she went her way and called Mary her sister secretly, saying, "The Master is come, and calleth for thee." A secret restlessness made her fetch Mary. It is tiresome when we are excited and pee-vish to see others calmer in bearing our common anxiety, and I am inclined to think that Jesus had not called Mary, but Martha meant to say that His arrival in Bethany seemed to demand Mary's presence. She thought Mary ought to have been ready to meet Him and attend on Him. Mary, seemingly as zealous and devoted as Martha, rises quickly and goes to Him. Once again Martha speaks, and at what a moment! They were all standing round the grave—the cave with a stone laid against it. Cannot you imagine exactly how they all felt? The big lump of sorrow in the throat, which told of a big hollow space down in the heart—every nerve strained to its tightest with a vague wonderment as to what was going to happen next, and every breath held back till it came, and the only sense of relief being in the fact that there beside them stood that Friend to whom Lazarus had been dear—the strong Son of God. He says, "Take ye away the stone." Is it Martha's lips that utter that somewhat coarse exclamation? Is she going to interfere at that moment, and with Him?

How one fault tarnishes the glory of a dozen virtues! Poor warm-hearted, energetic Martha, don't despair. With all your faults Jesus loves you, and, it may be, felt more at home—felt less utterly lonely—in your house than ever He felt anywhere out of His Father's Home. How affectionately He would have defended you if Lazarus or Mary or any one else had blamed your zeal, your ministries, your fervent love! No less dear to His great heart than Lazarus or Mary are you. "Jesus loved Martha and her sister and Lazarus." He wept over Lazarus's grave as He would weep over yours. He wept to think of the anguish you and Mary have felt so keenly the last four days. Jesus knows you love Him, and He wants you to love everybody else for His dear sake.

These conversations of the gospels enforce and illustrate in a most striking way the maxims preached by our Lord in His sermons. "Judge not, that ye be not judged," [Matt. 7:1] and "Why beholdest thou the mote that is in thy brother's eye, but considerest not the beam that is in thine own eye?" [Matt. 7:3]. And with almost Christlike gentleness St. Paul exhorts his followers: "Brethren, if any of you be overtaken in a fault, ye which are spiritual, restore such an one in the spirit of meekness, considering thyself, lest thou also be tempted" [Gal. 6:1]. I fear there are Meddlesome Matties among us at the present day. There is nothing more gratifying to our vanity than to listen to sermons and discourses about the faults and follies of others. Why do we not remember that if we have not their sins we have our own? And why is it so much pleasanter to confess our general depravity than to own to one little fault specially indicated? When we are brought clearly face to face with a fault which is too glaring to be any longer hidden, even from our own sight, we are occasionally weak enough to think of some one who is still more addicted to it than we are; like the hare in the fable, timid, frightened, trembling always, and bound to confess he was a terrible coward; but finding, to his great consolation, one day that he was as great a terror to some frogs in the neighbourhood as large animals were to him, he came to the conclusion that he must be a great hero after all.[21] No one should eagerly find fault with the arrangements and methods of others. There is no cleverness in that. Critics (in secular matters) have been defined as "those who have failed in literature or art," and critics of other men's piety and theology are probably those who have failed to be holy and sound in doctrine themselves. We are told in Earl Stanhope's History[22] that some noblemen and gentlemen were one day discussing the Duke of Marlborough, and one said he had been a very stingy man. "Ah! well," said Lord Bolingbroke, "he really was so great a man that I had forgotten that he was guilty of that defect."

How can we with our deceitful hearts, our strong prejudices in favour of ourselves, and leniency to our own views and actions, be impartial arbiters

21. Versions of this brief fable appear in many editions of Aesop's Fables. See, for example, *Three Hundred Aesop's Fables*, translated by George Fyler Townsend (London: George Routledge & Sons, n.d.), 97–98.

22. Philip Henry Stanhope, 5th Earl of Stanhope (1805–1875), a British politician and historian, wrote *The History of England from the Peace of Utrecht to the Peace of Versailles* (1839–53), *The Life of William Pitt* (1861–1862), and *The History of England, Comprising the Reign of Queen Anne to the Peace of Utrecht* (1870).

of others' doings? No one is in a position to judge of his neighbour's conduct till he has stood in his place; and no one knows the weight of another's burden. Imitating others and measuring others against ourselves are equally injurious. In running a race, to have the head turned in the right direction is as important as speed; and many an Asahel for lightness of foot has lost his chance of winning by looking back to see how far behind the next man was [2 Sam. 24:13]. We come to Jesus not to be made better than other people, but better than ourselves; and while we hold out our hand to pull our friends up the hill of holiness we must take good care not to slip back ourselves.[23] We do not want all to serve God in precisely the same way, nor expect all to agree with us on every point of Christian doctrine; nor do we wish to get stupid and narrow-minded, "like the parson of Saddleworth who could read in no book but his own."[24] But we claim Christian brotherhood with all who take the Bible as the standard of truth and who trust in Jesus Christ for their salvation and their righteousness. For every train in the largest and most confusing of junctions there is a pair of rails to travel on; and it is when Christians want all to be travelling on the same pair of rails, and either to meet each other or to follow each other, that they come to collisions. A prince and a peasant if each is a child of God will work every day from the same motive, but will serve God in totally different ways, as becoming his station in life.[25]

When you are studying the characters of men and women remember always to look out for their strength; the weaknesses are sure to discover themselves later on without your seeking them, but the later the better. Have we not enough to do with fighting against our own besetting sins without devoting our leisure to the correction of others? Let each exercise the special gifts which God has given. He has classes in His school for all types of character and for all degrees of capacity. He has in the material world endless variety. The various trees and fruits are grown, each for a special use, and even flowers have their purpose, for they touch our hearts and we can but love them as we do little children for their own sweet sakes. God has given

23. Here Woosnam alludes to an image from John Bunyan's *Pilgrim's Progress*.

24. According to a note explaining this proverb, it predates 1295, when the patronage of Saddleworth belonged to the Cistercian Abbey of Stanlawe in Cheshire, which sent "less learned" priests, who would only be familiar with Cistercian rites, to remote chapels. Since they could not use the rites locally used, they read no book but their own. J. H., "A Note on a Yorkshire Proverb," *The Yorkshire Archaeological Journal* 7 (1882), 142.

25. At this point Woosnam cited the hymn "O God, whose thoughts are brightest light," by Frederick William Faber (1814–1863).

"to every man his work."* Some of you, dear girls, will be clever and thoughtful nurses of the sick; some will have a gift for music, or drawing; some will excel in the management of money matters; some will be persuasive teachers of children; some will organise households, and set others to work; some will have, perhaps, no special gift, but that best one of all, the genuine sympathy which wins the love of friends, soothes their sorrows, shares their cares, and knows how to speak a word in season to him that is weary. For each one of us on earth there is work enough, which no one, else can do as well. Only let not Martha condemn Mary for idleness, nor Mary accuse Martha of restlessness. And when the task of life is over and the lesson-books are closed, will there not be for all of us Heaven enough?

Source: Etty Woosnam, *Women of the Bible: New Testament* (London: S. W. Partridge, 1885), 29–38.

M. G. (FL. 1893)

....

Work and Devotion

M. G. wrote anonymously. Her only known publication, *Women Like Ourselves: Short Addresses for Mother's Meetings, Bible Classes, etc.* (1893), contains some hints about her life.[26] She delivered the addresses or sermons printed in her book in an Anglo-Catholic parish. Her sermons reveal that she valued the importance not only of church attendance, the liturgy, and sacraments, but also a personal relationship with Jesus. M. G. wrote with authority, as an experienced teacher, for the benefit of those who wished to learn to teach. In her introduction, M. G. provided suggestions for presenting the sermons contained in her book.[27]

Women Like Ourselves contains twenty-five addresses beginning with Eve and ending with the Virgin Mary. It includes twenty addresses on Old Testament women and five on New Testament women, focusing especially

---

26. M. G., *Women Like Ourselves: Short Addresses for Mother's Meetings, Bible Classes, Etc.* (London: SPCK, 1893).

27. For more on M. G. as a preacher, see her sermon on Anna in the next chapter.

*St. Mark 12:34

on characters M. G. felt were not frequently discussed in sermons or publications. As the title, *Women Like Ourselves*, suggests, M. G. saw the biblical characters as real people, people like herself and her audience, people who provided an example to be followed.

The chapter on Mary and Martha excerpted here reveals M. G.'s sacramental theology, her approach to interpreting Scripture, and her views on piety. Like many Anglo-Catholics, she read Scripture literally and figurally. She suggested that just as Martha and Mary had Jesus visit their home, her audience could have Jesus visit the home of their heart, particularly as they participated in the Sacrament of the Lord's Supper. M. G. called her audience to imitate Mary of Bethany's piety. She also presented a very sympathetic reading of Martha, "a woman like ourselves." M. G.'s ideal of the spiritual life combined outward and inward devotion. She suggested that her readers practice both outward devotion to Jesus in acts of public worship, and inward heart devotion during daily activities. In this way she advocated a spiritual life that combined "Martha's work with Mary's devotion."

MARY AND MARTHA.

About three miles from Jerusalem, hidden in a little valley among the hills, lies the village of Bethany. To reach it you must cross the brook Kedron, and go up past the most sacred garden of Gethsemane, where the ancient olive trees are still standing beneath which we believe that Jesus must have knelt on the night of the Agony; and then you go up the Mount of Olives till you come to that turn in the road from which that striking view of the holy city is obtained, which wrung from our Lord's lips the sorrowful cry, "O Jerusalem, Jerusalem!" [Matt. 23:37]. The Feet of Jesus have often trodden that road, for in the village a little further on lived a family, the members of which Jesus loved with a very special affection (S. John 11:5). We often find that when He had been teaching in Jerusalem all the day, He would retire to Bethany for the night, sure of a welcome there (S. Matt. 21:17; 26:6); and the two days before His betrayal were spent in seclusion there.

Our dear Lord had but few earthly friends, and even they were not all true, for He chose to feel all our sorrows, and loneliness and want of friends is one heavy sorrow, while for friends to prove false is a heavier trial still; and these griefs He shared with us. At the same time He had a few whom He loved and trusted, for He would taste—just taste—earthly joys for our sakes, as He tasted the wine and myrrh offered to Him in pity on the cross, to show us that He did not despise, much less disapprove of, the good gifts which God has given to His children.

What a happy family that must have been where Jesus was a frequent and a welcome guest! The knowledge that others hated and despised Him would only make Lazarus and his sisters the more anxious to show Him every loving honour and attention in reparation for the insults He received elsewhere. With what care and watchfulness they would be ever on the alert, knowing that at any hour He might walk in!

Would you like Him to open the door of your cottages and to walk in at any moment? He is standing knocking even now. Not at the outer door of the house, for since He rose from the dead He can pass through earthly doors even if they are closed and barred; but He cannot, at least He will not, enter the door of your heart unless you let Him. "Behold," He says, "I stand at the door and knock" (Rev. 3:20); but how few respond to His gentle knocking! Some doors are barred fast against Him, while others are only open just so far as to give Him grudging entrance, such as He received in the houses of the Pharisees. Will not you, at least, open wide to Him, and try to make up to Him for the rudeness of others? If you open to Him He will honour you by coming to dwell with you and sup with you, making His home in your heart, as He comes back to you again and again in the Sacrament of the Lord's Supper. Because others despise His Presence there and turn their backs upon Him, should not we try to make amends the more, by all the loving reverence that we can show?

The Sisters at Bethany seemed as if they could not do enough to show their intense adoring love. On one occasion (S. John 12:1–9) Mary took a box of very costly ointment and poured it upon His sacred Head as an offering of love, as Mary Magdalene had done once before.[28] Others murmured at the "waste," as they called it, but it only won praise from the Lord Himself, and the sweet odour of that offering of the best and most precious thing that she had went down into the grave where the sacred Body was laid within the week, and has spread through the whole Church to teach us that the best that we have should be devoted to the Master's service.

"Mary had chosen the good part" (Luke 10:42), the part of sitting at the Saviour's Feet, seeing and caring for none but Him, wrapped up, heart and soul, in loving adoration, and listening to His Word. "Blessed are they," Jesus

---

28. See the chapter on Mary Magdalene for a discussion of the conflation of Luke 7 and Luke 8.

once said, "who hear the Word of God and keep it" [Luke 11:28]. Oh, if we could but choose that good part, not only with our lips but in our hearts—listening ever intently for His Voice, gazing upwards to catch a glimpse of His Face (marred as it was more than any man's [Isa. 52:14]), kneeling in lowliest adoration at His Feet, regardless of what the world might think or say,—we too might win the praise from His Lips, "She hath done what she could. She hath chosen the good part, which shall not be taken away from her."

The time came when the outward presence of Jesus was withdrawn from the home at Bethany, but He still dwelt on there in the heart of Mary, as He would fain dwell now in your heart and in mine, if we would only welcome Him there.

Jesus loved Martha too. Hers was a different nature to Mary's, but it was none the less lovable in the Eyes of the Saviour, who could see into her devoted heart. She was one of those whose love displays itself in busy active work, and when so great a Guest came to her house she wanted to show Him all the loving honour and respect in her power. You know how much extra work the preparation for an honoured visitor involves. Cooking has to be done, the best china carefully got down and dusted, the choicest linen looked out from the press, the table decked with flowers and fruit, the bed prepared,—all this takes much time and thought. Have we not sometimes had to do all this when we have known that the guest was in the parlour, and longed to be with him so as not to lose any of his society, and yet been hindered by all these little household duties from being with him? Then we can sympathize with Martha, and we shall perhaps not be very much surprised that she got flurried and vexed, and we might almost say that she got into a little bit of a temper at last (for she was only a woman like ourselves) when she saw her sister sitting there so calmly without offering to help her. At last she could bear it no longer, and burst out with the indignant remonstrance, "Lord, dost Thou not care that my sister hath left me to serve alone?" (ver. 40) Under other circumstances Mary's conduct would have been selfish, but here she had had to choose (and our Lord tells us she had chosen well) not to lose the precious moments of communion with Jesus for the sake of outward demonstrations. However much we may have to do for Christ's sake, we must not let it hinder us in our devotions. See how gently and tenderly the Lord showed Martha her mistake. "Martha, Martha" (can we not imagine the finger raised in gentle warning), "thou art careful and troubled about many things for My sake, and thy loving service is very acceptable to Me. But thou must not forget among all these things that one thing is needful; namely, to spend some moments at least in speaking to Me and listening to My voice, and thou must not interrupt thy sister in this."

Might He not say the same to us? We are most of us apt to get cumbered with the burden of duties which we cannot, must not neglect. Some among us are called especially to "service," and S. Paul tells you that you must do it well (Col. 3:22–23), "heartily, as unto the Lord." Ah, there lies the secret, not to get fussed or worried or impatient over it, but to do it quietly and gladly as if the Lord Himself were being waited on by us. Doubtless, after she had sat awhile at Jesus' feet, Mary would joyfully rise and take her turn in serving, to give her sister the opportunity of taking her place; and she would go about her work with double energy after being thus refreshed with the dew of heaven [Gen. 27:28].

There are few who can spend all their time in outward devotion—there are none who cannot spare a few minutes daily at the Feet of the Lord. Let us keep this "one thing needful" in our minds amid our daily toil, and not forget or neglect our times of regular worship. And not only at those times, but even when our hands and feet are busy, we may still keep speaking and looking to our Lord, when He is dwelling in us.

A French servant-girl, who had slaved hard all her life, was so holy and wise that many looked up to her as a saint, and came to her for teaching. One day some one asked her to teach them how she had gained such heavenly wisdom. "Why," she said, "I never had any time to study. I was only thinking always as I went about my duties how I could love God more." That is the great secret, not to let ourselves get "cumbered," as Martha did, with what we have to do, but since now we have our Saviour with us everywhere, and not in one room alone, we can, if we keep our hearts free, be ever learning from Himself how to love Him more.

There was a lady, also in France, who had a large family and an important household, which at one time was always at sixes and sevens through the neglect of the mistress. All at once a change came over everything, and some one asked the reason. Her maid could easily give it. "Before," she said, "Madame used to go and spend long hours in prayer, and everyone was made uncomfortable by her neglect; but now since the good Bishop has told her of it, she says her prayers all day long and looks after us as well, and no one is made miserable, but we are all much happier." She had learnt, you see, to combine Martha's work with Mary's devotion.[29]

---

29. It is clear from her book that M. G. read broadly and picked up stories to use from many sources. In other places she quotes the devotional works of Francis de Sales (1567–1622), the

There is one other lesson I want to help you to see from the story of this family. Where was the father of Martha and Mary and Lazarus? He, poor man, could not join them. Somewhere outside the town he was hiding in caves and crying, "Unclean, unclean," for he was a leper (S. Mark 14:2). Does it not occur to us at once that Jesus had healed so many lepers, that surely if He had chosen He could have healed Simon? We feel sure that Martha and Mary would often with tears entreat Him that He would do so, and yet it seems that their prayer remained unanswered, although "Jesus loved Martha and her sister and Lazarus."

Yes, perhaps it was because He loved them that He chastened them [Prov. 3:12] with this bitter trial, and would not give them all they wanted in this world. Again, we read in S. John 12:5, 6, Lazarus was sick and sent for Jesus, but because the Lord loved him, therefore He remained two days without going to him.

We see now why He stayed away so long, because He was going to give them a special proof of His love in raising Lazarus from the dead when all hope was over; but at the time it must have seemed strange and hard to the anxious sisters watching for Him so long in vain. So we may believe that if He did not heal their father, it was for some good purpose which one day they would fully understand and bless Him for.

And if our prayers seem to remain unanswered—if some troubles remain with us all through our lives, and other dreaded blows fall upon us, though we entreat Him to remove them—do not let us for a moment think that Jesus does not love us and does not listen to our prayers. Did He not love S. Paul, who besought again and again that his thorn in the flesh might depart from him (2 Cor. 12:7–10), and only received the answer, "My grace is sufficient for thee: My strength is made perfect in weakness"? Nay, did not our Blessed Lord Himself fall on His Face on the ground, praying, "If it be possible, let this cup pass from Me," [Matt. 26:39, 42] and yet He had to drink it to the very dregs? Oh, then, don't let Satan ever tempt you to despair of the love and favour of Jesus, even if He seem to tarry long, without sending you the answer you look for. We read His promise in Rev. 3:20, to come in and dwell with those who love Him sufficiently to open the door of their hearts to Him. But in the verse which immediately precedes it (v. 19) He warns us that we must not expect all to go smoothly with us even then. "As many as I love I rebuke and chasten"—"For whom the Lord loveth He chasteneth" (Heb. 12:6).

French Roman Catholic Bishop of Geneva, and a well-known spiritual director. De Sales and other Catholic spiritual writers were popular in the nineteenth century.

Trust Him, then, even when His Face is hidden. Yes, even if, most mysterious of all, He should suffer some we love to live and die in the leprosy of sin. It needs perhaps more faith to trust His love in such a trial than in any other; but this we know, that He Who loved Martha and Mary, and Who loves all His own even to the end, will wipe away all tears at last in the joy which He has prepared for those who love Him.

Source: M. G., *Women Like Ourselves: Short Addresses for Mother's Meetings, Bible Classes, Etc.* (London: SPCK, 1893), 132–138.

MARY ANN SMITH (FL. 1897)

Doing What We Can

Little is known about Scottish author Mary Ann Smith, who lived in the Anglican parish of St. Mark's, Edinburgh. She worked with women in the parish and, like M. G., drew lessons on the spiritual life for women in her Mothers' Meeting from the stories of women in the Old and New Testaments. Her book, *The Holy Women of Old*, consists of 17 chapters, eight covering women from the Old Testament and nine on women in the New Testament.

Smith devotes one chapter to each of the Bethany sisters in *The Holy Women of Old*. Both the chapters are included below. In the chapter on Martha, Smith was most concerned with discovering Martha's fault mentioned in Luke 10. Smith argued the fault could not be serving, as Jesus also served. Smith then suggested four faults Martha exhibited that were corrected through Martha's engagement with Jesus. Similarly, Smith argued, she and her readers could learn to correct their faults from Scripture. Smith also noted that Mary did not just learn from Jesus, she acted upon what she learned, particularly as seen in the supper described in John 12. On that occasion, Jesus said of Mary, "She did what she could." This is Smith's key lesson from Mary's life. In her application to herself and her readers Smith asked: have we done what we could? Like M. G., Smith drew a lesson on the importance of Holy Communion as a means of grace from the example of Mary's devotional life.

By attending to Martha and Mary separately, Smith did not primarily focus on the differences between the sisters, unlike Balfour and other writers excerpted in this chapter. For Smith, both Martha and Mary were holy women who could teach women of the nineteenth century spiritual lessons. By avoiding the direct contrasts between the sisters Smith allows each a depth and complexity of character that was often missed when the sisters were typecast as active or contemplative.

Martha

Martha first comes before us in St. Luke 10:38, where we read, "A certain woman named Martha received Him into her house." Now what was it in Martha's conduct on that occasion that called forth our Lord's rebuke? Certainly not her desire to serve. It is impossible to think that He who was among us as "one that serveth," who came not to be ministered unto but to minister (St. Matt. 20:28), ever found fault with any one for wanting to serve, and serve much. The best and greatest service we can render is as nothing compared to His own. Never let us think that Christ was here encouraging us to sit down and selfishly enjoy our own religious privileges without troubling ourselves about others, or about the work His father has given us to do. His own life was the most emphatic denial of such conclusion. "My meat is to do the will of Him that sent Me, and to finish His work" (St. John 4:34).[30]

There were perhaps four things wrong—First, Martha did not seem to realize that she had any need to learn. Even in earthly things, the Church Catechism so well reminds us, we need to learn as well as labour, and not only when we are young, but all through life. Wise people are always learning. Specially in heavenly things we need to sit at His feet and hear His words if we are to do properly the work He gives. We should not have so many "unhappy divisions," we should not be hindered by people quarrelling over work if they had learned of Him to be "meek and lowly in heart;" nor should we find people desponding, and thinking everything a failure if they could but learn to be "steadfast, unmovable, always *abounding* in the work of the Lord, forasmuch as they *know* that their labour is not in vain in the Lord" (1 Cor. 15:58).

Then she worried over her service, instead of feeling the blessedness of it; she wanted to serve in her own way and at her own time, she had not the

---

30. For a similar discussion of the service of Jesus and the service of women, see Elizabeth Rundle Charles's poem "Ministry," found in Elizabeth Rundle Charles, *Sketches of the Women of Christendom* (New York: Dodd, Mead & Co., 1880), iii-iv.

patience to wait. A very common fault even in our service of our fellow-creatures; some one has been ill, a kind friend with the best possible intentions calls, stops and fusses and talks far beyond what the slowly returning strength can bear, and then goes away, either pleased with herself for the good she has done, or fancies she has done; or, Martha-like, rather put out because the visit was not appreciated as she considered it deserved. Had the visitor been less taken up with self, the symptoms of weariness on the invalid's face would not have passed unnoticed. We need a "heart at leisure from itself" if we would serve well. And in the Lord's work how often we find women grumbling at the work He gives them to do; they would like something else so much better; very like Martha who wished to serve when her Master wished her to learn. Then there was a certain jealousy, and finding fault with her sister, who had gained more approval than she; and that led to the fourth fault, murmuring against the Lord Himself. "Lord, dost Thou not care?" Of course He cared. "Jesus loved Martha and her sister and Lazarus" (St. John 11:5). "Careful and troubled about many things" was Martha. We also may sometimes experience the same feeling, yet we may be sure He cares, and may "cast all our care upon Him" (1 St. Peter 5:7).

But this is not our only sight of Martha—a great trial of her faith came. In their care and trouble over their brother's illness, Martha and Mary sent to Jesus saying, "Lord, behold, he whom thou lovest is sick." Martha seems to have learned one lesson. No suggestion that He did not care; simply the trouble laid before Him, with the perfect certainty that He would deal with it best of all. But the faith of both sisters must have been sorely tried when the Lord made no sign, and they saw their brother die. Both seemed to be convinced had the Lord been there it would not have been so, for both greeted Him when He did come to them, with the same words, "Lord, if Thou hadst been here, my brother had not died." Yet it was in love He delayed. "Jesus loved Martha, and her sister, and Lazarus. When He had heard, *therefore*, that he was sick, He abode two days still in the same place where He was." Something greater was to be shown them. So, answer to our prayers is often delayed for our good. The trial of our faith is so precious, that God, if we trust in Him and wait for Him, will give us, as He did to the sisters of Bethany, "exceeding abundantly above all we ask or think" [Eph. 3:20]. They thought He would have cured their brother's sickness alone, but over death itself He has all power. Martha, when she heard the Lord was coming, hastily went forth to meet Him with still some hope apparently, for she added to the words we have noticed, "But I know, that even now, whatsoever Thou wilt ask of God, God will give it Thee." She made, too, a remarkable declaration of her belief in the final resurrection of the dead. "Jesus saith unto her, Thy brother shall rise again. Martha saith unto Him, I know that He shall rise again in the resurrection at the last day." Perhaps she had heard His own words, "The hour is coming in which all that are in the graves shall hear His voice, and shall come forth" (St. John 5:28, 29). And her answer to Him called from Him those cheering words, with which our Church greets the bodies of her members when brought by sorrowing relatives and friends to the House of God, in which they have offered their prayers and praises, "I am the resurrection, and the life: he that believeth in Me, though he were dead, yet shall he live: and whosoever liveth and believeth in Me shall never die."[31] And one of the earliest confessions of faith is that which Martha gave in answer to His question, "Believest thou this?" "Yea, Lord; I believe that Thou art the Christ, the Son of God, which should come into the world." Then she went and called her sister, and together they accompanied the Lord to the grave. For a moment Martha's strong faith seemed to waver, for she hesitated at the command to take away the stone. Not until He had said unto her, "Said I not unto thee, that, if thou wouldest believe, thou shouldest see the glory of God?" was the stone removed; and then to their joy and wonder, the dead heard the voice that cried "Lazarus, come forth." "Women received their dead raised to life again" (Heb. 11:35), through faith in him who is the Resurrection and the Life.

Our last sight of Martha, like our first, is at service. Jesus came to Bethany before the Feast of the Passover. "There they made Him a supper, and Martha served," served, we may think, in a humble, less self-conscious spirit, for her service was accepted. There was no reproach then. Let us copy Martha, in her desire to serve, only trying to do all in un unselfish spirit, not simply to please ourselves, wanting to do only the work we like, remembering, too, that we are always needing to learn. "Blessed Lord, who has caused all Holy Scriptures to be written for our learning, grant that we may in such wise hear them, read, mark, learn, and inwardly digest them." Yes, learn in such a way that "by patience and comfort of His Holy Word, we may embrace, and ever hold fast the blessed hope of everlasting life, which He has given us in our Saviour Jesus Christ."[32]

Source: Mary Ann Smith, The Holy Women of Old (Edinburgh: John Anderson, 1897), 45–48.

---

31. In the rubrics for funerals in the Anglican Book of Common Prayer, clergy are directed to meet the corpse at the entrance of the church-yard and recite a series of Scripture texts, beginning with John 11:25–26.

32. The prayer quoted in two parts is the collect for the second Sunday of Advent in the Book of Common Prayer.

Mary of Bethany

Like her sister Martha, Mary first comes before us in the tenth chapter of St. Luke's gospel, where we find her "choosing that good part which will not be taken away from her." Choosing the Lord's will rather than her own, humbly "sitting at His feet and hearing His word," willing to take the learner's place, she seems to have been more thoughtful than her sister. The same quiet spirit showed itself at the time of Lazarus's death and when he was raised from the grave. "Mary sat still in the house" (St. John 11:20), when the more impulsive Martha went to meet our Lord; yet as He defended Mary when her sister grumbled at being left "to serve alone," so now He seemed to have no word of blame for her. He honoured her by sending for her, and waiting till she came, before He went to the grave and called Lazarus back to life.

But we must not think that Mary simply passed her life in learning the will of God, or in sitting still dreaming about it. We must never forget it was to the quiet, meek-spirited Mary of Bethany our Lord gave that high praise, "she hath done what she could" (St. Mark 14:8). What was the secret of Mary's doing? Did it not spring from the fact that she had so truly learned. She did not rush into service to please herself, nor for the sake of excitement, or of liking some faith occupation. No, she had quietly learned at Jesus' feet. She had deeply drunk of His loving spirit, and self-sacrifice came as a pleasure to her. There might be so much said of this act of Mary's, when "she did what she could." It was a costly gift, worth a far, far greater sum in those days than in ours, and we may imagine that many a little act of sacrifice and self-denial had been necessary for Mary to save so large an amount, but what a delight she must have taken in such sacrifice. Then she seemed to show so much common-sense, so much of the "forethoughtfulness" that love inspires when she came "aforehand." One always wishes respect and attention shown to the remains of the departed, but is it not sometimes sad to know that the love and care bestowed on the unconscious dead would have brought healing and joy to the living hearts? Too late, sometimes, comes the thought for others, too late the kindly word of reconciliation, too late the penitent comes to plead for forgiveness, too late the gentle treatment or the skilful aid—the life that might have been comforted, that might, perchance have been saved has gone—no tears, no care, no effort now can bring it back again. Oh! if we had only thought, only known sooner! While we have time, therefore, let us be ready to do what we can. St. John tells us that the "house was filled with the odour of the ointment," and is there not a lesson for us here? It is in the house which she is making her home that a woman's sweetness should be known—it matters little whether it is heard of elsewhere. But how was her act received? The lookers-on (the disciples) murmured; one especially (Judas), "who was a thief and kept the bag," said, "To what purpose is this waste, for this ointment might have been sold for much and given to the poor" (St. Matt. 26:8, 9). A remark we often hear now. Some loving, grateful hearts, find a joy in presenting a beautiful gift to the house of God: and what do some disciples say, Christians, true Christians, not imitators of Judas—"What a waste, when there are so many poor people wanting food." Well, there are many answers to be made to that. First, it is very doubtful if it is a good thing to give money unless we know all about the case. More often than not, the money given without proper enquiry goes to support the public-house, and to increase the troubles of the poor, instead of lessening them. There are men and women too lazy to work, they prefer telling some pitiable and perhaps untrue tale, in a whining voice, and people are taken in and give, thus oftentimes encouraging vice. It would be interesting to know what amount is given to beggars in a single day in London alone. Probably the sum might go a long way to helping some struggling charity which is really doing good; but to give people work is helping them in the best way, so that if a church is built, or restored, or decorated, it really is in that sense giving to the poor, or preventing poverty, which is better still.

There are ways in which it is right and wise to give to the poor, and generally it is found that those who are most ready to give to the more immediate glory of God are the most ready to give to His poor; but they will not do it, lazily or selfishly to save themselves the trouble of enquiring, or to get rid, like the unjust judge, of a wearisome beggar. No. the Scriptures say, "Blessed is he that considereth the poor" (Ps. 41:1). But above all Mary's heart was overflowing with love and gratitude to Him who had taught her things no other could, to Him who had brought back to life the brother she so tenderly loved. Nothing now was too great a sacrifice for her to make, she could not do enough to prove the depth of her devotion.

Men might despise her loving offering, not the Lord—"Jesus said, Let her alone, why trouble ye her? she hath wrought a good work on me. For ye have the poor with you always, and whensoever ye will, ye may do them good: but me ye have not always. She hath done what she could, she is come aforehand to anoint my body to the burying. Verily I say unto you, wheresoever this gospel should be preached throughout the whole world, this also that she hath done shall be spoken of for a memorial of her" (St. Mark 14:6–9). Nothing we may be sure was further from Mary's thoughts than that her act should be made known to all generations, yet her Lord willed it so, for her sake partly, no doubt—He loved to honour her who had honoured Him—and for our sakes too, that we may follow her example. The gifts we can bring may seem insignificant to ourselves, may seem insignificant in the eyes of men, but if they come from a true and loving heart, they are "an odour of a sweet smell, a sacrifice acceptable, well pleasing to God" (Phil. 4:18). We must take care that we give, as we are able, and give too as she did, of that which costs us something.

And now let us ask ourselves, Could our Lord say this of any one of us, "She hath done what she could," can any one of us say it honestly of herself, as we look back on our many opportunities and means of grace—the greatest of all, the Holy Communion—have we profited thereby even if we have been as regular as we ought to be in the outward observance, have we learned to know God better, have we "increased in His Holy Spirit more and more," if so it must have shown itself in our behaviour—in our greatest kindness to others, in our thinking less of ourselves and in our greater diligence in our business? Can we think that we have done what we could in the service of God? Surely we must all feel "we have left undone those things which we ought to have done,"[33] those things which perhaps we ourselves intended to do. Any one who carefully attends to the daily lessons given by our Church, must surely be humbled when she reads that passage and thinks of her own shortcomings. Yet we may take courage. God sees our feeblest efforts, His strength is made perfect in our weakness [2 Cor. 12:9].

"Wherefore work out your own salvation with fear and trembling. *For* it is God that worketh in you both to will and to do His good pleasure" [Phil. 2:12].

And if, as we look back, we can feel that, spite of our feebleness, our little faith, God has graciously crowned any effort we may have tried to make with success, to His Holy Name be the praise. "Hitherto hath the Lord helped us," [1 Sam. 7:12] so let us thank God and take courage, resolving in His strength to strive more earnestly in the future "to do what we can."

Source: Mary Ann Smith, *The Holy Women of Old* (Edinburgh: John Anderson, 1897), 49–53.

---

33. From the confession in the *Book of Common Prayer*.

STUDY QUESTIONS

1. What adjectives do these interpreters use to describe Mary and Martha? Which ones are used most consistently? Compare the nineteenth-century descriptions with adjectives used to describe Mary and Martha today.

2. Most of these excerpts emphasize hospitality. How was hospitality understood in the nineteenth century? How is hospitality understood differently in our day? How do the writers present Mary and Martha as examples of hospitality? Is this reading still relevant?

3. How are the spiritual lives of Mary and Martha portrayed by the writers? How are Mary and Martha held up as examples of spirituality?

4. What other Scripture passages do these interpreters draw on to fill out their portrayals of Mary and Martha? How well do these other Scriptures fill in the gaps in the gospel narratives?

5. Compare and contrast the account of Jesus' anointing in John 12 with the account in Matthew 26. Are the interpretations presented here successful in harmonizing these two accounts? Why or why not?

PART 2

UNSEALED LIPS:
WOMEN PREACHING

Introduction

Women Preachers?

Though it was highly controversial, nineteenth-century women preached sermons in a variety of settings, and made arguments for their ability and authority to preach.[1] We define a sermon in a broad sense, to mean an orally delivered interpretation of a biblical passage, given to an audience gathered to hear such a message. Preaching is the act of delivering a sermon so defined.[2] Further, a sermon usually has a point of application to the hearers' lives. The sermon has the "purpose of moving them [the audience] by the use of narrative analogy and other rhetorical devices to accept that application and to act on the basis of it."[3] The examples found in this chapter clearly show the use of rhetorical devices by preachers (or writers) to move hearers (or readers) to apply the Bible to their lives.

Generally women were officially barred from preaching in mainline churches in North America and Great Britain during the nineteenth century. What is not often remembered is that nineteenth-century women did preach. They preached in some churches, particularly young denominations. They

---

1. Olive Anderson, "Women Preachers in Mid-Victorian Britain: Some Reflexions on Feminism, Popular Religion and Social Change," *The Historical Journal* 12, no. 3 (1969): 467–84.

2. For a helpful discussion of the definition of a sermon and its limitations, see Joni S. Sancken, "Calling Forth More Witnesses: Claiming the Voices of Preachers Silenced by History," *Toronto Journal of Theology* 26, no. 1 (2010): 47–58. See also Beverly Kienzle and Pamela J. Walker, eds., *Women Preachers and Prophets Through Two Millennia of Christianity* (Berkeley and Los Angeles: University of California Press, 1998), xiii-xiv.

3. O. C. Edwards, Jr., *A History of Preaching* (Nashville: Abingdon Press, 2004), 4.

preached in evangelistic contexts at missionary gatherings. They preached without a pulpit in churches and meeting halls.[4] Many women spoke at meetings meant only for other women—though a few men sometimes attended these gatherings.[5] Olive Anderson documents women who preached to large mixed audiences in Britain in the 1860s. By the end of the century, women were officially recognized as preachers in the Salvation Army, in some Methodist denominations, and some Congregational churches.[6]

Sermons initially delivered orally were often published, as witnessed by the sermon collections of men such as Charles Spurgeon and Henry Parry Liddon.[7] In a similar way, women such as M. G., Mrs. Donaldson, and Hannah Locker-Lampson published their sermons. Sermons published by both men and women reached a larger audience than could fill a church or hall. Some women, such as Harriet Beecher Stowe and Anne Brontë, included sermon-like speeches in their novels.[8] Some women, such as Esther Cop-

---

4. Many works recovering the history of women preaching from the early church to the present day have been published over the last fifteen years. These include Susan Hill Lindley, *"You have Stept Out of Your Place": A History of Women and Religion in America* (Louisville: Westminster John Knox Press, 1996); Catherine A. Brekus, *Female Preaching in America: Strangers & Pilgrims 1740–1845* (Chapel Hill and London: The University of North Carolina Press, 1998); Rebecca Larson, *Daughters of Light: Quaker Women Preaching and Prophesying in the Colonies and Abroad 1700–1795* (New York: Knopf, 1999); Beverly Zink-Sawyer, *From Preachers to Suffragists: Woman's Rights and Religious Conviction in the Lives of Three Nineteenth-Century American Clergywomen* (Louisville: Westminster John Knox Press, 2003); Eunjoo Mary Kim, *Women Preaching: Theology and Practice Through the Ages* (Cleveland: Pilgrim Press, 2004). In Kim, see particularly chapters 2–4 which trace the history of women preachers from the time of the early church to the early twentieth century.

5. Anderson, "Women Preachers," 481. See also J. Ramsey Michaels, "A Washington Bible Class: The Bloodless Piety of Gail Hamilton," in *Strangely Familiar: Protofeminist Interpretations of Patriarchal Biblical Texts*, ed. Nancy Calvert-Koysis and Heather E. Weir (Atlanta: SBL Press, 2009), 191–92.

6. Methodist churches in the holiness tradition were precursors of Pentecostal denominations which appeared in the early twentieth century. Practices varied in African American churches; all the examples of women who preached found in this chapter are white. See Kim, *Women Preaching*, 98, for a fuller discussion of women's ordination in the nineteenth century.

7. For examples of Spurgeon's published sermons see *The Metropolitan Tabernacle Pulpit: Sermons Preached and Revised during the year 1865* (London: Passmore & Alabaster, 1866); examples of Henry Parry Liddon's published sermons can be found in *Sermons Preached Before the University of Oxford* (London: Rivington's, 1869). "The publication of sermons was a practice from earlier periods that continued through the nineteenth century" (Jennifer M. Stolpa, "Preaching to the Clergy: Anne Brontë's *Agnes Grey* as a Treatise on Sermon Style and Delivery," *Victorian Literature and Culture* 31, no. 1 (2003): 228).

8. "Arguably, Harriet Beecher Stowe had a ministerial career—she preached with her

ley and Florence Nightingale, wrote sermons for men to preach.[9] Scholars of English literature have long recognized that nineteenth-century women barred from public preaching opportunities often preached with their pen.[10] Written sermons were an established literary form that women as well as men practiced.[11] Some of the excerpts included in this section are written sermons.

Preaching and Women in the Gospels

In this section we provide examples of women's sermons as well as their arguments for women's ability and authority to speak a word from the Lord. Two of the gospel women in this section provided examples of women who testified about Jesus: Anna and the Samaritan woman. Herodias and her daughter provided subject matter for sermons on the social ills of dance, and the misuse of power by women.

Anna and the Samaritan woman testified about Jesus. Anna testified to those in Jerusalem who looked for the Messiah, and the Samaritan woman to the people of her town. Testimony, as Anna Carter Florence reminds us, "is an old, old word for homelitics."[12] The testimony Anna and the Samaritan

---

pen. Her text was the Bible; her congregation was the world." Marion Ann Taylor, "Harriet Beecher Stowe and the Mingling of Two Worlds: The Kitchen and the Study," in *Recovering Nineteenth-Century Women Interpreters of the Bible*, ed. Christiana de Groot and Marion Ann Taylor (Atlanta: Society of Biblical Literature, 2007), 100. On Brontë: "The formation of her novel [Anne Brontë's *Agnes Grey* (1847)] as an exemplary sermon represents her entrance into an exclusively male genre of the time—theological treatises and handbooks on sermon style." Stolpa, "Preaching to the Clergy," 225.

9. For Copley see Marion Ann Taylor and Heather E. Weir, eds., *Let Her Speak for Herself: Nineteenth-Century Women Writing on the Women of Genesis* (Waco: Baylor University Press, 2006), 32. For Nightingale, see Lynn McDonald, ed., *Florence Nightingale's Spiritual Journey: Biblical Annotations, Sermons and Journal Notes,* volume 2 of *The Collected Works of Florence Nightingale* (Waterloo, ON: Wilfred Laurier University Press), 325–26. Nightingale is one example of a woman who wrote sermons as literary works, without the certain expectation that they would be preached.

10. See, for example, Christine L. Krueger, *The Reader's Repentance: Women Preachers, Women Writers, and Nineteenth-Century Social Discourse* (Chicago: University of Chicago Press, 1992).

11. See Joni Sancken, "Deverell, Mary," in *Handbook of Women Biblical Interpreters: A Historical and Biographical Guide*, ed. Marion Ann Taylor and Agnes Choi (Grand Rapids: Baker Academic, 2012), 159–62.

12. Anna Carter Florence, *Preaching as Testimony* (Louisville: Westminster John Knox

woman bore of Jesus provided women who wrote about them, particularly Baxter, Wilson, and Palmer, with evidence to support arguments that women could and should preach in the nineteenth century as they had done in the first century. Baxter found the Samaritan woman a helpful counter-example to the argument that required preachers to have a certain kind of education and official standing in the church. Locker-Lampson's sermon on the Samaritan woman exemplifies the kind of rhetoric preachers used to convince their audiences to change their behavior.

Clara Lucas Balfour also noted the model of the Samaritan woman as a preacher and evangelist, but used her primarily as an example of repentance and forgiveness. She was a repentant sinner fully accepted by Jesus. Balfour's written sermon drew a moral lesson from the behavior of Jesus for the women of her own time. Balfour did not dwell on the Samaritan woman as a preacher, finding a more pertinent practical life lesson in the story for her audience.

In a similar way, Herodias and her daughter provided nineteenth-century women with moral examples, in this case, of how not to live. Herodias and her daughter (unnamed in the biblical text, but named Salome in Josephus[13]) provided the subject matter for sermons on social ills such as dancing. The stern moral tone of the sermons in this section provides a glimpse into the mindset of the Victorian middle class. Like many Victorian sermons, each excerpt begins with a text around which the preacher focused her thoughts.[14] In Margaret Black's very short devotional sermon, the moral application, addressing specific behaviors and attitudes, immediately follows the Scripture text. Donaldson's sermon is much longer; she used the story of Herodias and her daughter as a springboard to preach the gospel of salvation found in Jesus Christ. E. J. Richmond and Harriet Beecher Stowe used their essays on Herodias and her daughter to preach on the power of women to do evil.

Anna and the Samaritan woman were examples to nineteenth-century women who felt called to preach. Those two women of the Gospels spoke "the very oracles of God" (1 Pet. 4:11), giving their nineteenth-century sisters courage to speak also. Herodias and her daughter, on the other hand, provided subject matter for nineteenth-century women's sermons. Whether as examples of preaching or occasions to preach, the women of the Gospels provided inspiration for the women of the nineteenth century.

Press, 2007), xx. Florence's entire book explores the relationship of testimony and preaching, particularly as found in women's traditions of preaching.

13. *Antiquities* 18.5.3
14. Solpa, "Preaching to the Clergy," 229.

3

Anna: The Vocation of a Woman Preacher

Anna is the only living prophet mentioned in the infancy narratives of Jesus. She is a minor figure in the New Testament, only appearing briefly in Luke 2:36–38, where she is introduced as an aged, widowed prophet, the daughter of Phanuel from the tribe of Asher, who spent her time in the temple, worshiping God with fasting and prayer. She appeared in the temple at the very time Simeon was talking to Mary and Joseph and began praising God and talking about the child Jesus to everyone who had been "looking for the redemption of Jerusalem" (Luke 2:25–38).

Anna's cameo appearance in Luke intrigued nineteenth-century women. Her status as a widow prompted them to reflect upon what it meant to live as a widow in the context of a community of faith. Anna's identification as a prophet, and her act of speaking about the Christ child in the temple, prompted reflection and argument about women's roles in church and society. The four selections on Anna in this chapter are representative of many other women's writings on Anna; they reveal nineteenth-century women's fascination with Anna's vocation as a prophet. With all interpreters of Luke 2, these women had to decide what it meant that Anna served in the temple "day and night"; the four writers excerpted here did not all agree on what this meant.

These excerpts also show that Anna's example was used to argue that women were called to preach. American writers Hale and Wilson used Anna to promote their views on the nature and roles of women in the church and society. British writers Baxter and M. G. also addressed the issue of women and preaching, but their contexts and audiences were different and their arguments were more nuanced and subtle.

Three genres are featured in the four excerpts on Anna. Both Hale and Baxter wrote biographical sketches of Anna; these biographies treated Anna in different ways. Hale's brief biography of Anna made a strong argument for women's equality with men on the one hand, and women's spiritual superiority to men on the other. Baxter fleshed out Anna's story and suggested her significance as a model preacher. Wilson's excerpt on Anna was part of a larger polemic for women's public roles in the church. The final author included here, M. G., preached a sermon for women on Anna.

SARAH HALE (1788–1879)

Anna's Spiritual Superiority

Sarah Josepha Hale was an accomplished American editor and writer, author of many periodical pieces, thirty-six books, and the nursery rhyme, "Mary Had a Little Lamb."[1] She was born in Newport, New Hampshire, the daughter of Captain Gordon Buell, a revolutionary soldier, and Martha Whittlesey, who educated her daughter at home. She learned Latin and philosophy from her brother, who studied at Dartmouth. She married David Hale in 1813 and gave birth to five children before her husband died in 1822. She took up writing to support her young family. In 1828, she was offered the editorship of the *Ladies' Magazine*; in 1837, she became editor of *Godey's Ladies Book*.

Hale's most ambitious publishing project was *Woman's Record: or, Sketches of All Distinguished Women from the Beginning Till A.D. 1850*.[2] This project took the form of an ideologically-framed biographical dictionary of women beginning with the biographies of women in Scripture. Throughout the work Hale argued for women's moral and spiritual superiority to men.

Hale emphasized Anna's spiritual superiority to Simeon as part of her grand argument for women's excellence. She noted that while Simeon lived in Jerusalem, Anna did not depart from the Temple. Hale also called Simeon and Anna "testifiers" to Jesus' mission. Since "testifying" is a term associated

---

1. Heather Macumber, "Hale, Sarah (1788–1879)," in *Handbook of Women Interpreters of the Bible*, ed. Marion Ann Taylor and Agnes Choi (Grand Rapids: Baker Academic, 2012), 240–42. See also Sherbrooke Rogers, *Sarah Josepha Hale: A New England Pioneer* (Grantham, NH: Tompson & Ruetter, 1985).

2. This work went through several editions. The edition excerpted here has the year 1854 in the title.

with preaching or proclamation throughout the history of the church, it could be argued that Hale regarded Anna as a preacher.[3]

ANNA

A JEWISH prophetess, the daughter of Phanuel, of the tribe of Asher. She had been early married, and had lived seven years with her husband. After his death, she devoted herself to the service of God, and while thus employed, finding the virgin Mary with her son in the temple, she joined with the venerable Simeon in thanking God for him, and bearing testimony to him as the promised Messiah. It is worth remarking, that these two early testifiers of our Saviour's mission being both far advanced in life, could not be liable to the most distant suspicion of collusion with Joseph and Mary in palming a false Messiah on their countrymen, as they had not the smallest probable chance of living to see him grow up to maturity, and fulfil their prophecies, and therefore could have no interest in declaring a falsehood. Thus we find the advent of our Lord was made known, spiritually, to woman as well as to man. The good old Simeon had no clearer revelation than the aged devout Anna. Both were inspired servants of the Most High; but here the characteristic piety of the woman is shown to excel. Simeon dwelt "in Jerusalem," probably engaged in secular pursuits; Anna, "departed not from the temple, but served God with fasting and prayers night and day." See St. Luke, chap. 2.

Source: Sarah Hale, *Woman's Record; or, Sketches of All Distinguished Women, from the Creation to A.D. 1854* (New York: Harper & Brothers, 1855), 71–72.

ELIZABETH BAXTER (1837–1926)

A Role Model for Female Ministry

Elizabeth Baxter was an English evangelist, preacher, teacher, and prolific author of some forty books and commentaries, booklets, tracts, Bible stud-

3. See Ronald E. Osborn, *Folly of God: The Rise of Christian Preaching*, vol. 1, *A History of Christian Preaching* (St. Louis: Chalice, 1999). See also Florence, *Preaching as Testimony*.

ies, and a guide to the Anglican Book of Common Prayer.[4] Baxter was the daughter of Thomas Nelson Foster (1799–1858), a Quaker, and his second wife, Elizabeth Gibbs. Baxter had a conversion experience in her late teens and became involved in the Anglican deaconess movement. After her marriage to end-times lecturer and evangelist Reverend Michael Paget Baxter (1834–1910), Elizabeth Baxter spent 15 years as a traveling preacher.[5] Later the couple was involved in the Moody-Sankey crusades in Great Britain where Baxter expounded Scripture to as many as 1500 women each week.[6] Her husband's purchase of *The Christian Herald* publishing company allowed Baxter's publishing career to flourish.

Most of Baxter's books grew out of her extensive preaching and teaching ministries. Some works focus on characters in Scripture (*The Women in the Word* [1897] and *The School of the Patriarchs* [1903]); others are commentaries (for example, *Ezekiel Son of Man: His Life and Ministry* [1902], *Portraits from Proverbs* [1891], and *Job* [1894]). As the subtitle, *A Few Simple Hints from Bible Portraits of Women*, suggests, Baxter intended *The Women in the Word* to provide spiritual advice to her readers. Most of the 46 chapters in the book focus on one particular woman or group of women, although Baxter includes two chapters on Deborah, and four on Mary. Her primary audience was women, although Baxter included all Christians in some of her applications.

Baxter's experience of a strong sense of call to evangelistic preaching and teaching influenced the way she understood the women of Scripture. As her discussion of Anna demonstrates, Baxter did not think that a call from God exempted women from household duties. Rather, she argued that a woman's usual service, to husband, children, and servants, was part of her spiritual vocation. Anna was one of many women of the Bible who provided Baxter with a role model for a life of prayer and proclamation.

---

4. Marion Ann Taylor, "Baxter, Elizabeth (1837–1926)," in Taylor and Choi, *Handbook*, 59–62.

5. On their honeymoon, Elizabeth Baxter experienced "a call from God, not to be disregarded or disobeyed" to join her husband in street preaching. Nathaniel Wiseman, *Elizabeth Baxter: Saint, Evangelist, Preacher, Teacher and Expositor* (London: The Christian Herald, 1928), 83.

6. For a summary of Moody and Sankey's evangelistic work in Britain see D. W. Bebbington, *Evangelicalism in Modern Britain: A History from the 1730s to the 1980s* (London: Unwin Hyman, 1989), 162–64.

ANNA: THE PROPHETESS.

Luke 2:36–38.

ANNA is one of the prophetesses mentioned in the Word of God as such. In early life she married, but we may well believe that the Lord was with her in all the commonplaces of housekeeping and household duties. The same God who afterwards gave her her vocation was her Counsellor and Strength. Whenever God gives to a woman a special spiritual vocation, it will generally be found that her home life was made of God a preparation for it.

In the early Church it was one of the necessities for the office of a Bishop that he should be "one that ruleth well his own house, having his children in subjection with all gravity; for if a man know not how to rule his own house, how shall he take care of the Church of God?" (1 Tim. 3:4, 5.) With how much more reason must a woman, whose ordinary vocation is in the house, be true and faithful in little things if God is to call her to any unwonted ministry in His vineyard!

Anna's married life was short—only seven years—and then came the deepest blow of all to the heart of a woman, and especially a Jewish woman— WIDOWHOOD. Sorrow hardens those who live a selfish life. They give themselves up to self-pity, bemoaning their lot, looking upon their God as hard, and jealously envying what seems the happier lot of others. But a widow who has accepted the Lord her God as her stay is perhaps one of the happiest, one of the most useful, one of the most gracious of God's creatures.

Anna's vocation was that of prayer. "She was a widow of about fourscore and four years which departed not from the temple, but served God with fastings and prayers night and day."

"What a dull life!" some young person might say, and seen from the outside it might seem so; but those who looked on the face of the aged prophetess would see nothing monotonous there. Living continually face to face with God, drinking in perpetually the thoughts which he would impart to her, losing the narrowness of self interest and absorbed in the continually widened interests which God would make known to her as she was able to bear them—there must have been a light upon the countenance of Anna which was a study in itself, for God and heaven shone there.

There are few who could be fitted for a vocation such as this—only those who understand that "a living sacrifice" [Rom. 12:1] means A LIFE OF PRAYER.

During the temple services, Anna would have no pre-eminent place, but in some quiet corner when the praises of the priests and Levites were going up to heaven, this still woman would be praying, and bearing up every worshipper upon her heart. When the children were brought into the temple that they might be presented to the Lord, the dedication of the parents would be buoyed up by the prayers of Anna. If Jerusalem were visited with a pestilence, perhaps no other had more to do than Anna with its removal, for she would bear upon her heart the sin of her people which God was rebuking, and would take case after case of those who were smitten, and inquire of the Lord concerning them. She was at home with those who were unworldly; she was not to be found at feasts or in worldly gatherings; but wherever there was a need for God, wherever there was a cry after God, there Anna found admission; it was just there that prayer was needed.

Surely it was no accident that brought her into the temple just when the Spirit of the Lord guided Simeon thither, and the parents of the Lord Jesus had brought Him, as an infant, "to do for Him after the custom of the law" [Luke 2:27]. The same instinct from on high which gave Simeon to see in Him the Lord's Christ, led Anna to "give thanks likewise unto the Lord." She, too, recognised her Redeemer "and SPAKE OF HIM to all that looked for redemption in Jerusalem." (Luke 2:38.)

It may be, she was a woman of few words; most people who pray intensely are so. But when she did speak, her one theme was Himself, and she knew who would understand her. Probably the majority of the population of Jerusalem did not know even of her existence, but Anna knew all those "who looked for redemption in Jerusalem," and probably, those in the hill country of Judea who laid up in their hearts all that was revealed concerning the vocation of John the Baptist. This little company, with their eyes upon the coming King, and the coming kingdom, lived in an atmosphere contrary to the world of their day. Herod and Jerusalem "were troubled" [Matt. 2:1] at the birth of Jesus: Anna's whole soul was filled with adoration for it; the aged intercessor saw the answer to her prayers.

The Lord raise up praying Annas in our day of whom it may be said, "She spake of Him."

Source: Elizabeth Baxter, *The Women in the Word: A Few Simple Hints from Bible Portraits of Women*, 2nd ed. (London: Christian Herald, 1897), 203–5.

ELIZABETH WILSON (FL. 1839–1849)

....

A Woman with a Vocation

Elizabeth Wilson was a women's rights activist and author of *A Scriptural View of Women's Rights and Duties, In All the Important Relations of Life.*[7] Wilson, who lived in Cadez, Ohio, was the daughter of a Scottish Presbyterian minister. She spent ten years researching and writing her 376-page book on women's rights and duties.[8] Wilson believed that woman remained the equal of man after the fall, retaining rights and dignities which she felt were not being honored in the church or civil society. With passion and authority, she criticized preachers, commentators, and civil authorities who circumscribed women's rights and roles in the family, church, and society.[9]

For Wilson, Anna was an important witness to the public and prophetic preaching ministry of women.[10] Wilson's brief comments on Anna are part of a larger discussion about what she called "woman's instrumentality in the church, from its first organization, including both Old and New Testament dispensations."[11] Her intention was "to see whether the apostle could possibly prohibit women from speaking in the church, (1 Cor. 14:34) considering the example and facts on scripture record."[12] She imagined Anna as a much more public figure than the other authors excerpted in this chapter. Wilson's involvement with the early women's movement in the United States influenced her reading of the Bible.

---

7. Philadelphia: Wm S. Young, 1849. For more on Wilson, see Joy A. Schroeder, "Elizabeth Wilson, the Bible, and Legal Rights of Women in the Nineteenth Century," *Postscripts: The Journal of Sacred Texts and Contemporary Worlds* 5, no. 2 (2009): 219–32.

8. Letter from Mott to Elizabeth Cady Stanton as quoted in Nancy Isenberg, *Sex & Citizenship in Antebellum America* (Chapel Hill: University of North Carolina Press, 1998), n. 127, 230–31.

9. Wilson, *A Scriptural View*, 374.

10. See also Wilson, *Scriptural View*, 231, 235, and 237. Wilson combined Anna with Deborah and Huldah as counter-examples to a male preacher's argument that it was immodest for women to speak publicly.

11. Wilson, *Scriptural View*, 167.

12. Wilson, *Scriptural View*, 167.

Woman's Instrumentality in a Religious Point of View, Under the Old and New Testament Dispensations

Anna, the prophetess, was the first who preached him [Jesus] publicly: she ministered in the temple; she served with fastings and prayers, night and day. These prayers were manifestly public, as she publicly gave thanks when she saw the infant Messiah make his appearance in the temple, and spoke of him to all that looked for redemption in Jerusalem, or (as the margin) in Israel. The word of the Lord was precious in those days among the Jews,— open vision had nearly ceased. Anna was the last established prophet under the Jewish dispensation. This devout woman spent her whole time in the service of the temple, and she had a favourable opportunity of speaking to Jews from all places, who resorted thither to worship, and they would thus be privileged to hear the discourses of this great prophetess, so famed for her deep-toned piety and rare gifts.

Source: Elizabeth Wilson, *A Scriptural View of Women's Rights and Duties, In All the Important Relations of Life* (Philadelphia: Wm S. Young, 1849), 167.

M. G. (FL. 1893)

A Widow's Vocation: A Sermon

M. G. was an Anglo-Catholic author of *Women Like Ourselves: Short Addresses for Mother's Meetings, Bible Classes, etc.* (1893).[13] Her published addresses delivered to Mothers' Meetings were to be used by women working in ministries to women.

While M. G. used the term "addresses" for her works, they can be called sermons.[14] Her published compositions in *Women Like Ourselves* clearly originated as oral presentations. M. G. is included in this chapter primarily as an example of a woman preaching about Anna, whom she regards as an

---

13. For more information on M. G., see "Work and Devotion" in the chapter on Mary and Martha.

14. See Joni Sancken's discussion of the sermon in "Calling Forth More Witnesses: Claiming the Voices of Preachers Silenced by History," *Toronto Journal of Theology* 26, no. 1 (2010): 47–58.

example to widows. In this sermon she used standard preaching rhetoric, asking questions such as "Did you ever notice?" and "Won't you sometimes come to Church?" to draw her listeners into the story and realize its practical relevance to their lives. She also preached with confidence, exhorting women to follow Anna's example and speak to others around them about Jesus.

Anna

DID you ever notice the tender way in which God always speaks of "the widow" in Holy Scripture? It would be an interesting occupation some Sunday evening, if you would take your Bibles and search through them to find how often the widow is spoken of with fatherly compassion, as being especially under God's protection. We have only time to turn to a few of those passages now. See in Exodus 22:22–24, how God declares Himself the champion of the widow and the fatherless when they are oppressed. In Ezekiel 22:7, we see how God reckons among the many sins of the city of Jerusalem, that there "they vexed the fatherless and the widow." In Proverbs 15:25, we read that while He casts down the proud, God will "enlarge the border of the widow," that is, make her little property increase. Did not He do this for the widow of Sarepta, whose story we have in 1 Kings 17:8–16, and for that other widow in 2 Kings 4:1–7.

You will remember, almost without turning it out (in St. Luke 7:12, 13), how when our Blessed Lord saw the widow at Nain mourning for her son, His heart was filled with great compassion for her. I see several widows here to-day; it is a comforting and beautiful thought for you, is it not, that now that your natural protectors are gone, you have Almighty God Himself taking special charge of you, and promising to fill your husbands' place, with all the love and sympathy and tender care that *they* had for you, excepting that with God all these are infinitely deeper and stronger than any human affections could be.

The idea among the heathen in many countries is that there is a different deity taking special departments in charge; for instance, that there is one god for farmers and another for sailors, and another, they think, is god of war, and a different one god of love. So that under different circumstances they pray to different gods. We know better than they. Our Creed teaches us to say, "I believe in one God."[15] And this "one God" styles Himself especially

---

15. The Apostles' Creed begins with this phrase.

"the God of the widow,"[16] as if she were more His care than all the rest of the universe beside.

As we might expect, since God sets us this example, we too are commanded to take particular charge of the widows amongst us. I will give you one precept, and one example. In St. James 1:27, we have sympathy and care for them mentioned as one of the chief characteristics of true religion. And for an example, we find in Acts 9:36–42, that the chief of the good works of Dorcas was her charity in making garments for the widows of Joppa. Among the heathens in India, widowhood is considered a lasting disgrace. It was the rule, till our Government forbade it, that the widow was always burnt alive on the same pile with her husband's body.[17] This cruel custom is abolished now, but many Indian widows still seek for death, to escape the bitter cruelty with which they are treated by their relations for the rest of their lives. What a contrast between heathenism and Christianity in this respect! When a great persecution arose in Spain, some of the persecutors came to the Church where a young deacon named Lawrence had been left in charge, and demanded to see the jewels for which they had heard that the Church was famous. "Our precious treasures?" said Lawrence. "Yes, you shall see them. Come this time to-morrow and I will have them set out for you to see." Next day they came again at the time appointed. Lawrence led them into the Church and showed them a number of aged and infirm widows. "Those are our precious jewels," he said, "of greater value than any gold and silver."[18]

In the early days of Christianity it was the practice to enroll the old and deserving widows upon a list, so that they might be looked after and relieved; they, on their part, engaging to devote the rest of their lives entirely to God's service, as the husband henceforward of their souls.

In 1 Tim[othy] 5 we find the regulations which St. Paul laid down for the sort of Sisterhood into which the widows of Ephesus were formed, when they were left without children or near relations to support them. These desolate ones, if they were truly "widows indeed" (vers. 3–6), *i.e.* if they were widows in heart, resolving to remain ever faithful to their husbands' memory, should henceforth have no thought for the things of the world. "The host who no longer wishes to receive guests," says a holy bishop "should pull down the

16. M. G. may be alluding to Ps. 146:9 or Ps. 68:5. In the Bible God is often portrayed as one who protects the widow and the fatherless, but is never called "the God of the widow."

17. This practice was formally banned in India beginning in 1829.

18. This story is part of the tradition surrounding St. Laurence, martyred in A.D. 256. See David Hugh Farmer, *The Oxford Dictionary of Saints*, 4th ed (Oxford: Oxford University Press, 1997), 295–96.

sign from his house. Seeing that she ought now to have no other love but God she ought scarce to have words for any other but God."* As St. Paul puts it, "she that is a widow indeed and desolate, trusteth in God, and continueth in supplications and prayers night and day" [1 Tim. 5:5].

We have a type of this sort of consecrated widowhood in the Gospel (St. Luke 2:36–38). We see an aged woman, Anna by name, who, after seven brief years of happy married life, had lost her husband eighty-four years before. Since his death, worldly pleasures had had no delight for her. Her home was the Temple, where, in the immediate presence of the God of the widow, and the companionship of His servants, she no longer felt desolate. Since she no longer had to care for the things of the world, that she might please her husband (1 Cor. 7:34), her delight was to "attend upon the Lord without distraction" [1 Cor. 7:35]. She "departed not from the Temple," that is, she was constantly to be found there, at every service, and often in private devotions besides, "serving God with fastings and prayers night and day."[19] Her self-denials and constant communion with God purified and enlightened the eyes of her soul, so that she could see and understand many of the deep things of God, which were hidden from the less spiritually minded, so that she was called "a prophetess." In her younger days, we may be sure, she had been "well reported of for good works" [1 Tim. 5:10] all of kinds. Now, in her old age, she could not do much else but pray, and by her continual intercessions she strengthened the servants of God and helped on the work of the Church.

Now could not those of you who are, like Anna, left desolate, follow her example in this respect? You have not the cares of a family to keep you away from God's House; you own that you have no ties to earth, your day for work seems over. Won't you sometimes come to Church on a week-day, like Anna, and pray for those who are too busy, or too idle, or too worldly-minded to pray for themselves? Won't you, as you sit with your hands folded by your fireside, or as you lie awake in the long dark nights, keep offering short prayers to God for yourself and for all around you, and for the welfare of

19. Compare "Anna" in Esther Hewlett Copley, *Scripture Biography: Comprehending All the Names Mentioned in the Old and New Testaments* (London: Fisher, Fisher & Jackson, 1835), 84–85. Like M. G., Copley understood the description of Anna serving in the temple day and night to mean that Anna attended morning and evening prayer and any other service available. Copley and M. G. were reading back into Anna's story the Christian discipline of attending services of morning and evening prayer.

*St. Francis de Sales. [M. G. has joined two sentences from different parts of de Sales's work together. Francis de Sales, *Introduction to the Devout Life* (London: Rivington's, 1864), 161, 201.]

God's Church? I have known some whose old age has thus become the most beautiful and most useful portion of their life. That good bishop I quoted before, says—"The true widow is in the Church a little March violet, who sends forth an inexpressible sweetness by the perfume of her devotions, and keeps herself almost always concealed under the broad leaves of her lowliness, while her dark colour tells of her self denial. She grows in cool and hidden places, not willing to be troubled with the conversation of worldly people."[20]

Such was old Anna, and such every Christian widow may be in God's sight. There came a day when, coming as usual to the temple, Anna found the long-desired Christ there, and could join with aged Simeon in heartfelt thanksgiving, that they had seen with their own eyes the Lord's salvation. We too, if we persevere in regular attendance at God's House, shall find Christ there. We may be almost the only worshippers, those who are there may not recognize Him, but He will manifest His presence to us, in the dim light, it may be, of the early morning, at His altar, and we too shall feel that now whenever He shall call us we are ready at last to depart in peace.

And, lastly, having found Him, Anna could not but lead others to recognize Him too. Not in idle chatter up and down the town, did she speak of her "experiences," but softly and reverently to those who she knew would love to hear of Him. "They that loved the Lord spake often of Him to one another" [Mal. 3:16 paraphrase]. But with us, even between those whose hearts are the most dearly attached to Him, there is sometimes too great a shyness in speaking and encouraging one another on religious matters. It is well not to chatter about them too much, but rather to keep them and ponder them in our hearts; but we may carry the reserve a little too far. Oh, having, like Anna, found the true undying object of affection and adoration, let us sometimes, at least, speak of Him to those who, like ourselves, are looking for redemption.

Who knows how those, whose journey is nearly over, may comfort and strengthen their brethren who are still toiling in the heat of the day? In many a busy parish there is the cottage of some old widow to which the Pastor often turns his steps for sympathy, and even for advice, when he is wearied and disheartened in his work. A word of comfort, a soft "God bless you," a whispered prayer after the visitor has left, do not sound much to give; the angels treasure them up though, and bear them to the throne of God, and the lonely priest and the wearied mother, the sinful wayfarer and the little

---

20. De Sales, *Devout Life*, 202.

child, all go their way cheered and helped by the poor widow's kindly words, and blessed more than she or they can ever know by her prayers.

Thus you see God has work for us all to do, the little servant-maid, the great queen, the old widow. And if we do that work faithfully to the last, then when He calls us hence it will be to go up to the Temple above, the heavenly Jerusalem, where those who have long looked for His redemption upon earth shall at length see His glory.

Source: M. G., *Women Like Ourselves: Short Addresses for Mother's Meetings, Bible Classes, Etc.* (London: SPCK, 1893), 126–31.

STUDY QUESTIONS

1. What is the difference between prophesying and preaching? How are they similar? How do these commentators see the relationship between the two? How is Anna portrayed as an example of prophesying or preaching?

2. What adjectives do these excerpts use to describe Anna? What do these commentators say is the significance of Anna's character within the text? How do they apply Anna's significance to their audience? Would their applications work today?

3. Compare and contrast these commentators' reflections on the importance of prayer. How is Anna portrayed as an example of a life of prayer in their context? Does this portrayal translate to the present? Why or why not?

4. Several of the commentators note that Anna had been a wife and then a prophet. Women often balance duties at home and duties in a career or vocation. Is Anna an example for women seeking balance? Why or why not?

4

The Woman at the Well: The First Samaritan Evangelist

The unnamed woman of Samaria met Jesus by Jacob's well outside of Sychar. John 4 records Jesus' conversation with the woman in some detail. The chapter also notes her invitation to the people of Sychar, "Come, see a man, which told me all things that ever I did: is not this the Christ?" (John 4:29). The Samaritan woman's testimony convinced many of the people of the city to believe in Jesus. John 4 also records that Jesus stayed in Sychar for two days at the people's invitation and many more believed after hearing his teaching during that time.

Nineteenth-century women writing on this story answered common interpretive questions arising from John 4. They discussed the geographical setting of the story, using both their own travel experiences, and the travel experiences of others. They addressed questions about the historical relationship between the Samaritans and the Jews, using published theological and historical works. They talked about the theological significance of Jesus' teaching about living water. They reflected on the way Christians should treat people with moral failings.

Significantly for the theme of this section, the women excerpted in this chapter also examined the Samaritan woman's role as an evangelist. They used the Samaritan woman as a model to encourage women to evangelize in the private and public spheres, by sharing their spiritual experiences with others and by preaching. All of the authors in this chapter were preachers. Not all of the excerpts included argue unambiguously for women's preaching—significantly Hannah Locker-Lampson did not mention that application in her sermon at all—but all demonstrate the reality of women preaching in the nineteenth century.

The first two selections in this chapter, Balfour's and Baxter's scriptural biographies, hold up the Samaritan woman as an example in her conversion and in her evangelism of the people of Sychar. Palmer's essay is a polemic for women's preaching, and focuses exclusively on the woman's evangelistic endeavours. The final two selections on the woman of Samaria are sermons. Taking the woman of Samaria who preached the gospel to her contemporaries as an example, two of the nineteenth-century, Locker-Lampson and Beck, preached her story, and the gospel, to other women.

CLARA LUCAS BALFOUR (1808–1878)

A Changed Woman

Clara Lucas Balfour was a popular British speaker, writer, and social justice activist.[1] Her life experience of battling poverty and domestic problems, including her husband's drinking, and her public career influenced how she read Scripture.

In *Women of Scripture* (1847), Balfour examined key women in Scripture, calling attention to their virtues and presenting them as examples to her readers. The woman of Samaria was one such woman. Balfour highlighted the importance of Jesus' caring attitude toward the erring woman, encouraging Christians, particularly women, to be less judgmental and more concerned for transformation in others. As a careful reader of the biblical text, Balfour picked up on textual details and possible contradictions in the story. She took the point of view of the Samaritan woman, emphasizing the intelligence she displayed in her conversation with Jesus. Balfour empathized with the woman, downplaying her culpability, noting differences in divorce laws between the world of the text and nineteenth-century England. She lauded the Samaritan woman's desire to invite others to listen to Jesus, naming her as a successful early preacher of the gospel.

---

1. For more information on Balfour and *Women of Scripture* see "Humility: The Noblest Virtute," in the chapter on Mary and "Action and Contemplation" in the chapter on Mary and Martha.

INQUIRY AND REPENTANCE—THE WOMAN OF SAMARIA

Among the many harsh prejudices which the holy system of the Gospel was designed to root out, none is so successfully exposed as the spirit of stern, contemptuous judgment against our weak and erring fellow-mortals, and an overweening estimate of ourselves. We are taught by that pure and benevolent system, to discriminate between sin and the sinner; while we are to shun and hate all evil, we are to compassionate and labour for the reclamation of evil-doers. In all our dealings with the erring, we are to be actuated by a desire for their real good, and never by a spirit of revenge. . . . According to some notions, tears cannot wash away her sin,—repentance opens no door of hope,—she is shut out of society, and forbidden to attempt to re-enter it. This has the effect of hardening the heart of some sinners, and driving others to despair. Woman is verily guilty towards her sister woman in this particular. It would correct many errors on this and all questions of morals, if we came to "the law, and to the testimony" [Isa. 8:20] of the great Teacher for instruction.

The Jews and Samaritans had long entertained a national feud with each other. The former despised the latter as their inferiors in every particular. The Samaritans had, at a remote period, set up a rival temple for the worship of God on Mount Gerizim, near to the town of Sychar, contrary to the institutions of the Jews; and many discontented or profligate Hebrews mingled with the Samaritans, instituting a form of worship, and an order of priesthood, in distinction from the Jews.* This was sufficient to account for the jealousy, though it could not excuse the prejudice, that subsisted between the people of each locality against the other. Our Lord, to avoid the persecutions of the Pharisees,† "left Judea, and departed again into Galilee, and he must needs go through Samaria:" he came to Sychar, where Jacob's ancient well was, and, being wearied, rested on the brink of that well. How affecting is the record, he was "wearied!"—hunger, thirst, poverty, weariness, every vexing and humiliating trial that flesh is heir to, was the daily portion of Him who was "Lord over all, blessed for ever!" [Rom. 9:5]. While the exhausted traveller thus sat, there came a woman of Samaria to the well to draw water; and Jesus, with condescending sweetness, said to her, "Give me to drink." The

*See Prideaux's Connexion, vol. ii. 553 [Humphrey Prideaux, *The Old and New Testament Connected in the History of the Jews and Neighbouring Nations from the Declension of the Kingdoms of Israel and Judah to the Time of Christ*, 4 vols. (London: R. Knaplock; J. Tonson, 1715–18). This standard reference work was republished several times in the nineteenth century.]
†John 4

woman, by his speech and garb, knew Him to be a Jew, and was startled at the request, for she was well acquainted with the strong dislike that subsisted between the Jews and her countrymen, and, instead of complying, she says, "How is it that thou, being a Jew, askest drink of me, who am a woman of Samaria? for the Jews have no dealings with the Samaritans." This remark appears to contradict a preceding verse, where it is said, "His disciples were gone away into the city to buy meat;" but the "dealings" which the woman referred to were probably the refusal of the Jews to owe any obligation, or to ask any kindness of the Samaritans, and not to dealings of exchange and barter. Our Lord, instead of being offended with the discourteous woman, who preferred parleying with a thirsty, exhausted stranger, to granting his simple request, gently replied, "If thou knewest the gift of God, and who it is that saith to thee, Give me to drink; thou wouldest have asked of Him, and He would have given thee living water." There was something in the tone of the mild impressive voice that thrilled to the depths of the woman's soul. She gazed again intently on the stranger. . . . [H]er manner became more courteous, and yet a kind of lurking incredulity mingled with her speech. "Sir, thou hast nothing to draw with, and the well is deep, whence hast thou this living water? Art thou greater than our father Jacob?" Then followed the sublime announcement "Whosoever drinketh of this water shall thirst again; but whosoever drinketh of the water that I shall give him shall never thirst." Ah! little did this woman of Samaria know of the renewing grace, that, like a perennial spring, is ever flowing in the pious heart, ever rising up to light and life, refreshing the soul, strengthening the spirit,—a spring coming from the "river whose streams make glad the city of God" [Ps. 46:4]. Again she considers, wonder and awe mingling with her doubts, and tempering the manner of her pertinacious questions. "Sir, give me this water, that I thirst not, neither come hither to draw." Then it was that our Lord sought to probe the depths of her heart, and to recall her to a salutary sense of degradation and sin. She was a skilful disputant—a sturdy inquirer; one remark shall call her thoughts home to her own life. Jesus said, "Go, call thy husband, and come hither:" in confusion the Samaritan made a brief reply, "I have no husband." Then our Lord displayed his knowledge of her affairs, "Thou hast had five husbands, and he whom thou now hast is not thy husband; in that saidst thou truly."

Confounded by this remark, we find the woman of Samaria rallying her scattered thoughts, and with something that looks like feminine tact and ingenuity to hide her confusion,—after, with all respect, owning Christ as a prophet,—seeks to call off his attention from her degrading domestic affairs by asking a solution of the national difference, "Our fathers worshipped in this mountain; and ye say that in Jerusalem is the place where men ought to worship." Then followed that hallowed reply, announcing the necessity of spiritual worship; not forms of faith, nor localized ceremonials, but the consecration of the heart. While he thus spake, the soul of the listener was aroused; who could this be that uttered such wonderous words? she had heard of the expected Messiah—this can be no other, and she exclaims, "I know that Messias cometh, which is called Christ; when He is come, He will tell us all things." It pleased the Redeemer in reply to this, to make a full announcement of Himself. Instantly the films of doubt are dispersed, and the woman of Samaria believes. It is so obvious throughout the whole conversation, that, however degraded this woman might be, she was not an ignorant person. She knew of the controversies of her people and the Jews; she had an intelligent desire to know the opinion of the remarkable individual she had met in reference to the right locality for worship: she knew the traditions of the ancient well and the prophecies relative to the Messiah; the fact of her having an informed mind only adds to her guilt, but there is this to be borne in mind, that if intellectual attainments do not prevent people from falling into sin, they have a decided tendency to keep them from being happy in guilt, and to restrain them from sinking to the lowest depths. Nor must we forget that the social customs of that ancient time will not bear to be viewed in the light of Christianity. The facility of divorce may account for the repeated marriages of the woman of Samaria, and she might not have lost caste among her people in consequence of her circumstances.

The way in which our Lord alludes to the domestic character of this woman marks his sense of its revolting nature, yet, he shows his compassionate sympathy for the individual. He does not rebuke or revile her, but calls her thoughts from earthly and sensual pursuits to the beauty of spirituality, the sublimity of truth. He tells her of the character of God, and shows that there must be an affinity (however great the disparity) between the worshipper and the worshipped. In the midst of all her degradation, the heart of this woman was not utterly seared; she had felt the bitterness of remorse—the struggle with convictions; she knew too much of good to be happy in evil,—she possessed a mind

"Not all degraded
even by the crimes through which it waded."[2]

2. Lines from Lord Byron, "The Giaur, a Fragment of a Turkish Tale." Reprinted in *The*

Hence her restless, inquiring, arguing spirit. Anything is better than supineness—the guilty who sink down to the level of their deeds, uninquiring, listless, are in the most hopeless state of moral degradation. . . .

The faith of the woman of Samaria was ardent as well as sincere: it is an interesting incident that she "left her waterpot and went her way into the city," so absorbed in the gracious and glorious tidings that had fallen upon her ear, that she forgot the purpose which had brought her to the well. Her soul had been purified in communion with the hallowed source of all purity. The degrading chains that bound her to sin had been broken, and she arose in the freedom of the gospel, and hastened to communicate to others the good news of the coming of Christ. "Come, see a man who told me all things that ever I did: is not this the Christ?" It is plain that this woman of Samaria must have been held in estimation by her townspeople; we have seen that it could not be for her moral excellence; it must, therefore, have been for her intelligence. The people would not have left the city at the words of a foolish woman. We find that many of the Samaritans "believed on him for the saying of the woman," "and many more believed because of his own word." It is a beautiful trait in her regenerated character, that she so actively sought to bring others to Jesus—the best evidence of the sincerity of her change, both of heart and life. Her communication also was as brief as any invitation could be—enough to arouse attention and stimulate a wholesome curiosity, not to satisfy either: Christ, and Christ only, could complete the work of faith in the heart; therefore her grateful townspeple said, "We believe, not because of thy saying: for we have heard Him ourselves, and know that this is indeed the Christ, the Saviour of the world."

It would be well if all who call themselves Christians, when they are giving over some erring mortal to reprobation, would for awhile suspend their judgment, and be more ready to hope, and pray, and labour, for the amendment of the sinner, than to call for his punishment—remembering that one of the most successful early preachers of the Messiah, through whose instrumentality numbers were converted, was this poor erring daughter of Samaria.

Source: Clara Lucas Balfour, *Women of Scripture*, 2nd edition (London: Houlston & Stoneman, 1850), 303–14.

Works of Lord Byron Complete in One Volume, 3rd ed. (London: John Murray, 1837), 49–60. These lines found on page 56 of this edition.

Elizabeth Baxter

....

The Gospel Preacher

Elizabeth Baxter (1837–1926) was a preacher, teacher, and author.[3] Baxter's book *The Women of the Word* included a three-part chapter on the Samaritan woman; the final two parts that focus on John 4:13–42 are included here. Baxter spent time preaching the gospel to crowds of people; this experience influenced her understanding of this text.

Baxter framed the second part of her exposition of the story of the Samaritan woman with a discussion on conversion, contrasting what she judged as the "superficial conversions" of many in her day with the conversion of the woman of Samaria. Baxter concluded the second section by naming the woman as Jesus' first Samaritan disciple and evangelist, just as Balfour did. In the third part of her chapter on the Samaritan woman, Baxter made a strong argument for the ability of women to preach the gospel. She emphasized the simplicity of the Samaritan woman's sermon, and adapting an anti-clerical tone, she suggested that women can leave theological wrangling to men and simply testify or preach about their experiences of Jesus.

THE WOMAN OF SAMARIA.

John 4:[13]-42.

PART II

THERE are many superficial conversions in our days. There are those who profess to belong to the Lord, and yet their experience is by no means described by the words of Jesus to the Samaritan woman, "Whosoever drinketh of the water that I shall give him shall never thirst," for they thirst for amusement, for admiration, for money, for power, for pleasure, for fame, and for other earthly things, just exactly as though they were not converted at all![4] "If any man love the world, the love of the Father is not

3. For more details on Baxter's life and preaching, see "A Role Model for Female Ministry," in the chapter on Anna.

4. See Baxter's written sermon on Herodias and her daughter in the next chapter for similar language and arguments.

in him" (1 John 2:15). What does this thirst prove? Surely this—that they are not drinking of the water which the Lord Jesus gives; they may have once sipped a little, but it is not their habit to "draw water out of the wells of salvation" (Isa. 12:3), and, therefore, the eternal life which Jesus gives to those who follow Him has never yet become a well of water springing up within them.

Such converts are dependent upon prayer meetings and preaching services, special ministers and Christian friends, to keep the little life they have alive. And, in addition, they must needs have, in order to make their lives tolerable, a large slice of the world! It is a miserable kind of conversion; it is that of the wheat where the thorns grew up and choked it, and it became unfruitful [Matt. 13:24–30]. These are the believers who do no good in the world, and about whom it is absolutely necessary to ask the question whether they have been converted or not! There is not enough light in their lives for people to distinguish whether they are the children of light or the children of darkness! [1 Thess. 5:5].

Everyone who drinks continually of the water which Jesus gives ceases to thirst for the world's pleasures, or for anything which it has to give. God is their satisfying Portion. But the Samaritan woman had begun to thirst:

"Sir, give me this water." Instantly Jesus met her as a Prophet. Looking fully into her eyes, with His eyes, which are as a flame of fire, He said unto her:

"Go, call thy husband, and come hither." This was the open wound; this was the sore point; this was the sinful thing which needed setting right. There is no true conversion until the Lord Jesus has laid His finger upon the sore place, the source of sin within. If we would drink of the living water, our lives must be pure and without spot before our God, and all that is wrong must come out and be judged, forgiven and set right in His sight.

"I have no husband."

"Thou hast well said, I have no husband; for thou hast had five husbands; and he whom thou now hast is not thy husband; in that saidst thou truly."

The woman did not attempt a denial; she did not begin to excuse herself; startled by finding herself known as she really was, she bowed before Him whom she recognised as Prophet and Master:

"Sir, I perceive that thou art a prophet."

It was as though she had said: "Thou hast found me out; Thou hast disclosed the deep wickedness of my heart; I know that Thou art right and I am wrong; Thou art holy and I am sinful"; and then, just like all those who are not enlightened by the Holy Ghost, she fell back on the little rag of religion which she had, and spoke of the differences between the Samaritans and the Jews:

"Our fathers worshipped in this mountain; and ye say that in Jerusalem is the place where men ought to worship."

"Woman, believe Me," was the answer of Jesus, taking her out of her depth, "the hour cometh, when ye shall neither in this mountain, nor yet at Jerusalem, worship the Father. Ye worship ye know not what; we know what we worship; for salvation is of the Jews. But the hour cometh, and now is, when the true worshippers shall worship the Father in spirit and in truth; for the Father seeketh such to worship Him."

Here was the secret of the living water; it was a changed life which she needed; a new heart, and a new spirit, new motives, new aims, and new impulses. The convicted sinner was at the end of all her resources; nothing could extenuate the past; nothing could justify the present; her only hope was in the coming One:

"I know that Messias cometh, which is called the Christ; when He is come He will tell us all things" (R. V.). It was the instinct of an awakened soul. There is no hope for such outside of Jesus. But she was unprepared for the declaration:

"I that speak unto thee am He."

She was ready to receive Him; doubts found no place as a nonconducting influence between her convicted soul and her Saviour. The sinner and the Saviour had met. Old things were already passed away, all things were become new (2 Cor. 5:17).

Jesus had conquered, and won unto Himself His first Samaritan follower and His first Samaritan evangelist.

PART III

John 4:27–42.

God so ordered it that no interruption should occur in the conversation of Jesus with the Samaritan woman until the critical moment when He revealed Himself as the Messiah, and she accepted Him as her Saviour. But just then "the disciples returned, and marvelled that He talked with the woman," and yet none of them questioned Him on the matter.

But the woman had got what she wanted. Perhaps for long years there had been the yearning of her soul for something satisfactory, something which she felt her need of, and which would make it possible that her dark life should be made light, her sinful life clean; and now that she had found it, all else was left. She "left her waterpot, and went her way into the city" to tell about Jesus. It was a simple sermon:

"Come, see a Man which told me all things that ever I did; is not this the Christ?"

A woman preacher who is sent of God does not need to become a Doctor of Divinity. Let her leave the knotty points which scholars wrangle over to others, but let her testimony be: "Come, see a Man," come and look at Jesus, come and receive of Him what I have received of Him. He has told me all things that ever I did, He has searched my heart as no human being could: "is not this the Christ?"

The woman's character was so well known in Samaria that everyone was conscious that if Jesus had told her all things that ever she did, He had told her what was not much to her credit. In her simple testimony there was no assumption of being herself anything remarkable; it was Jesus she sought to honour; He was the subject of her discourse.

And it was effectual. "Many of the Samaritans of that city believed on Him for the saying of the woman which testified, He told me all that I ever did." Is it not a dangerous thing that one so recently converted, and converted out of such sin, should be allowed to preach to others as though she had been an example of holiness for years? Jesus Himself not only suffered it, but rejoiced to see her testimony, and spoke of it as the promise of a harvest.

Source: Elizabeth Baxter, *The Women in the Word*, 2nd ed. (London: Christian Herald, 1897), 224–29.

PHOEBE PALMER (1807–1874)

Women's Preaching Justified

Phoebe Palmer was a Methodist evangelist, preacher, theologian, and author. She is remembered as the Mother of the Holiness Movement.[5] Her parents, Henry Worrall and Dorthea Wade Worrall, were members of the Method-

---

5. See also Renee Kwan Monkman, "Palmer, Phoebe (1807–74)," in Taylor and Choi, *Handbook*, 390–93.

ist Episcopal Church in New York. At nineteen she married Walter Clarke Palmer, a homeopathic physician. Questions arising from the deaths of their first three children led to a spiritual experience that became the basis for her writings and ministry. Palmer began a weekly women's prayer meeting with her sister in 1835, and was soon asked to speak and write about her spiritual experiences. In 1842, she collected the articles she had previously published into *The Way of Holiness with Notes By the Way*, a book that sold more than 20,000 copies in the first six years of its printing. Palmer was a very effective speaker and she traveled extensively, often speaking to large audiences. Her preaching stirred up controversy over the issues of women's public speaking and preaching. In response to negative attitudes toward women speaking publicly in the church and society, she wrote a defense of women's public ministry, *The Promise of the Father* (1859).[6]

In *The Promise of the Father*, Palmer argued that women, who she claimed were spiritually equal to men, could be called to speak God's word in "these last times."[7] She likened her own spiritual experience of sensing God's call to the experience of Mary and the other women disciples who "received the tongue of fire in answer to the Promise of the Father . . . [and] at *once used* the gift and spake as the Spirit gave utterance [Acts 2:4]."[8] Palmer described herself as "a Spirit–baptized Mary . . . [upon whom] the tongue of the fire" had descended.[9] Adhering to a traditional separate-spheres ideology, she argued that God may occasionally bring women "out of the ordinary sphere of action, and occupy in either church or state positions of high responsibility."[10] Palmer cited examples of women in leadership from both the Bible and church history. She supported her position with testimonial letters from well-known figures who had experienced women in ministry and who recognized the legitimacy of their calls.

The excerpt below comes from the end of the first chapter of *Promise of*

---

6. Lucy Lind Hogan, "Negotiating Personhood, Womanhood, and Spiritual Equality: Phoebe Palmer's Defense of the Preaching of Women," *American Transcendental Quarterly* 14.3 (2000): 212. For a further discussion of Palmer and feminism, see Diane Leclerc, "Two Women Speaking 'Woman': The Strategic Essentialism of Luce Irigaray and Phoebe Palmer," in *Being Feminist, Being Christian: Essays from Academia*, ed. Allyson Jule and Bettina Tate Pedersen (New York: Palgrave Macmillan, 2006), 111–26.

7. See Hogan's discussion of Palmer's use of the topos of spiritual equality in her argument. Hogan, "Negotiating Personhood," 212.

8. Phoebe Palmer, *Promise of the Father* (Boston: H. V. Degen, 1859), vi.

9. Palmer, *Promise of the Father*, vi.

10. Palmer, *Promise of the Father*, 1–2.

the Father, and is part of Palmer's introductory argument in favor of women prophesying or preaching in public. Palmer argued that women should be able to speak if God calls them to speak. In support of her argument she quotes Mary Bosanquet, a renowned Methodist deaconess and preacher.[11] By citing Bosanquet's words, Palmer also invokes her example. Palmer continued her argument by using examples of biblical women, including the woman of Samaria.

Chapter 1

Says the devoted philanthropist, Miss Bosanquet, afterwards the wife of the distinguished Vicar of Madely, Rev. J. Fletcher, who felt herself called to proclaim the power of saving grace to others, "Some think it inconsistent with that modesty the Christian religion requires in women professing godliness. Now, I do not apprehend Mary could in the least be accused of immodesty when she carried the joyful news of her Lord's resurrection, and in that sense taught the teachers of mankind [John 20:1–2, 18]. Neither was the woman of Samaria to be accused of immodesty when she invited the whole city to come to Christ. Neither do I think the woman mentioned in 2 Sam. 20 could be said to sin against modesty, though she called to the general of the opposing army to converse with her, and then went to all the people to give them her advice, and by it the city was saved. Neither do I suppose Deborah did wrong in publicly declaring the message of the Lord, and afterwards accompanying Barak to war because his hands hung down at going without her [see Judges 4]. But says the objector, All these were extraordinary calls; sure you will not say yours is an extraordinary call? If I did not believe so, I would not act in an extraordinary manner. I praise God, I feel him near, and prove his faithfulness every day."[12]

That Christ was successfully preached to the Samaritans through the instrumentality of a woman is manifest, John 4:39. "Many of the Samaritans believed on him for the saying of the woman." This woman was the first apostle for Christ in Samaria. She went and told her fellow-citizens that the

11. Mary Bosanquet Fletcher (1739–1815) was a Methodist deaconess and preacher. She married Rev. John Fletcher, John Wesley's designated successor, in 1781. Fletcher died in 1785, and his widow carried on his ministry for thirty years after his death.

12. See Henry Moore, *The life of Mrs. Mary Fletcher: consort and relict of the Rev. John Fletcher, Vicar of Madeley, Salop, compiled from her journal, and other authentic documents* (London: Wesleyan Methodist Book Room, nd).

Messiah was come, and gave for proof that he had told her the most secret things she had ever done.

But Providence, under ordinary circumstances, assigns woman a sphere of action both suited to her predilections and her physical and mental structure. Indeed, can we conceive of a work more important than that which in the general orderings of Providence falls to woman? "The future destiny of the child is always the work of the mother," said the sagacious Napoleon.[13] The training of the human mind irrespective of sex, as it comes forth fresh from the hand of the Dispenser of life, is, for the most part, committed to woman. What a high and holy trust! It were difficult to give a just presentation of the magnitude of this work. Immortal minds are to be trained for immortality and eternal life; and all the minutiae of future life, whether for good or evil, are to show the result of these early trainings. And to all eternity, as millions on millions of ages pass away, the result of those early motherly trainings will influence largely the destiny of that deathless spirit. Not only will the women of this age have to do with the women of the future age, but, as the men of the future age will have had their early training mostly from the women of the present age, how greatly have women to do with the destinies of the moral and religious world! Wonderful indeed is the work to which woman has been called in the social relation. Says Mrs. Hale, "But with the privileges we must take the position of women; leave the work of the world and its reward, the government thereof, to men; our task is to fit them for their office; and inspire them to perform it in righteousness."[14]

It is not our aim in this work to suggest, on behalf of woman, a change in the social or domestic relation. We are not disposed to feel that she is burdened with wrong in this direction. But we feel that there is a wrong, a serious wrong, affectingly cruel in its influences, which has long been depressing the hearts of the most devotedly pious women. And this wrong is inflicted by pious men, many of whom, we presume, imagine that they are doing God service in putting a seal upon lips which God has commanded to speak.

It is not our intention to chide those who have thus kept the Christian female in bondage, as we believe in ignorance they have done it. But we feel that the time has now come when ignorance will involve guilt; and the

13. Napoleon Bonaparte (1769–1821), military and political leader of France, was renowned (among other things) for his pithy sayings.

14. Sarah Josepha Hale, *Woman's Record; or Sketches of All Distinguished Women from the Creation to A.D. 1854* (New York: Harper & Brothers, 1855), xlv.

Head of the church imperatively demands a consideration of the question
proposed in the following pages.

Source: Phoebe Palmer, *Promise of the Father; or, A Neglected Speciality of the Last Days*
(Boston: H. V. Degen, 1859), 11–13.

HANNAH JANE LOCKER-LAMPSON (C. 1840–1900)

Empathetic Evangelistic Preaching: A Sermon

Hannah Jane Locker-Lampson was a wealthy author and educator. She was
born to American parents who later became British subjects. Her father, Sir
Curtis Miranda Lampson, was a fur merchant and telegraph cable promoter
from Vermont and her mother was Jane Walter of Massachusetts.[15] Hannah
Lampson became the second wife of Frederick Locker in 1874, who took
on the Lampson name in order to inherit the family estates. They had two
sons and two daughters. Hannah Locker-Lampson wrote stories for children
and published two collections of Bible readings for Mothers' Meetings, *Bible
Readings from the Acts of the Apostles* (1879) and *Bible Readings from the
Gospels* (1877), from which the excerpt on the Samaritan woman is taken.

Bible Readings from the Gospels is a collection of sermons published as a
resource for women who wanted to hold Mothers' Meetings but were un-
able to produce lessons of their own. Locker-Lampson pitched her sermons
to an audience of uneducated women, having chosen to talk about simple
subjects "couched in the easiest language."[16] Her book is very similar to the
other collections of addresses given to Mothers' Meetings exerpted in this
book, including M. G's *Women Like Ourselves*, Mary Ann Smith's *The Holy
Women of Old*, and Mrs. Donaldson's *Home Duties for Wives and Mothers*.

Locker-Lampson's sermon on the Samaritan woman invited her audience
to imagine the setting of the story of the woman of Samaria. She used travel
accounts and commentaries to provide her audience with the background

15. G. C. Boase, "Lampson, Sir Curtis Miranda, First Baronet (1806–1885)," *Oxford Dictionary of National Biography* 32:353.

16. Hannah Locker, *Bible Readings from the Gospels for Mothers' Meetings, etc.* (London:
The Religious Tract Society, 1877), vi.

they needed to understand the encounter between Jesus and the Samaritan woman. She drew her audience into the story by connecting their experiences to those of both the Samaritan woman and Jesus, thus minimizing the distance between her audience and the gospel text. She concluded her message with an evangelistic appeal to her audience to come to Jesus and experience the living water he offers.

The Woman of Samaria

The chapter I have just read seems to me one of the most interesting of the Gospel histories. It is the account of one afternoon in our Saviour's life. Jesus had been in Judea, and had now determined to go to the poor people of Galilee.

Galilee was a country in the north of Palestine, and Jesus was in the south in Judea. Samaria lay between Galilee and Judea, and there were two roads to Galilee. One was by the Jordan Valley, and this was the way which all the strict Pharisees went, to avoid meeting the Samaritans; the other road was through Samaria, and it was this way that our Saviour chose. Now, is not the fourth verse of this chapter very striking, "And He must needs go through Samaria?" How often we all have read this fourth chapter of St. John; but have we paused over that fourth verse, to think how much it means, and what a deep lesson it has for us?

Jesus "must needs" go through Samaria because there was work for Him to do there, because His Father wanted Him to go there. I wonder how many of us in this room feel a "must needs" when we get up each morning? I have no doubt we all feel a "must needs" of some kind,—one of us, our work for the children; another, household work, and so on; but right as all this is in its proper place, there is a great "must needs" for us all every day of our lives, a work to be done for God.

Every one of us here, young and old, has a *daily* work to do for God. How few of us, however, when we wake in the morning, think of it! Do we get up a little earlier because we want an extra half-hour to do some work for God? Perhaps it may only be to visit a sick neighbour, and say a little word of counsel and comfort; perhaps it may be to spend a few minutes longer in prayer to God; perhaps it may be a little work done for a neighbour poorer and busier than ourselves, or it may be to do a work for God in our own home. In fact, it may be any or all of these, differing according to our circumstances.

One thing is certain,—a work there is for each of us, a great "must needs" for us all. On this occasion, therefore, our Saviour went through Samaria, though, no doubt, the way through the Jordan Valley would have been quieter and pleasanter.

There were in Samaria two beautiful hills, where, in the olden days, the law had been proclaimed by Joshua; and between these hills was a valley called Sychar, and in this valley there was a well, which Jacob had dug many hundred years before the birth of our Saviour. Strange to say, that well exists to this day: it is cut in the solid rock, and is seventy-five feet deep.

It was midday when our Saviour arrived there. We know, even in England, how hot it is sometimes at noon, and how glad those who are working in the fields are to sit quietly under the trees and rest. In the East, where our Saviour lived, it was much hotter than it is here, and we can fancy how tired and weary He was with His hot, dusty journey. When He reached the well He was quite exhausted, and could go no further. The disciples went on to the nearest city to buy meat, and Jesus was left alone by the well. The water of the well was cool and sparkling; but He had nothing to draw it with, and He sat there faint and tired.

At last, in the distance, a woman is seen approaching with a water-jar on her head. She is coming to draw water, and is it not most natural that Christ should ask her for some water? Would she not pity Him? Christ asks her for water. What a simple request! A cup of cold water! We all feel we could not refuse so small a thing. And yet see the unkindness of this woman who refuses our Saviour's request. The reason she gives is that she is a Samaritan, and our Saviour is a Jew, and that the Jews and the Samaritans had no dealings with each other.

I think you will understand this better if I tell you why the Jews and the Samaritans hated each other. The Jews were the real children of Abraham, and descended from him, and the Samaritans were foreigners. The Samaritans, however, settled in Palestine, and built a temple at Mount Gerizim. They declared that God ought to be worshipped at Mount Gerizim; while the Jews said the real Temple was at Jerusalem.

The Samaritans refused shelter to the Jewish travellers, and often waylaid and robbed them; and on one occasion they robbed the Temple at Jerusalem, and defiled it by scattering bones about. On the other hand, the Jews publicly cursed the Samaritans in their synagogues, allowed them no privileges, and despised them as foreigners.

When, therefore, our Saviour asked the Samaritan woman for water she refused it, as we have seen. I wonder, if such a thing happened to ourselves, what we should do? If a neighbour, or if anyone we passed on the road, refused to give us water, what should we say? Would not very unkind, hard thoughts come into our hearts, and rise to our lips? Look at Jesus, weary and thirsty, with no means of getting water, yet no impatient exclamation drops from His lips, and listen to the gentleness of His reproof: "If thou knewest the gift of God, and who it is that saith to thee, Give Me to drink; thou wouldst have asked of Him, and He would have given thee living water."

Her surprise is great. From whence could He get water? and did He think there was better water than the water of Jacob's well?

But Jesus shows that there are two defects in this earthly water. First, it cannot satisfy for ever. Do we not all feel this? Are any of us quite contented? Are we not always wanting something we have not got,—a little more money, a little more pleasure? Things may be very good, but we thirst again. Sooner or later we all feel that nothing merely earthly can satisfy.

As we grow older our friends fall around us; we follow our dear ones to their graves; our homes, once so happy, become silent and sad; and each day we ourselves become older, weaker, our sight fails, and we feel our end drawing near. Then the worthlessness of all our earthly joys and possessions, of all earthly life, comes up before us, and we "thirst again."

A second want in the earthly water is that it cannot always be obtained. We cannot always get what we want of earthly things. We often long for a thing; and then, when we can no longer enjoy it, it comes to us. One of our children leaves us, goes abroad; we long to see him. Perhaps the end draws near, and the parent passes away; and when the child comes home it is only to stand by the grave of the one who longed so dearly to see him.

With the heavenly water it is so different: if once taken, it satisfies for ever. One draught from that fountain, and we thirst no more. And then we can always have it, wherever we are. It will be "*in* us" a well of water.

Think of this, my dear friends. Here is something offered to us, which will make us happy for ever, take away our thirst, take away our weariness. Oh, why do not we take it? Can we not hear the beautiful words of Isaiah: "Ho, *every* one that thirsteth, come ye to the waters, and he that hath no money; come ye, buy and eat; yea, come, buy wine and milk without money, and without price?" [Isa 55:1].

We have now come to a most important part of this interview. The poor woman feels a great longing for this gift, though, as we see by verse 15, she does not yet fully understand it, and she begs Jesus to give her this water. But before she can receive it, a great work must be done in her heart. While she is standing, waiting for our Saviour, can we not think what that work is? She *must be convinced of her sin*; and with us it is just the same. Everyone of us in this room who has not gone to God is being kept back because we have never properly felt our sins. It matters not who we are, what age we are, whether we are mothers of large families, or young girls just starting in life, or old women just tottering on the edge of the grave,—for us, one and all, the same thing is necessary for salvation,—we must be convinced of our sin. And why is this? Because until we feel our sins we shall never go to God.

Would a man who was quite well send for the doctor? Certainly not. The hundreds of people we see around us who have no care for the future, and no love for God, are just people who have never felt the weight of their sins.

Let a man just once feel the terrible load of his own sinful nature, feel it thoroughly, and I will defy him to rest till he has gone to God and got rid of it. Would any of us go about with a heavy burden weighing us down to the ground, impeding our progress, if we could get rid of it? No, indeed. And yet each of us who are here met together, in fact, everyone in the world, is on a journey; and, alas! how many of us are loaded with this terrible burden of sin, which is preventing our getting on, tripping us up, making us wander out of the way, and to many will at last prove such a stumbling-block that it will prevent their ever reaching the golden gates at all, and will drag them down and down till they are lost for ever!

Is not this terrible to think of, particularly when we know that we can all get rid of our burdens if we like? Oh, my dear friends, let me beg of you to *begin to-day*, and pray daily and earnestly to God to let you feel this burden of your sin, and to take it away to Jesus, who bears our burdens for us.

I think that to everyone a feeling of sinfulness sometimes comes. No doubt all who are here assembled lead busy lives; and a very good thing a busy life is, if it is lived in the fear of God. But a busy life is sometimes made an excuse to keep us from God. As we get up in the morning we say we have no time for prayer; then we go down and prepare a breakfast which we have no time to give God thanks for; and so the day goes by,—a busy morning, a busy afternoon, and an evening when we do all that we have not had time to do in the day; and we go to bed too tired and hurried to say even *one* prayer to God.

Now, is this a picture of anyone's life here? and if any of you are leading such a life, has it ever struck you what a terribly lost life it is? How can we get up every morning, and live through the day, enjoying God's bright daylight, eating the food He has provided for us, surrounded by the children He has sent us, without giving Him thanks? Let us think this carefully over, and upon our knees to-night let us pray God that He will give us of His strength, that we may never again pass a day without Him, without thankfulness to our Father who has given us everything.

In the case of this poor Samaritan woman, we find that in order to convince her of her sin Christ gave her a command: "Go, call thine husband;" and see her answer: "I have no husband." We can well fancy with what faltering lips and shame-stricken face this reply was given. Then hear what our Saviour says—how He exposes her life to her, and how He makes her look back through the long past years upon her sins. He cannot spare her, He must convince her of sin before He can save her. "Thou hast well said, I have no husband: for thou hast had five husbands; and he whom thou now hast is not thy husband."

Now, for the first time, the woman feels that she is in the presence of a great prophet, and, at the same time, she feels the great sinfulness of her life; and then it comes into her mind how can she be better, how can she worship God truly? Then, also, she remembers the old discussion as to *where* God should be worshipped; and as this Man appears to be a prophet, she asks Him where God ought to be worshipped, at Gerizim or Jerusalem.

We have now come to a second part of this conversation, at which I should like to pause for a moment, for Christ here declares God to this woman.

Is not this a most important subject; for if Christ had only convinced the woman of her sins, and then left her to go home, would she not have been more wretched than ever? But God never stays His gracious work there,—He convinces us of our sins, and then reveals Himself, *and then* points us to our Saviour, who died to save us from those very sins which we feel such a burden.

Instead, therefore, of telling this poor woman on which mountain to worship God, Christ told her a great and most comforting truth—that God is a Spirit, and therefore *everywhere.*

Is not this a most blessed thing for us to know, that wherever we are, or whatever we are doing, we can worship God? We need not wait to worship on Sundays, or only on our knees, for we can worship Him every day, and all day long. Our work can all be done to God's glory; so that instead of being a hindrance to our loving God it may help to lead us to Him.

As we prepare our food we may think of the kind Father who has provided it for us, and may thank Him for it; as we send our children away to school, or out into the world, we may most earnestly pray that God may bless them, and may make us instruments in His hands to lead them in the right path.

As we rise in the morning we can pray to God to strengthen us for all the temptations of the day; and as we lie down at night we should commend ourselves to Him, and ask Him to keep us during the night, and prepare us, when our time comes, to lie down peacefully in the long sleep of death.

We can be continually praising and blessing God. Paul says, "Pray without ceasing" [1 Thess. 5:17]. The Old Testament tells us that Nehemiah, when asked by the king what his request was, even before answering the question, made a short fervent prayer to God; and then when he made his request the king granted it, for God had softened the king's heart. Nehemiah's prayer was granted [see Neh. 2:1–6].

God is a Spirit, therefore we do not see Him; but He is with us in the house, He is with us all through the busy day, and through the long dark night,—loving us, waiting for us, pleading with us.

Such knowledge, we may well say, is too wonderful for us: how shall we understand it all [Ps. 139:6]? It seemed as though the woman could not at once take it in. She shows in her next words that she feels the need of some great instructor who would set her right on this and all other matters. "I know that Messias cometh, who is called Christ." Messias and Christ are words meaning the same thing, in two different languages: the Anointed One, the Saviour-King.

Then was the time for Jesus to declare Himself. He was the Instructor, the Saviour, the King. It was for Him that this woman, and thousands of needy ones besides, had been waiting, although she knew it not.

"I THAT SPEAK UNTO THEE AM HE."

This last part of the conversation was the most important of all. We might feel our sins, we might even feel God near us, and yet if we did not know our Saviour we might be afraid of approaching God. God said if we sinned we should die; and we did sin, and we should have been lost for ever, but Christ came and died for us; and He leads us to God, and washes away all our sins, and saves us for ever! So Christ revealed *Himself* to this poor suffering, sin-stained woman. He told her He was the Messias, that He had come to save sinners. He was going to die to save her, and such as her. She was safe for ever if she would believe in Him, and accept His salvation, and all her past sinful life would be blotted out and forgiven.

And so by that well-side, at the noon-tide hour, many hundred years ago, there came into that poor Samaritan woman's heart all the joy and comfort of the glad gospel tidings, and the sin-load of years was taken away for ever; and, today, to us poor suffering sinners, comes the same message, the same Messias. The same kind Friend is standing waiting, pleading with us to-day, who eighteen centuries ago stood by the well at Sychar.

He asks us to come to Him, to lay upon Him the weight of our sins. He begs us to drink of this heavenly water, that we may thirst no more. Let us all go to Him, lay our burdens at His feet, take Him as our Saviour; so may it be said of us, as of those blessed ones of whom we read in the Revelation: "They shall hunger no more, neither thirst any more; neither shall the sun light on them, nor any heat. For the Lamb which is in the midst of the throne shall feed them, and shall lead them unto living fountains of waters: and God shall wipe away all tears from their eyes" [Rev. 7:16–17].

Source: Hannah Locker, *Bible Readings from the Gospels for Mothers' Meetings, etc.* (London: The Religious Tract Society, 1877), 31–44.[17]

MARY ELIZABETH BECK (FL. 1872–1892)

Bearing the Words of Life: A Sermon

Mary Elizabeth Beck was a writer of poetry, articles, and books on the Bible, church history, travel, and theology. She was also a prominent member of the Society of Friends in London. Beck wrote under her initials M. E. B. and also as Mary E. Beck. She documented her travels to the Holy Land and America in her popular 1872 publication, *East and West*. Her other books include *Heavenly Relationships* (1885), *Fresh Diggings in an Old Mine* (1885), *Collateral Testimonies to Quaker Principles* (1887), and *Turning Points in the Lives of Eminent Christians* (1888).

Bible Readings on Bible Women (1892) consists of seventeen short chapters, fourteen of which tell the story of a woman or group of women from the Bible. The first three chapters provide introductory material on the Bible, sin, and redemption. Each chapter was designed to be read aloud to a group of women gathered to study the Bible. These addresses undoubtedly grew out of Beck's preaching and teaching in London.

Beck's chapter on the woman of Samaria, excerpted here, is an example of a sermon preached by a woman to other women. Quaker women had a long history of preaching to both women and men.[18] Although Beck may

---

17. Note that Hannah Locker-Lampson published using the name Hannah Locker.

18. See for example Rebecca Larson, *Daughters of Light: Quaker Women Preaching and Prophesying in the Colonies and Abroad, 1700–1775* (New York: Knopf, 1999).

not have preached as widely as Methodist Phoebe Palmer or Salvationist Catherine Booth, she did presume to preach and encouraged others to do the same. Beck identified herself as a "messenger" with "a most blessed office." Although she herself preached with confidence, she stepped back in her conclusion when she talked of women being "permitted to take a little message from our Lord" to our families and the sick or afflicted and stressed women's meekness citing 1 Peter 3:4.

The Woman of Samaria

"She left her pitcher at the well, and to her home returned,
The welcome words of life to bear, that in her full heart burned.

       *   *   *

Like her of Sychar, hast thou drank of that blest fount. Then go,
Let others learn the priceless gifts that from the water flow;
Go forth! and in thy Saviour's strength thy voice shall yet be heard,
And wandering hearts shall turn and bless a feeble woman's word."[19]

Read aloud, John 4:1–42.

MANY years ago I sat by that well.[20] It was the hour of noon, and very hot, being about the same time of the day as that when our Lord, weary and thirsty, sat there, for we must add six hours to Eastern time, making it twelve o'clock. I remember that our horses were left under care as we went into the field, and we clambered over the ruins of an old mosque that we might sit quite near to the mouth of the well. Then Newman Hall, whom perhaps you know by name as a London preacher, read this chapter, and very glad we were to hear it on the spot.[21] The Bible is so true in the little

19. Lines from Anna Shipton, "The First Missionary." This poem was reprinted in *A Library of Religious Poetry: A collection of the best poems of all ages and tongues; With biographical and literary notes,* ed. Philip Schaff and Arthur Gilman (New York: Dodd, Mead, and Company, 1881), 228–29.

20. For another woman who used her first-hand experience of travel in the Holy Land directly in her interpretations of Scripture, see below, "Traveling to Tyre" by Elizabeth Rundle Charles in the chapter on the Canaanite woman.

21. Christopher Newman Hall (1816–1902), a renowed English Nonconformist, traveled

particulars it gives us about places. The well is still "deep," that is, between seventy and eighty feet in depth; the fields, on which doubtless the eyes of our Lord rested when in a figurative sense He spoke of fields "white unto harvest" [John 4:35], are still there. The Samaritans had for centuries been hostile to the Jews. They were the descendants of the Assyrian people whom the King of Babylon had brought with him from his own country to live in the land when he carried the ten tribes into captivity (2 Kings 17). They were at first idolaters, but afterwards they built a temple for the worship of the true God on Mount Gerizim. The Jews disliked them, not only because they were a foreign people, but also because they had a rival worship; and the Samaritans returned their hatred, showing their opposition by many acts of wrong-doing. . . .

These strong prejudices will help us to understand the astonishment of the Samaritan woman when Christ asked her for water. But He was far more earnest to supply her with the "water of life" than to have His own thirst relieved, and He began to unfold to her some of the most wonderful and blessed truths which He ever taught to mankind. He brought home to her first the conviction of her own sinfulness, and with it came the assurance that He who could thus read her past history could be no less than a Prophet! Now, then, she might obtain an answer to the contested point of where men ought to worship. Were the Jews right in worshipping at Jerusalem, or the Samaritans in choosing Mount Gerizim? How wonderful was the answer! The time had come when even the sacred temple, where God had commanded His chosen people to worship, was no longer the only sanctuary acceptable to Him; neither had the temple at Gerizim any virtue in itself. The heart of the worshipper, and not the place, was to determine whether or not the worship was true or false. "God is a Spirit, and they that worship Him must worship Him in spirit and in truth." We may differ very much about the mode of our worship, and we may worship in very different places, but we are told "God looketh at the heart," [1 Sam. 16:7] and to go to church or chapel will not be worship to us unless our hearts are sincerely lifted up to God. Neither is true worship confined to those *times* when we worship with others. Wherever we are, even in the midst of our occupations, we can send a glance upward to our Father in Heaven, and feel the sweetness of His presence. A poor servant girl being asked what was the meaning of the text, "Pray without ceasing" [1 Thess. 5:17] replied that when she was dressing herself in the morning

---

to the Holy Land twice with other pilgrims. See *Newman Hall, an Autobiography* (London: Cassell, 1898), 145–58.

she prayed that she might be clothed in Christ's righteousness; when she washed she asked to be cleansed from her sins; and in this way she could turn her common pursuits into prayer. I have read of a good man, whose name was Nicholas Herman, who was converted at eighteen.[22] He lived as cook in a kitchen, a business he very much disliked, but he said that having accustomed himself to do everything there for the love of God, and with prayer upon all occasions for His grace to do his work well, he had found everything easy during fifteen years that he had been employed there. He added that he was very sensible of his faults, but not discouraged by them; that he confessed them to God, and when he had so done, he peaceably resumed his usual practice of love and adoration.

"We ought," he said, "without anxiety to expect the pardon of our sins from the blood of Jesus Christ, only endeavouring to love Him with all our hearts. When I fail in my duty, I readily acknowledge it, saying, '*I am used to do so; I shall never do otherwise if I am left to myself.*' If I fail not, then I give God thanks, acknowledging that it comes from Him."[23] Surely this poor Frenchman, who is described as a "mean and unlearned man," and who lived about two hundred years ago, understood much of the spirit of true worship.

But let us return to the Samaritan woman. When, like Andrew (John 1:41), she was conscious that she had "found the Messias," she did the very same thing as he did. She left her waterpot by the well forgetting everything else in the grand discovery, and called her own people to come and see for themselves. Nothing that we hear about Christ can satisfy us; we must hear His gracious words spoken in the secret of our own souls: "Thy sins are forgiven, go in peace."[24] Nevertheless, the messenger has a most blessed office, and we find that many "believed on Him for the saying of the woman, and many more believed because of His own word." See how the love of Christ melts the heart, and removes prejudices; these Samaritans, who would not have eaten out of the same dish as a Jew, now welcomed their Lord under this character, and "besought Him that He would tarry with them," making

22. Nicholas Herman is more commonly remembered as Brother Lawrence (c. 1614–1691), whose letters and spiritual advice are collected in *The Practice of the Presence of God*. The account of Br. Lawrence related here is found in that text, which is often reprinted. One nineteenth-century edition was published in London by J. Masters in 1855.

23. This quote comes from the end of the second conversation in *The Practice of the Presence of God*. Beck has used excerpts from the last three paragraphs of that conversation.

24. Beck has compressed two speeches of Jesus to the unnamed woman in Luke 7:36–50 who washed his feet with her tears. See Luke 7:48 & 50.

the noble confession, "We have heard Him ourselves, and know that this is indeed the Christ, the Saviour of the world."

We, women, are often permitted to take a little message from our Lord, to speak of His goodness in our own families, and at the bedside of the sick and afflicted. Let those of us who have found Him for ourselves, watch our opportunities for making Him known; and above all, let us seek to adorn His Gospel by our own lives, and by "the ornament of a meek and quiet spirit" [1 Pet. 3:4].

Let us repeat together, John 4:13, 14.

Source: Mary E. Beck, *Bible Readings on Bible Women* (London: S. W. Partridge, 1892), 55–60.

STUDY QUESTIONS

1. How do the writers describe the Samaritan woman's proclamation or preaching about Jesus? How is she portrayed as an example of a preacher in their context? Does this portrayal translate to the present? Why or why not?

2. Provide examples of the ways theological, hermeneutical, and cultural assumptions shape nineteenth-century readings of the Samaritan woman's story. How are these assumptions different in the present? What kind of readings of this story result from present assumptions?

3. Compare and contrast the explanations these commentators give of the relationship between the Jews and the Samaritans. How do the interpreters help their audiences understand the division? What moral lesson or lessons do they derive for their nineteenth-century readers from the interaction between Jesus and the Samaritan woman? Would these applications work today? Why or why not?

4. How do these commentators fill in the gaps of the Samaritan woman's story? How do they make her accessible to their audiences? Are these readings compelling? Why or why not?

5. How is the Samaritan woman portrayed as an outsider? What is the theological significance of outsiders? How do these interpreters apply ideas of outsiders to their audiences? Would this work in the contemporary context?

5

Herodias and Salome:
The Royal Tigresses Judged

The gospel story of the death of John the Baptist at the request of Herodias and her unnamed daughter is found in Mark 6:21–28 and Matthew 14:6–11. Most interpreters in the nineteenth century followed Josephus in naming Herodias's daughter Salome.[1] The story is told as a flashback in both Mark and Matthew: Herod hears about Jesus and associates him with John, whom Herod had killed. In the context of this association, the story of John's death is told. On Herod's birthday, Herodias's daughter danced for the king at a banquet. Herod was so pleased with this performance he promised the girl anything, up to half his kingdom. At the prompting of her mother, the girl asked for the head of John the Baptist. Herod kept his promise and presented the head to her.

This gospel narrative particularly intrigued interpreters in the late nineteenth century.[2] They viewed Herodias and her unnamed daughter as the embodiment of women who were dark and dangerous. The daughter went from an unnamed minor character in the gospels to a named woman with dangerous desires in the writings of both men and women. Salome has also been famously represented as a seductive woman in many other art forms, in paintings, as well as in dramatic productions. The women excerpted here embraced this reading of Herodias and her daughter.

The nineteenth-century women selected for this chapter used the story as a platform for exposing the ability of women to influence men for ill. By

---

1. Josephus, *Antiquities* 18.5.4.

2. For discussions of the interpretation of this story during this time period see Alice Bach, "Calling the Shots: Directing Salomé's Dance of Death," *Semeia* 76 (1996): 103–4, 107. See also Jennifer A. Glancy, "Unveiling Masculinity: The Construction of Gender in Mark 6:17–29," *Biblical Interpretation* 2, no. 1 (1994): 34–50.

accenting women's power, the writers were implicitly empowering women, encouraging them to use their influential power for good and not evil. The four excerpts included in this chapter were written by women who desired to provoke moral and spiritual change. The writers used words carefully, drawing readers into the drama of the event. The essays written by Stowe and Richmond are part of larger works on biblical women; both display feminist motivations. Donaldson's sermon is part of a larger collection of sermons preached to women at Mothers' Meetings, and endorsed by her bishop. Black's devotional homily uses rhetoric effectively in its call for spiritual and moral conversion.

HARRIET BEECHER STOWE (1811–1896)

It's All about Power

Harriet Beecher Stowe was an abolitionist, biblical interpreter, and the best-selling author of *Uncle Tom's Cabin*, the book reputed to have started the American Civil War.[3] The seventh child of Lyman and Roxanna Beecher, Stowe was raised in a home where hermeneutics, theology, and preaching were dinner-table conversations. Stowe's father and brothers were all ministers and she herself felt that she was born to be a preacher.[4] Although Stowe was not able to pursue a formal vocation in the ministry, she did preach with her pen.[5] Her novels and essays contain biblical interpretation and sermonic elements. Her husband, Calvin Stowe, a renowned biblical scholar, provided

3. See also Marion Ann Taylor, "Stowe, Harriet Beecher, (1811–96)," in *Handbook of Women Biblical Interpreters*, ed. Marion Ann Taylor and Agnes Choi (Grand Rapids: Baker Academic, 2012), 482–87. Further, see Marion Ann Taylor, "Harriet Beecher Stowe and the Mingling of Two Worlds: The Kitchen and the Study," in *Recovering Nineteenth-Century Women Interpreters of the Bible*, ed. Christiana de Groot and Marion Ann Taylor (Atlanta: Society of Biblical Literature, 2007), 99–115.

4. In a letter to her brother dated December 1828 she wrote: "You see My dear George that I was made for preaching—indeed I can scarcely keep my letters from turning into sermons . . . Indeed in a certain sense it is as much my vocation to preach on paper as it is that of my brothers to preach viva voce." Cited in Joan D. Hedrick, *Harriet Beecher Stowe: A Life* (New York: Oxford University Press, 1994), 64.

5. Joan D. Hedrick, "'Peaceable Fruits': The Ministry of Harriet Beecher Stowe," *American Quarterly* 40, no. 3 (1988): 307–32.

her with the biblical and theological resources that allowed her to engage with texts in a very sophisticated way.

Woman in Sacred History (1873) contains Stowe's biographical sketches on selected women of the Bible, as well as poetry, works of art, and essays by other authors. Stowe's purpose in writing this book was not simply biographical; she conceived of her book as "a history of Womanhood under Divine Culture, tending toward the development of that high ideal of women which we find in modern Christian countries."[6] Stowe divided the women of Scripture into three eras: the women of the patriarchal age, the national period, and the Christian era. She began with Sarah and ended with an essay on women of the apostolic church.

In her sermon-like essay on the daughter of Herodias, Stowe used information drawn from Josephus, art history, and other parts of Scripture. She recreated the drama of the scene, with a particular focus on the power of women. Her message was one of Christian morality as she railed against the power of dance, drawing parallels between the reactions of men to dance in her own times and the response to the dancer in the gospel story. Using rhetorical language, she invited her audience to contrast the types of women found in the gospels. Stowe regarded Herodias and Salome as types of evil womanhood, contrasting them with Elizabeth and Mary, the mother of Jesus. She invited readers to ponder the irony that in the biblical record, evil women were a part of the upper class, whereas poor women were models of virtue; Stowe associated poverty with vice, and virtue with the middle and upper classes of society.

THE DAUGHTER OF HERODIAS

In the great drama of the history of Jesus many subordinate figures move across the stage, indicated with more or less power by the unconscious and artless simplicity of the narrative. Among these is the daughter of Herodias, whose story has often been a favorite subject among artists as giving an opportunity of painting female beauty and fascination in affinity with the deepest and most dreadful tragedy.

Salome was the daughter of Herodias, who was a woman of unbridled passions and corrupt will. This Herodias had eloped from her husband

---

6. Harriet Beecher Stowe, *Woman in Sacred History* (New York: J. B. Ford and Company, 1873), 11.

Philip, son of Herod the Great, to marry her step-uncle, Herod Antipas, who forsook for her his lawful wife, the daughter of the king of Arabia. Herod appears in the story of the Gospels as a man with just enough conscience and aspiration after good to keep him always uneasy, but not enough to restrain from evil.

When the ministry of John powerfully excited the public mind, we are told by St. Mark that "Herod feared John, know[ing] that he was a just man and holy, and he observed him, and when he heard him he did many things and heard him gladly."

The Jewish religion strongly cultivated conscience and a belief in the rewards and punishments of a future life, and the style of John's preaching was awful and monitory. "Behold the axe is laid at the root of the tree, and whatsoever tree doth not bring forth good fruit shall be hewn down and cast into the fire."[7] There was no indulgence for royal trees; no concession to the divine right of kings to do evil. John was a prophet in the spirit and power of Elijah; he dwelt in the desert, he despised the power and splendor of courts, and appeared before kings as God's messenger, to declare his will and pronounce sentence of wrath on the disobedient. So without scruple he denounced the adulterous connection of his royal hearer, and demanded that Herod should put away the guilty woman as the only condition of salvation. Herod replied, as kings have been in the habit of replying to such inconvenient personal application of God's laws: he shut John up in prison. It is said in St. Mark that Herodias had a quarrel against him, and would have killed him, but she could not. The intensity of a woman's hatred looks out through this chink of the story as the secret exciting power to the man's slower passions. She would have had him killed had she been able to have her way; she can only compass his imprisonment for the present, and she trusts to female importunities and blandishments to finish the vengeance. The hour of opportunity comes. We are told in the record: "And when a convenient day came, Herod on his birthday made a supper to his lords and high captains and chief estates of Galilee."

One of the entertainments of the evening was the wonderful dancing of Salome, the daughter of his paramour. We have heard in the annals of the modern theatre into what inconsiderate transports of rapture crowned heads and chief captains and mighty men of valor have been thrown by the dancing of some enthroned queen of the ballet; and one does not feel it incredible,

---

7. Matthew 3:10 with a parallel verse in Luke 3:9. Stowe's wording reflects neither of these exactly.

therefore, that Herod, who appeared to be nervously susceptible to all kinds of influences, said to the enchantress, "Ask me whatsoever thou wilt, and I will give it thee; and he sware unto her after the pattern of Ahasuerus to Esther, saying, Whatsoever thou shalt ask of me I will give it thee, to the half of my kingdom."[8] And now the royal tigress, who has arranged this snare and watched the king's entrance into the toils, prepares to draw the noose. Salome goes to her mother and says, "What shall I ask?" The answer is ready. Herodias said, with perfect explicitness, "Ask for the head of John the Baptist." So the graceful creature trips back into the glittering court circle, and, bowing her flower-like head, says in the sweetest tones, "Give me here John the Baptist's head in a charger."

The narrative says very artlessly, "And the king was sorry, but for his oath's sake, and for the sake of them that sat with him at meat, he would not refuse her, and immediately the king sent an executioner and commanded his head to be brought, and he went and beheaded him in prison!"

What wonderful contrasted types of womanhood the Gospel history gives! We see such august and noble forms as Elisabeth, the mother of the Baptist, and Mary, the mother of Jesus, by the side of this haughty royal adulteress and her beautiful daughter. The good were the lower, and the bad the higher class of that day. Vice was enthroned and triumphant, while virtue walked obscure by hedges and byways; a dancing girl had power to take away the noblest life in Judæa, next to that which was afterward taken on Calvary.

No throb of remorse that we know of ever visited these women, but of Herod we are told that when afterwards he heard of the preaching and mighty works of Jesus, he said, "It is John the Baptist that I slew. He is risen from the dead, therefore mighty works do show forth themselves in him" [Matt. 14:2].

In the last scenes of our Lord's life we meet again this credulous, superstitious, bad man. Pilate, embarrassed by a prisoner who alarmed his fears and whom he was troubled to dispose of, sent Jesus to Herod. Thus we see the licentious tool and slave of a bad woman has successively before his judgment-seat the two greatest men of his age and of all ages. It is said Herod received Jesus gladly, for he had a long time been desirous to see him, for he hoped some miracle would be done by him. But he was precisely of the class of whom our Lord spoke when he said, "An adulterous generation seeketh a sign, and there shall no sign be given them" [Matt. 16:4]. God has no answer

---

8. See Mark 6:22b-23. Stowe added the comment "after the pattern of Ahasuerus to Esther" to the gospel quotation. See also Esther 5, particularly verse 3.

to give to wicked, unrepentant curiosity, and though Herod questioned Jesus in many words he answered him nothing. Then we are told, "Herod with his men of war set Jesus at naught, and mocked him, and arrayed him in a gorgeous robe, and sent him again to Pilate" [Luke 23:11]. And this was how the great ones of the earth received their Lord.

Source: Harriet Beecher Stowe, *Woman in Sacred History* (New York: J. B. Ford and Company, 1873), 321–23.

EUPHEMIA JOHNSON RICHMOND (1825–C. 1900)

Voluptuous Dancing

Euphemia Johnson Richmond was a successful career writer of prose and poetry. She was born near Upton, New York, in 1825. Her parents and grandparents were professional and literary people who valued education and encouraged her literary endeavors. She published poems in the New York *Tribune* and some early novels under the penname Effie Johnson. A temperance history based on the lives of people she knew, called *The McAllisters*, launched her successful publishing career under her own name. Like Harriet Beecher Stowe, Richmond preached with her pen. An *Illustrated Scripture Primer* (1888) and *Woman, First and Last: And What she has Done* (1887) reveal her approach to interpreting Scripture, her passion for the equality of persons, and her use of the rhetoric of the pulpit.

In her two-volume work, *Woman First and Last*, Richmond appealed to Scripture, history, and biography to show that the sphere of woman is the world itself and that since women have the power for good and evil, intellect has no sex. Each of the sixty-five chapters in her book is devoted to a woman of either good or evil repute. Richmond began with Eve, and included twelve other women from the Bible, one of whom is Salome, excerpted here. Her review of women continued to her present; she included such figures as Cleopatra, Joan of Arc, Catherine de Medici, Lady Jane Grey, Queen Mary of Scotland, Queen Elizabeth, Hannah More, Charlotte Corday, Charlotte Brontë, Florence Nightingale, and Harriet Beecher Stowe.

In *Woman First and Last*, Richmond introduced Salome as the first dancer in Scripture. She contrasted her dancing with Miriam's and David's which she thought was connected to worship. Richmond expanded the account of Herod's birthday party recorded in Matthew 14, using extra-biblical sources, such as Josephus, contemporary sources on dancing, as well as her flair for writing historical fiction. She set the scene with care, noting that at the height of the wine-induced "gayety and mirth," Salome, Herodias's daughter, "executes one of the voluptuous dances of the East." Richmond described the dancer and the dancing in detail, arguing that dance exerted a powerful influence over "the immortal part" of the mind; its evil influence on Herod proved her point. Like Stowe, Richmond preached to her readers about the evil schemes of Herod's wife and her daughter to illustrate the power of woman for evil.

SALOME, THE DAUGHTER OF HERODIAS.

A royal feast in the palace. The occasion is the anniversary of the birth of Herod the king; and the "lords, high captains, and chief estates of Galilee" are all invited to a supper by the king. Wine flowed freely at this feast; and when the gayety and mirth which it inspired had reached their height, Salome, the daughter of Herodias, the wife of King Herod Antipas, appears before them and executes one of the voluptuous dances of the East.

She is the very personification of grace, as her lithe form sways hither and thither and floats airily to the dulcet strains of music, while the king and his courtiers look on in undisguised admiration. The "poetry of motion," as dancing has been called, has so bewildering and fascinating an influence that many people are ready to apologize for it, if they do not directly approve and practice it. They quote, in support of their opinion, the authority of the divine word even. We believe, however, that this is the first instance in which this practice is recorded in the Bible, if we except the act of worship of Miriam, when she led the women in praise and devotion [Exod. 15], and the leaping, and dancing of King David before the ark of the Lord when it was restored again to the royal city [2 Sam. 6:14–16].

The influence which this graceful pastime exerts over the mind—the immortal part—is the true test by which to judge of its character. It caused Herod to make a rash promise, a promise which led to the commission of a fearful crime, at which the nation stood aghast. He first promised Salome, "Ask of me whatsover thou wilt, and I will give it thee;" and, as if this were not enough, he sware unto her, "Whatsoever thou shalt ask of me, I will give it thee, unto the half of my kingdom."

The crafty Salome is a true descendant of the wicked Salome, the sister of Herod the Great;[9] and now she has attained what she has so long desired—the opportunity of revenge. Wicked men and women hate those who dare reprove them for their crimes. The proud Herodias could ill brook that her actions should be judged in the light of the word of God, as other people's were; and there is now in one of the dungeons of the castle a prisoner, thrown there at the instigation of this wicked woman. The bold and fearless prophet, who openly denounced King Herod for marrying his brother Philip's wife while he was yet alive, inspired the king with respect and veneration. The record tells us that "Herod feared John, knowing that he was a just man and a holy, and observed him; and when he heard him, he did many things, and heard him gladly" [Mark 6:20]. No greater evidence of the power of woman for evil is wanting than the fact that, at the solicitation of this proud, beautiful woman, the good and true servant of God was cast into prison.

Herodias greatly desired his death, but waited patiently, like her blood-thirsty grandmother, Salome, till she could accomplish it in safety. Here was the long-desired opportunity for revenge. Mother and daughter had doubtless often consulted together over this favorite plot, and now when Salome comes into her mother's presence flushed and triumphant, saying eagerly, "What shall I ask?" the answer is ready, "The head of John the Baptist."

King Herod and his lords are still reclining at the banquet, perhaps discussing the merits of the pretty dancer, and wondering what brilliant bauble she will ask of the king who has given her such a lavish promise.

Hark! that is the sound of her footsteps approaching, and with crimson cheek and flashing eye she appears before the assembly again. She is speaking to the king. Can it be that they hear aright?

"I will that thou give me by and by in a charger the head of John the Baptist!"

With sorrow and dismay the king hears the cruel request, but his oath has been given, and those who sat with him are waiting to see if he will dare to behead him whom "all men count as a prophet." Cowardice prevails; fear of the anger of his wife and the comments of his courtiers pushes him on to the commission of a fearful crime.

The order is given to the executioner. The gory head of God's holy prophet is brought to the cruel maiden. The cold eyes are fixed in death. The lips are silenced; they will never reprove the sins of the wicked mother again; but

9. Richmond included a chapter on "the blood-thirsty" grandmother Salome in *Woman First and Last*, 94–101.

she has planted the sting of remorse in the heart of King Herod which shall endure throughout the ages of eternity.

The cruel daughter bears the charger with its dreadful burden to her mother, and she gazes in triumph on her hated accuser. The assembly breaks up in silence, for a dread of divine retribution has fallen upon them. Will not God avenge his own? We see here the sins of the parent "visited upon the children to the third and fourth generation" [Exod. 20:5]. The sanguinary character of the first Salome is mirrored in her descendants until the judgments of God sweep them from the face of the earth.

With a sensation of relief we take our final leave of these women, who, though belonging to a people whom God had blessed with peculiar favor, were yet his enemies and the enemies of their race. It is sad to think that Salome and the wicked Herodias used their power over King Herod only to excite him to deeds of evil, and thus bequeathed to the world the deathless power of an evil example.

Source: E. J. Richmond, *Woman, First and Last: And What she has Done* (New York: Phillips & Hunt, 1887), 117–20.

MRS. DONALDSON (FL. 1882)

The Great Danger of Worldly Amusements: A Sermon

The little that is known about Mrs. Donaldson comes from the preface to her only book, *Home Duties for Wives and Mothers, Illustrated by Women of Scripture*. Donaldson preached to large numbers of poor women who attended the Mothers' Meetings she led in her husband's parish of St. Stephen's, Spitalfields, in East London. In the preface to her book, William Walsham How (1823–1897), the suffragan bishop for East London, commended Donaldson's teaching and evangelistic ministry to women. He claimed this book was "just what one wants," for use in Mothers' Meetings. "Poor weary women, in such a population as East London, want very plain teaching, and very kind loving words."[10]

---

10. Mrs. Donaldson, *Home Duties for Wives and Mothers, Illustrated by Women of Scripture* (London: William Hunt, 1882), vi.

In *Home Duties for Wives and Mothers*, Donaldson wrote about twenty-five women of Scripture who faced the same kind of difficulties, joys, and sorrows that women she knew experienced. How the women in Scripture responded to their duties and life's challenges provided positive or negative examples for contemporary women to follow. Positively, Hannah provided an example of prayer, Abigail of prudence, the widow of Zarephath of the reward of obedience; Hagar was a negative example of fleeing from duty, Sapphira of the punishment for lying; and Herodias, excerpted below, an example of the great danger of worldly amusements.

Like Stowe and Richmond, Donaldson used the story of Herodias and Salome as a platform for preaching about women's power and influence. The oral quality of Donaldson's sermon is evident: she asked her audience to "listen to the fearful request from the lips of one so young and so fair!" Donaldson herself modeled the kind of positive influence women could have both in her oral preaching and in writing.

Herodias; or, the great danger of Worldly Amusements

Matthew 14:3–11.

The little that is recorded of this woman shows us that she was very wicked in every sense of the word. She had forsaken her own husband Philip, and was living with his half-brother Herod. Enraged beyond measure at the reproofs of that holy man John the Baptist, she determined to compass his ruin. But she could not achieve this for some time. At first she only induced her wicked partner to imprison the prophet. He would gladly have done more, but, though he laid hold on John and put him in prison to gratify Herodias, yet he dared do no more "for fear of the multitude," because they counted John as a prophet. . . .

Now, though John was in prison, and therefore certain not to be able to rebuke the king any more, still that wicked woman Herodias was not satisfied with this measure of revenge.

A woman will do many things to get her own way. She will wait and wait, contrive and plan, till at last she brings about her own ends. It is well indeed when this intense and firm determination to conquer circumstances, and bend them to her will, is accompanied by goodness, purity, and love.

Unhappily, however, she is not always patient or persevering in a right cause. She is capable of an implacable hatred, which will carry her through all obstacles to the attainment of that which she purposes. Such an instance is before us. John being in prison was not enough. He had dared to rebuke her unfaithfulness to her husband, and her present evil life. Her implacable revenge thirsted for his blood, and would not rest till it was shed. . . .

Herod's birthday came. It was kept, as was usual, with great pomp and feasting; doubtless drunkenness and riot were abounding.

To please such a licentious king as Herod all was done that could gratify the eye and grace the solemnity. In honour of the day the daughter of Herodias came and danced before them. Such an exhibition cannot be too strongly condemned. At such a scene, during such a time of debauchery, no modest girl would have been willing to be present, much less to have exposed herself to the gaze of such an audience.

But Herod, as both the mother and daughter probably knew, was just the man to be pleased at such a performance.

Times of mirth and feasting are often the convenient opportunities for carrying on bad designs, and this was just what this wicked woman wanted. She had, doubtless, inspired her daughter with a kindred feeling of hatred to the prophet, and they had planned the request she was to make.

The dance brought about just what they had anticipated, and, his heart being merry, the king entered into an extravagant obligation to give her whatever she would ask, confirming it by an oath. Now the time had arrived to which Herodias had looked forward, and for which she had waited so long!

But listen to the fearful request from the lips of one so young and so fair! "Give me here John Baptist's head in a charger!" And the deed must be done at once: no time for relenting when soberness should return. No space for trial or forms of justice which might, and surely would, terminate in his acquittal and freedom. No, it must be done on the spot; and, to be sure of its performance, the head must be brought in on a charger. It is stated that the king was sorry, but we cannot tell whether from a feeling of his old reverence for John before he had sunk so low in sin, or whether he only pretended to be so. At any rate, "for the oath's sake he commanded it to be given her."

He made a specious show of honour, but it is a great mistake to suppose that a wicked oath will justify a still more wicked action.

It was not, however, so much for the sake of the oath, but for those that sat with him that he granted the demand. It is probable that, if she had demanded a vast sum of money, or extensive possessions, he would have found some way out of the difficulty. But John the Baptist's head was of far less value to him than wealth or property, so he immediately issues a warrant for beheading John: "He commanded it to be given her." Thus was that voice silenced, that "burning and shining light" [John 5:35] extinguished, only to shine brighter, and for ever before the throne of God. He was now released from his long imprisonment, and was sent to his rest, and his great reward. "And his head was brought, and given to the damsel, and she brought it, to her mother." So closes this awful tragedy.

That wicked woman had got her own way, and accomplished that upon which she had set her heart! We hear nothing of her end, but we feel sure that great bitterness of spirit must have followed her as long as she lived. That ghastly head, those grave reproachful eyes, would haunt her day and night. Whether she died repentant, or whether her heart was hardened, by sinking deeper and deeper into sin, to hush the voice of conscience and the pangs of remorse, we cannot tell. But if unrepented of, we are sure this fearful deed must have sunk her soul into the deepest abyss of destruction.

Here I would say a few earnest words of warning against places of worldly amusement, such as dancing saloons, which are full of peril to the young. Teach your children, as you value their souls, to shun such places. Keep them pure in body and in mind, or, like the damsel of whom we have read, you will be as morally guilty of their soul's death as she and her mother were of John the Baptist's murder.

And, let me conclude by pointing out here as forcibly as I can, how sad, how dreadfully sad a case is that of a child whose parents are, like Herodias, their counsellors to do evil; who instruct them; and encourage them in sin, and set them bad examples. The evil nature that is born in them will be only too readily quickened by bad instructions. "Children, obey your parents," it is said, but *"in the Lord,"* [Eph. 6:1] not against Him and His precepts. If a parent commands a child to do what is wrong, the child must obey God first.

Are you ever guilty of this sin, my dear mothers? I mean the sin of causing your children to obey you in what you know to be wrong, helping you to carry out some unlawful practice, such as breaking the Lord's Day for some possible gain or profit. And even if you do not force them into sin by your direct command, there are many, I fear, who allow it without check. Oh, sorely we are bound by the sacred responsibility of motherhood to *restrain* our children from all sin, not only by advice, persuasion, and reproof, but, if needs be, by correction also.

But, above all, let your own life of devotion to God's honour, and to His service, be seen by them and they will soon tread with you the narrow road that leads to everlasting life.

Source: Mrs. Donaldson, *Home Duties for Wives and Mothers, Illustrated by Women of Scripture* (London: William Hunt, 1882), 93–99.

Margaret Black (1844–c. 1907)

....

Pleasing the Tyrant

Margaret Black was born in Ireland. She later lived in Scotland with her husband John James Black, the minister of the Free High Church in Inverness. Little else is known about Black's life. Her *Woman's Daily Text Book* is a collection of thirty-one short devotional reflections, each on a single Bible verse. The devotionals apply the verse to the reader's life using sermon-like language. In her introduction, Black stated that she intended her work: "to help forward a religion which will go down into every detail of woman's life, sanctifying it, and making it full of the power of Christ."[11]

Black devoted one of her daily meditations to reflections on Matthew's description of how the daughter of Herodias pleased Herod with her dancing (Matt. 14:6). Black preached with eloquence and confidence, implicitly drawing parallels between herself as a "faithful reprover" and John the Baptist. She moved from a literal reading of the story of Herodias's daughter's dancing to a typological reading in order to make a spiritual and moral application of the text to her audience. Black's homily is both evangelistic and moralistic in that it calls for the conversion and personal transformation of her audience. She suggested that pleasing Herod to gain his smile might be a laudable goal if this world were all there is, but since it is not, she commended pleasing God.

14th Day.

The daughter of Herodias danced before them, and pleased Herod.

Mat. 14:6.

Of course she did. And this was the grand point with this girl and her mother—to please Herod, and silence for ever the faithful reprover.

So it is today. How many daughters are instructed, and willing, to please the tyrant—Fashion, he is called now. No sacrifice of feeling, or modesty, or time, is too great to lay on his altar. And should the bold servant of God speak words of warning, slay him with sneers and contumely and contempt.

O my sisters, who live in what you call Society, and God calls the world,

11. Margaret Black, *Woman's Daily Text Book* (Paisley: J. and R. Parlane, n.d.).

I would my voice could reach you as I cry, The friendship of the world is enmity with God [James 4:4]. Herod only mocked Christ, and Christ spoke never a word to Him. You may make great sacrifices to please society like this girl, who, at the expense of modesty and good report, bought a tyrant's smile and a prophet's life; but what shall the end be? Is not the price you pay too high?—gaining the world, but losing yourself [Luke 9:25]. Were you only mortal, I might say, Please your Herod; gain his smile. Being immortal, I say, *Please God*. This is an aim worthy of you. The first step is to turn with all your heart to His Son for pardon. Until sin is put away by Christ, there is no pleasing God.

Source: Margaret Black, *Woman's Daily Text Book* (Paisley: J. and R. Parlane, n.d.), n.p.

STUDY QUESTIONS

1. The excerpts on Herodias and Salome are presented as examples of women preaching. How do these selections fit into the sermon genre? Is a nineteenth-century sermon different from a twenty-first century sermon? In what ways? Would these published sermons be considered part of the sermon genre today?

2. Which other Scripture passages do the writers use to illuminate the story of Herodias and Salome? How effective is their use of these passages? What does the use of these other biblical texts imply about their understanding of the use of Scripture in sermons?

3. What kinds of adjectives do these commentaries use to describe the characters of Herodias and Salome? Are there key descriptors that you see across all the excerpts? Based on these adjectives, what virtues did nineteenth-century British or American culture prize in women? What vices were women to avoid? Does contemporary culture think similarly about virtue and vice?

4. How have Herodias and Salome been portrayed in paintings, books, movies, or plays? How has this broad cultural tradition informed the readings of Herodias and Salome presented in this chapter?

PART 3

Unveiled Eyes:
Women and the Biblical Text

Nineteenth-century women used standard methods of biblical interpretation, and wrote in accepted interpretive genres. While not all of them had the same access to academic books on the Bible, many used the same resources male interpreters used. Women wrote devotional reflections, detailed commentaries, and sermons just as men did. Women and men alike interpreted the Bible in their particular cultural context, thus many of their interpretations of Scripture were similar. The three chapters in this section, however, contain excerpts that show that women wrote at the edges of biblical scholarship. While working with the same texts, and writing in the same genres, they did something different with the biblical text than men did. They engaged in acts of critique and reinterpretation of the biblical texts as interpreted and preached by men in established and church-authorized positions.

In her discussion of the long history of women interpreting the Bible, Gerda Lerner trivialized the traditional interpretations written by women.[1] Some of the interpretations included in this section might too easily be classified by Lerner and others as "traditional interpretations" which "do little or nothing to challenge the patriarchal tradition."[2] However, even apparently traditionalist works by women often contain indications of discontent, of different ways of thinking about the text, of different questions asked of the text, and thus different conclusions drawn from the text. Where men might see only a woman with a questionable past in the unnamed Samaritan woman at the well (John 4), women also found an example of a preacher and evangelist (see chapter 4 above). This simple

---

1. See Gerda Lerner, "One Thousand Years of Feminist Biblical Criticism," in *The Creation of Feminist Consciousness* (Oxford: Oxford University Press, 1993), 138–66.
2. Lerner, "One Thousand Years," 139.

move could empower women to think about what they were enabled to do in their own situations and contexts.

In *Bread Not Stone: The Challenge of Feminist Biblical Interpretation*, Elisabeth Schüssler Fiorenza proposed a model of biblical interpretation that includes four aspects: a hermeneutics of suspicion (because the biblical text supports patriarchal structures through androcentric language), a hermeneutics of proclamation (because the biblical text functions as Scripture for Christians in the present), a hermeneutics of remembrance (reconstructing Christian women's history from the biblical text), and a hermeneutics of creative actualization (leading to liturgical praxis emerging from women's biblical story).[3] We do not want to suggest that the nineteenth-century women examined in this section had the same understanding of the task of feminist biblical interpretation as Schüssler Fiorenza. Her categories, however, do provide a helpful way of discussing the work of earlier women interpreters.

Hermeneutic of Suspicion

Schüssler Fiorenza briefly defines a hermeneutic of suspicion as "critically entering the biblical worlds and the work of scholars in order to detect their ideological deformations."[4] This section features several examples of women who were suspicious of the work of male scholars and male biblical writers. One obvious example is Elizabeth Cady Stanton, also Schüssler Fiorenza's primary example of an early feminist interpreter. Stanton was unhappy that only the women, including Mary Magdalene, were portrayed in the gospels as incredulous enough to see the angels at the tomb of Jesus. Other women did not question the value of the biblical text as Stanton did; instead, they questioned the motives and conclusions of male scholars working with the text.

In reading these chapters, a hermeneutic of suspicion will not always be obvious. It can be seen in the ways the writers questioned traditional understandings of the biblical text, as well as in the ways women challenged conclusions men had drawn about a biblical passage. As will be seen in the chapter on the Canaanite woman, Charles suggested that the unnamed woman understood Jesus better than the male disciples. In the chapter on

---

3. Elisabeth Schüssler Fiorenza, *Bread Not Stone: The Challenge of Feminist Biblical Interpretation* (Boston: Beacon Press, 1984), 15.

4. Schüssler Fiorenza, *Bread Not Stone*, 148.

the adulterous woman, Charlotte Bickersteth Wheeler, Josephine Butler, and Elizabeth Baxter, all writing at the end of the century, provide clear examples of a hermeneutic of suspicion. Each of them explicitly challenged the way men understood or used the passage. In the final chapter on Mary Magdalene, the hermeneutic of suspicion can be most clearly seen in the work of Anna Jameson and Harriet Beecher Stowe, who challenged the critical academic (traditionally male) reading of the Bible.

Hermeneutic of Proclamation

Elisabeth Schüssler Fiorenza briefly defines a hermeneutic of proclamation as assessing "the Bible's theological significance and power for the contemporary community of faith."[5] All of the nineteenth-century women wrote for a particular audience with a particular goal in mind. They intended to teach their readers not only historical facts, but the theological and moral significance of a biblical text. Their approach to the text meant that the significance they drew from a text was not always the same as that traditionally deduced by men. They preached their applications of the texts, possibly first orally to an audience, but certainly through their written texts to their readers.

Three women writers excerpted in the chapters that follow, Caroline Pridham, Lucy Barton, and Amelia Gillespie Smyth, taught the Bible to children. Barton used a particularly adult story to talk with children about the gospel. Pridham, Barton, and Smyth were concerned to help children and teenagers understand and apply the biblical texts in their present. Stowe and Jameson embraced the tradition identifying Mary Magdalene as a prostitute, even if they were not sure the tradition was accurate, because that long tradition still spoke to women and men in their day. Mrs. Donaldson and Elizabeth Baxter preached their texts and drew clear applications for their readers. Nineteenth-century women writing on the Bible were very concerned with what the text meant for them and for their audiences; they practiced a hermeneutic of proclamation.

---

5. Schüssler Fiorenza, *Bread Not Stone*, 18. Note that Schüssler Fiorenza expands this definition to include the action of "critically evaluating what can be proclaimed and taught today as an inspired vision for a more human life and future" (148). With the clear exception of Elizabeth Cady Stanton, the nineteenth-century women in this book would probably not have endorsed the kind of revision of the lectionary that Schüssler Fiorenza envisions.

Hermeneutic of Remembrance

Schüssler Fiorenza uses this phrase for the reconstruction of women's history, a history hidden by the male-selected and male-transmitted biblical texts. The reconstruction of women's history is "facilitated by literary and historical critical reconstructions."[6] This hermeneutic of remembrance works hand in hand with the hermeneutic of suspicion. It looks for more information about women. It considers unnamed characters, the possible later fate of the women encountered in the text, and women whose presence in some gospel scenes is not mentioned. This recovery process is clearly evident in the work of the nineteenth-century women featured in this section. It has already been seen in this volume in many ways, including the naming of characters such as Jairus's daughter, and the imagining of the way gospel women might have talked with each other in the absence of men. In this section, two unnamed women are featured, along with Mary Magdalene, one of the female gospel characters given the most room in the biblical texts.

Sarah Hale and Harriet Beecher Stowe wrote works that specifically set out to recover women's place in history. Stowe's essay on Mary Magdalene is a part of her redemptive history of women. Elizabeth Rundle Charles connected the Canaanite woman and her daughter into the history of the church as related in Acts—although these women were not specifically mentioned in a description of the church at Caesarea, Charles placed them there. Most of the women writing about the adulterous woman speculated about the missing or hidden parts of her history. A hermeneutic of remembrance, that filled in the gaps in women's history, was an important part of nineteenth-century women's interpretation of the biblical text.

Hermeneutic of Creative Actualization

Schüssler Fiorenza defines a hermeneutic of creative actualization as the forward movement of biblical interpretation, one that imaginatively engages "in story and song, in ritual and meditation."[7] Nineteenth-century women creatively retold the biblical stories using language and genres appropriate to their audiences. In one example, found in the chapter on Mary Magdalene,

6. Schüssler Fiorenza, *Bread Not Stone*, 148.
7. Schüssler Fiorenza, *Bread Not Stone*, 148.

the story of Mary Magdalene meeting Jesus after the resurrection is told by Elizabeth Rundle Charles in both prose and poetry.

Nineteenth-century women told and retold stories from the Bible expecting lives to be changed just as their own lives had been changed. Josephine Butler dedicated her life to social justice for women, particularly those who turned to prostitution for survival. Her activism was based on her understanding of the Bible. As nineteenth-century women imaginatively engaged the biblical text, they practiced a hermeneutic of creative actualization and expected lives to be transformed because of their work.

Women and Biblical Criticism

In her essay "Women and Biblical Criticism in Nineteenth-Century England," Marion Ann Taylor suggests that over the course of the century women interpreters engaged with biblical criticism in similar ways to male biblical scholars.[8] The changing patterns of engagement can be seen in this section: works published before 1857 show little engagement with criticism, works published between 1858–1879 show an increasing awareness of critical ideas and methods, and in the last two decades of the century (1880–1900), critical ideas were broadly known and discussed by interpreters.[9] Women consumed, criticized, popularized, and practiced biblical criticism.[10]

The three chapters in this section highlight three aspects of women's interpretive work in the nineteenth century: their experience of the biblical text, the way they taught troublesome texts, and their engagement with the long tradition of understanding the Bible. The excerpts in these three chapters are examples of blended hermeneutics. Nineteenth-century women combined methods that were considered "womanly" with those considered "manly" to produce something different.

8. In *The Bible and Women: An Encyclopedia of Exegesis and Cultural History*, volume 8.2 edited by Ruth Albrecht and Michaela Sohn-Kronthaler (Atlanta: SBL Press, forthcoming).

9. Note that the time-scale listed here for engagement with biblical criticism applies to British women and men. In North America, the popularization of critical methods began later in the century.

10. Taylor, "Women and Biblical Criticism," 1–2.

6

A Woman of Canaan:
Experiencing the Text

The story of the Canaanite woman is found in Matthew 15:21–28 and Mark 7:24–30. The accounts in Matthew and Mark differ in details; the women excerpted below did not highlight the differences, but merged the two texts, using details from both accounts.[1] The woman, described as Canaanite in Matthew and Syrophonecian in Mark, asked Jesus to heal her daughter who was demon-possessed. Jesus ignored the woman's initial cries; his disciples asked Jesus to send her away. Jesus explained that his mission was to Israel. The woman entreated Jesus again and revealed her faith in the dialogue that followed. Jesus responded to her great faith by healing the woman's daughter.

Careful readers of these texts wondered about the identity of the woman, the source of her knowledge about Jesus, the delayed and seemingly rude response of Jesus to the woman's request, and the meaning of the dog imagery.[2] The authors excerpted in this chapter gave attention to these common questions as they taught the story to children and adults. They interpreted the story within its context, recognizing differences between its setting and their own. To unpack meaning from the text, they drew on information gleaned from history and travel, both parallel gospel accounts, and intertexts from other parts of Scripture.

The women highlighted in this chapter used experience, both their own and that of their audience, to interpret the biblical text. Caroline Pridham carefully explained cultural differences using concrete examples of dogs for

---

1. The most obvious merging of the two stories without noting the difference between them is in Mrs. Donaldson's work. She titles her sermon "The Syrophonecian Woman; or, The Reward of Faith and Humility" but gives her text as Matthew 15:21–29. It is Mark who identifies the woman as a Syrophonecian; Matthew calls her a woman of Canaan.

2. For a history of the interpretation of this story see Roy A. Harrisville, "The Woman of Canaan: A Chapter in the History of Exegesis," *Interpretation* 20, no. 3 (1966): 274–87.

her young readers. While in Tyre and Sidon, Elizabeth Rundle Charles reflected on this story in her travel journal. Mrs. Donaldson preached on the story from a woman's perspective, using a motherly hermeneutic of experience. She called her readers and listeners to empathize with the mother of the sick child. All three women use a hermeneutic of experience to understand the biblical text: their own experiences helped them read the text well, and they in turn helped their readers understand and apply it well.

Caroline Pridham (1809–1900)

Gentile Dogs?

Caroline Pridham was a children's writer born in Chester, England.[3] In 1839 she married Thomas L. Pridham, a surgeon who worked as a coroner in Devon. The Pridhams had four children, only one of whom survived his parents. Pridham remarried after her husband's death, becoming the third wife of Lewis Gorham Wait. While she wrote as Caroline Pridham, some of her books also identify her as Mrs. Wait. Pridham was aware of developments in biblical studies, science, and archeology that were changing the way the Bible was interpreted and understood. Although she did not specifically engage historical criticism, her approach to biblical interpretation reflects the widespread shift in the nineteenth century toward a historical approach to the Bible.

Pridham began writing for children in 1883, with *Peeps at Palestine and its People* (1883),[4] followed by *Twilight and Dawn or Simple Talks on the Creation* (1892), *Domestic Pets: Their habits and Treatment* (1893), *Little Elsie's Book of Bible Animals* (1895), and *Peasblossom: The Story of a Pet Plant* (1896). Pridham's book about Bible animals includes stories about sheep, goats, dogs,

---

3. Pridham's familiarity with the geography, customs, and artifacts of the Middle East suggests that she might have travelled to the Holy Land. Travel to the Holy Land became widely available after 1869 through the tours of Thomas Cook. See Timothy Larsen, *Contested Christianity: The Political and Social Contexts of Victorian Theology* (Waco, TX: Baylor University Press, 2004), 29.

4. Pridham had some access to theological books, as evidenced by her references in the text of *Peeps at Palestine* (1883). For example, *The Land and the Book*, by W. Thomson (1859), is referred to frequently in the text, and the characters are encouraged to look at Thomson's book.

camels, asses, and swine. Each chapter provides information about the animals before retelling various Bible stories featuring them. By linking biblical animals to animals children were familiar with, Pridham made the biblical world concrete and real for children.

In her chapter, "About Dogs," Pridham contrasted the treatment of dogs in Britain and the Middle East. She discussed several negative Old Testament references to dogs, then used these negative images as an introduction to the story of the Canaanite woman. She bridged her readers' experience of dogs and the reference to dogs in this Bible story to help children understand the depth of the unnamed woman's faith.

About Dogs

[Pridham began her chapter on dogs with several stories about dogs in British households.] But why do I tell you all these nice stories about English and Scotch dogs?

I do so, that you may see how great the difference is between them and the dogs of Eastern countries. Dogs are never praised or spoken well of in the Bible, and we should be surprised at this if we did not know that, while *our* dogs are our friends and companions, the dogs in Bible lands are despised and treated as unclean animals. I do not know, but it seems to me the poor dogs in those countries would not be so *very* different from our own if they had been better treated, but it has so long been the fashion to neglect and ill-use them that they can hardly understand it when anyone tries to be a little kind to them.

These dogs have no master to serve and love, no house to guard, no little children to play with; they just live as best they can in the streets of the large towns, a troop of hungry, savage-looking creatures, much more like wolves than dogs, from whom you would run in terror if you met them, and with very good reason, too.

An Italian gentleman, who lived for some time in Jerusalem, noticed that the dogs seemed to go about in companies, each company keeping to its own part of the city; but wherever he went they all growled savagely at him as he passed. At last he thought he would try what kindness would do, and so began to feed some of them during the winter; and how do you think these wolf-like dogs showed their gratitude? They used to come round him when he went out, but not now to worry him by barking and yelping and whining; no, they just liked to follow him about, and would walk home with him when he allowed them to do so, and come whenever he beckoned to them.

So you see they *do* care for kindness, and I wish they got more of it, for certainly much good cannot be expected from wild dogs which have never had any masters.

Poor creatures, they are generally more than half starved, and are always prowling about in the hope of finding something to eat, and very short work they make with whatever comes in their way. If a horse or a camel drops down by the road-side and dies, there is a rush of dogs to the spot, and the bones of the poor beast are picked quite clean. I daresay now you can better understand that dreadful story of the dogs of Jezreel eating the body of the wicked queen Jezebel [2 Kings 9:10, 30–37]. We can imagine of how fierce a nature those dogs must have been thus to devour a dead body in the open street; and the punishment of the haughty queen seems even more terrible when we remember, that to be eaten by these unclean animals was considered by Jews the most dreadful thing that could happen to anyone. It was a solemn lesson for all who passed by that day to see how exactly God's word, spoken by Elijah long before, had come to pass: "In the portion of Jezreel shall dogs eat the flesh of Jezebel" [1 Kings 21:23].

Knowing that dogs were counted unclean and hateful animals, helps us to understand the tone of contempt with which they are spoken of. When Goliath saw David coming to him he disdained him, and he said, "Am I a *dog* that thou comest to me with staves?" [1 Sam. 17:43].

So Mephibosheth, Jonathan's lame son, to whom David showed kindness for his father's sake, said to him in his gratitude, "What is thy servant, that thou shouldst look upon such a *dead* dog as I am?" [2 Sam. 9:8].

The Jews constantly spoke of all who were not Israelites as "Gentile dogs," and this was the most contemptuous name they could give them.

You remember how the Lord Jesus answered the poor woman who came from the sea-coast and cried, "Have mercy on me, O Lord, Thou son of David!" He said, "I am not sent but to the lost sheep of the house of Israel." *She* was a Gentile, and might not ask the Lord as *Son of David* to have mercy on her; that was taking the place of the Jews, a place which did not belong to her.

How sad it must have been for her to hear the disciples asking their Master to send her away! Yet she felt only the more that He alone could heal her daughter, so she came and worshipped Him, saying, "Lord, help me!"

She knew she was not one of God's chosen people, but only a "dog of the Gentiles," yet when Jesus said, "It is not meet to take the children's bread, and to cast it to dogs," instead of going away thinking, "Then there can be nothing for *me*," she spoke those beautiful words which showed that she understood that, while it was true, she had no *right* to ask for anything, there was such love in the heart of Jesus that He could not send even such an one as she was away without an answer of peace—"Truth, Lord; yet the *dogs* eat of the crumbs that fall from their masters' table." (The broken bits of bread left on the table after dinner were generally thrown to the dogs in the street.) "Then Jesus answered, and said unto her, O woman, great is thy faith, be it unto thee even as thou wilt. And her daughter was made whole from that very hour."

Source: Caroline Pridham, *Little Elsie's Book of Bible Animals,* 3rd edition (London: A. S. Rouse, 1903), 34–38.

ELIZABETH RUNDLE CHARLES (1828–1896)

Traveling to Tyre

Elizabeth Rundle Charles was an English author of poetry, spiritual and devotional reflections, and commentaries.[5] In 1851, Charles and her husband traveled due to his ill health. They visited the Holy Land, Egypt, Turkey, the Greek Islands and Italy; Charles documented their travels in *Wandering over Bible Lands and Seas* (1862). Her book was much more than a travel journal, however, as Charles wove together the stories of Scripture related to the places they visited into her descriptions of her experiences of those same places so many years later.

Charles's retelling of the story of the Canaanite woman follows her exposition of the story of the widow of Sarepta (1 Kings 17:8–16). Her retellings of both stories were shaped by her experience of being in the place where the stories happened. She concluded her discussion of the Canaanite woman with a reference to the apostle Paul's experiences when he landed at Tyre as described in Acts 21:1–6. Charles imagined the woman and her healed daughter in the crowd welcoming Paul to Tyre. Her travel experiences influenced the way she connected these biblical stories.

---

5. For a fuller discussion of Charles, see "Communion and Sacrifice" in the chapter on Mary and "Hidden Depths" in the chapter on Mary Magdalene.

"The Shores of Tyre and Sidon"

There was a home—a heathen home—on this coast once, where lived a mother and her young daughter. But between the mother and the child, and between that young maiden and peace and heaven, had intruded another inmate, desecrating all. "An unclean spirit" possessed the child; and of the anguish, the degradation, the separation implied in those words how little can we conceive! The most loathsome disease can but touch the body, but this impure and malignant spirit touched and soiled the maiden's soul.

Then came the rumour of the arrival of a mysterious Galilean in the land, whose power evil spirits acknowledged—"for He could not be hid." Mighty to heal and gracious to help in this world of hopeless and helpless need, how, indeed, could he be hid? The mother found him. And the rapid dialogue seems to echo along these shores, a lesson to all ages of what God means by delaying answers to prayer, and how infinitely more tender the Saviour's heart is to the suppliant than that of any disciple.

The cry of anguish—"Have mercy on me, O Lord, thou son of David; my daughter is grievously vexed with a devil!" But he answered her not a word. Strange silence on the lips usually only silent on his own sorrows, and so ready to speak words of pardon and peace! How she must have watched his countenance! But whatever *she* read there, the disciples read its expression wrong.

"Send her away," they said; "she crieth after us." *Us!* How soon Pharisaism creeps into the heart but just healed from its own self-condemning sorrow. These disciples, so lately called from the publican's seat or the broken fish-nets—so lately crying, "Depart from me, a sinful man, O Lord!" [Luke 5:8]—so soon to need faithful rebuke and tender intercession, and to prove all the depth of forgiveness in the heart they understood so little now. Happily for her, it was *not* "after *them*" she cried. But he answered and said (not to them, but to her), "I am not sent but unto the lost sheep of the house of Israel." The words had little encouragement. The look and tone must have explained them, for she was not repelled by them. "She *came* and" (attempting no argument) simply "worshipped him, saying, Lord, help me"—the best argument a needy human creature can use. She cast herself, helpless and needy, on his grace.

"But he answered and said, It is not meet to take the children's bread, and to cast it to dogs."

Dogs! What words from his lips! She was of the human nature he had taken on him never more to lay it down—of that race he had come to redeem, yet she made no remonstrance. She was not, in the Jewish sense, "a child," she admitted it. She had no claim to the privileges of the household—no claim at all but her misery and His mercy. Crumbs must fall from that plentiful table, and he would not refuse them even to the "dogs."

Then what a change! The searching test was over. No more humbling epithets; but commendation to crown her through all time: "O woman, great is thy faith: be it unto thee even as thou wilt." There had been no limit to her humility and trust; there was no limit to his gift.

She went back to her house, and found her child, no longer roaming hither and thither with the aimlessness of insanity or the restlessness of a lost spirit, but "laid on the bed," peacefully resting, and able to meet her mother's eyes with the conscious smile of recognition and love.

What intercourse must have followed between them!

Once more, however, the veil is drawn; and those two lives, one fragment of which stands out in such vivid light for us, are again withdrawn into the darkness.

Not thirty years afterwards, the apostle Paul "landed at Tyre," and, "finding disciples, tarried there seven days." "And when those days were accomplished, we departed and went our way; and they all brought us on our way, with wives and children, till we were out of the city: and we kneeled down on the shore and prayed. And when we had taken our leave one of another, we took ship; and they returned home again" [Acts 21:3–6].

They knelt together on these Tyrian sands, Jew and Gentile, no more "dogs" and "children," but one family, God's one household. The disciples had learned much since that "send her away."

Were the Syrophoenician, an aged, grey-haired woman, and that restored daughter among that kneeling, weeping company? We cannot tell. It is enough service for one woman to render, to hand down with her memory, from generation to generation, that one lesson of humility and trust, and of the unfailing answer to every faithful prayer, "Be it unto thee even as thou wilt."

The narrative of the Syrophoenician was the last association of Gospel story which was to illuminate our Syrian journey.

Source: Elizabeth Rundle Charles, *Wanderings Over Bible Lands and Seas*, New Edition (London: T. Nelson, 1887), 262–65.

MRS. DONALDSON (FL. 1882)

Dealing with Our Demons: A Sermon

Mrs. Donaldson taught Bible studies and published her lessons as *Home Duties for Wives and Mothers, Illustrated by Women of Scripture*. Her book is a collection of sermons given to "poor weary women" in East London.[6] Donaldson used a feminine or maternal hermeneutic to analyze the stories of women in Scripture. She not only interpreted from a female perspective, but also taught her audience to enter into the story as women, to empathize with the issues the women in Scripture faced and thus feel the truth of the story. Like all good preachers, Donaldson made clear applications of the stories to the experiences of her audience.

One of the twenty-five women of Scripture featured in *Home Duties for Wives and Mothers* is the Canaanite, or Syro-Phoenician, woman. In her sermon on this woman, Donaldson retold Matthew's account of the story from a mother's perspective for mothers. After addressing common interpretive questions, Donaldson applied this story to current demons. She explored the issue of women's personal demons or besetting sins, including the demon drink, suggesting that deliverance from demons can still be found in Jesus.

THE SYRO-PHOENICIAN WOMAN;
or, The Reward of Faith and Humility

Matthew 15:21–29.

We have in these few verses an account with which we all, as mothers, can fully sympathize. Let us examine closely all the incidents connected with the circumstance.

Far away on the Phoenician coast, perhaps in a small cottage by the sea, that poor woman dwelt with her afflicted daughter. We are not told whether she had a husband, or other children, nor is her name mentioned, doubtless to bring out into stronger notice the plain facts of the case,—the deep cause of her distress, and the miracle that was wrought in her behalf.

---

6. For more information on Mrs. Donaldson and her work, see the "The Great Danger of Worldly Amusements: A Sermon" in the chapter on Herodias and Salome.

She had, at least, one daughter, this we know; and *she* was afflicted and "grievously vexed with a devil."

This possession by an evil spirit we read of as having been frequent in the days of our Lord's sojourn upon earth. From the time when our first parents hearkened to the voice of the tempter, and the Devil became prince of this world, he had kept his dominion undisturbed over the souls and bodies of men. But now that the promise was about to be fulfilled, that "the Seed of the woman" should "bruise his head," [Gen. 3:15] the Evil One appeared to make a more marked, and, as it were, final struggle, to maintain that power which he knew would soon be wrested from his grasp.

Think then, my dear mothers, what that poor woman's sufferings must have been, as she witnessed the awful power which so controlled and overcame her child, rendered helpless by that unseen enemy, who often led her to injure, and perhaps almost to destroy, herself.

We can judge by our own feelings when we see *our* little ones suffering from far smaller maladies, be it some wound, or burn, or perhaps, some sad accident. Which of us would not far rather suffer it all herself, if only her child might be spared?

With what surprise, then, and hope, must that poor sorrowing mother have heard of a wonderful Stranger, who was passing from city to city, effecting such marvelous cures. In the neighbouring land of Gennesaret persons were crowding to Him from all parts, to touch even the hem of His garment, and all were made whole [Luke 8:43–48]. Let us fancy what such news would be to us, dear friends, just now. Do we each think of some loved one at home,—a husband, parent, child, or sweet babe. How we would take them to be cured by this gracious Physician! No money to be paid, and therefore none too poor to go to Him! He bade all welcome, nor turned away from the worst case ever presented to Him. With what feelings, then, must this Canaanitish mother have hastened to find Him. Her child was too bad to be taken to Him, it is true, but she would go herself, and plead on her behalf for help.

Nor had she far to go. See her with eager haste, as she inquires of each passer-by whether they could tell of hope for her miserable daughter, and guide her to Him whom she sought. At last her efforts are crowned with success! Along the dusty road she sees a multitude approach, and as she draws near,—though she cannot get very near Him for the crowd,—her despairing voice is heard again and again, lest the opportunity so eagerly sought should be lost. Hear her word as she lays her trouble before Him: "O Lord, Thou Son of David, my daughter is grievously vexed with a devil!" Mark, she asks no favour, she claims no mercy, she simply casts it all into His hands to heal as He sees best.

But what is this we see? He heeds her not, but passes by! Can it be that He heard her not? Or is it that He *will* not notice her? Again, as she follows the crowd, she utters her piteous cry, till those nearest the Lord came and besought Him to stop and give her what she wanted, so that her troubled voice might cease to disturb them.

Her anxiety tells her that they are pleading in her behalf, and she gathers courage as hope returns, and pushes her way through the crowd of bystanders. Not heeding the response of the Master as He replies to his disciples, "I was not sent but unto the lost sheep of the house of Israel," she falls at His feet in the utmost despair, fearful lest He should even now pass her by.

Can you picture her as she lies prostrate and clasps Him by the feet, with tears streaming down her eyes, uttering her bitter wail, "Lord, help me"?

Notice, she does not say my daughter, but *me*, "Help *me*." Yes, *we* are helped in the persons of our children, their troubles are ours, their joys are ours: when they receive any good, do not our hearts rejoice? I see by your faces, my friends, that you echo this thought, you feel the truth of it.

Listen, then, to the manner in which her petition is received, fancy yourselves in her place, and learn a lesson from her faith.

Is it a rebuke that falls from those gentle lips? Can that tender heart refuse to hearken to the cry of woe? It would *seem* so, for He replies discouragingly, "It is not meet to take the children's bread, and cast it to the dogs:"—as though He would say, the Jews are my people, my children. I have come to save and to cure them, for they are my own and have a right to my aid, but *you*, you do not belong to the Jews, but to the Greeks: you have no claim upon Me; we despise all who are not of our religion as dogs; it would not be fitting to waste my mercy on such as you! Oh strange, unlooked-for words! How they would stagger the poor trembling, anxious mother!

But let us listen to the sequel. Love is strong; a mother's love strongest of all, and well-nigh unquenchable! Once more she pleads; she stays not to contradict the declaration; she resents not the comparison with the dogs. For her child's sake she will put up with ignominy and contempt, so that her request be granted. And she replied, "Truth, Lord, yet the dogs eat of the crumbs that fall from their master's table;" and if even they, in their low estate, are allowed the crumbs, this is all *I* ask: one crumb out of thy fullness, Lord, one word from thy lips, and my daughter shall be healed. Marvelous faith! Wonderful importunity! Well dost thou deserve the object of thy intercession!

"Oh woman, great is thy faith: be it unto thee even as thou wilt."

And now, O ye mothers, are ye like this woman, strong in faith? do you take your requests to the great Hearer of prayer, feeling, as she did, the reality of your need, and urging your case with that earnestness that knows no denial, and heeds neither delay nor rebuff? Perhaps you say you have no such need. Some there are, I see as I look at your harrowed faces, who know what it is to have just such a need as this Canaanitish woman: you have loved ones at home, lying perhaps incurable, of one or other of the many forms of sickness to which our flesh is subject. Upon such I would urge the necessity of taking your case to Him who alone can help you. He does not always see fit to answer your prayer at once, any more than He did the mother of whom we have been speaking. But do not give up. In His own time and His own way He will send you the needed help; and what He does not remove He will give you grace to bear.

But not alone to such as have these temporal sorrows do I now address myself. To *all* of you, my dear friends, nay, to myself also do I speak. Have we not *all* a malady? Are we not all, not only in a *general* sense, but in some *particular* sense, possessed, even "grievously vexed, with a devil"? Some homes too often are rendered miserable, and their peace disturbed, by some demon or other. Methinks I see yonder a room, which tells of utter neglect and destitution, all brought on by the spirit of Drink,—that great demon of our land,—it may be, possessing the father, and thus rendering the mother hopeless and heartless, neglecting her home and children, or forced to leave them to seek a pittance from the hands of strangers.

But it is not the fathers alone who become possessed by this dreadful demon; for oh! sad to relate, and shame to our sex! too many are the cases in which the mothers—yes, and often quite young mothers—are to be seen fast chained by this hideous monster. What, then, must be the home? The father, if he follows not her steps, which so often leads to strife, and perchance even to crime, must almost inevitably be driven to other scenes of vice and self-indulgence, to the utter destruction both of body and soul. Let us then urge you most affectionately and most earnestly, as you value your own happiness, both here and hereafter, and not only your own, but that of those you love, wage war against this demon of strong drink, nor ever allow your children to yield to its wily charms.

But this is not the only evil spirit with which our homes are often devastated. His name is Legion. Each one of us has some *one* against which to struggle. It may be we have a violent and passionate temper, or perhaps a sulky one; an untruthful tongue, or perhaps love of backbiting others. I need not name more; these are enough to show you that when we are controlled by some evil tendency, or in the habit of yielding to some particular sin, *then* it is that we are led captive by the tempter, *that* is the evil spirit by which we are possessed. Search your own hearts, then, dear friends; you will find there, if you do it honestly, the demon that lurks within.

And having discovered your enemy, go in the spirit of this poor woman, not only with the general cry for deliverance from *all* your sins, but specially for deliverance from this, your most besetting sin. Jesus will not turn from you, even though He may try your faith. He loved you so much that He came to seek and to save you [Luke 19:10]. He knows the weight of your sins, because He bore them all, when He died for you on Calvary. And now He simply bids you come to Him with all your woes.

Cast yourself, then, low at His feet, tell Him you have no help but Him; He is able and He is willing to deliver you from all your sins, even the worst, and He will reply, "Be it unto thee even as thou wilt."

Source: Mrs. Donaldson, *Home Duties for Wives and Mothers, Illustrated by Women of Scripture* (London: William Hunt, 1882), 103–11.

STUDY QUESTIONS

1. Compare and contrast the parallel accounts of this story in Matthew 15:21–28 and Mark 7:24–30. Are the interpretations presented here successful in harmonizing these two accounts? Why or why not?

2. Caroline Pridham wrote for children. How did Pridham attempt to make the story accessible for children? Did she succeed? Are there portions of Scripture that are deemed too "adult" for children? How and why is that determined?

3. How did the experience of visiting the Holy Land influence the writers in this chapter? What other experiences shaped their readings of the Canaanite Woman?

4. How did these nineteenth-century commentators explain evil spirits? Is their understanding the same as current understandings?

5. What other Scripture passages do these commentators use to make sense of the Canaanite woman's story? Are these scriptural connections helpful? What do the connections tell us about the writers' view of the purpose, applicability, and unity of Scripture?

7

The Adulterous Woman:
Teaching Troublesome Texts

The account of the adulterous woman, John 8:1–11, is interesting in part because its legitimacy has been disputed since early Christian times. Although many scholars question its present placement in John's gospel, the story's authenticity as a well-established tradition is more certain.[1] English readers using the King James Version had no idea that the story's authenticity was disputed. After the Revised Version of the New Testament was published in 1881, readers encountered a story that was separated from what comes before and after by brackets and white space.[2] The explanatory footnote in the RV stated: "Most of the ancient authorities omit John 7:53–8:11. Those which contain it vary much from each other."[3] The general Bible-reading public was now faced with this textual issue. Preachers and Sunday school teachers had to think about teaching this story differently.[4] What did nineteenth-century women make of this story in the fourth gospel?

1. See Weil Eggen's discussion of the history of the text in "Jn 8:1–11, A Finger Writing Down the History: On Dialogues Beyond Canonicity," *Exchange* 27, no. 2 (1998): 98–120.

2. The revisers of the New Testament were commissioned in 1870 to update the language of the King's James Version and the text based on then current biblical scholarship. The Revised New Testament was published in 1881 and a revision Old Testament followed in 1885.

3. The New Testament in the Revised Version of 1881 (Oxford: Oxford University Press, 1910), 239.

4. In Charlotte Yonge's manual on how to teach the New Testament, she gave advice to teachers on the textual issue as highlighted in the Revised Version: "Again, in the case of St. John 8:1–8, the doubt is whether the narrative was really first written by St. John the Evangelist, not whether the event happened, nor whether the passage may be reckoned as part of the Word of Life. It is like the last chapter of Deuteronomy, which no one ever supposed to be written by Moses, but which has not the less authority on that account. The teacher should, therefore, inform himself from the revision, but never speak slightingly of the old one." *How to Teach the New Testament* (London: National Society's Depository, 1881), 52.

The five authors featured in this chapter assumed the authenticity of the story. Two of the five, Lucy Barton and Mary Cornwallis, wrote before the Revised Version (RV) was published. They did not mention the textual issue. Two of the three later authors addressed the issue of the text's authenticity head on. Charlotte Bickersteth Wheeler addressed the textual issue directly, proposing a theory for its exclusion from some of the earliest manuscripts, and defending its legitimacy. Josephine Butler made a similar argument, citing male bias as the reason the story was bracketed in the Revised Version. Elizabeth Baxter addressed the textual issue indirectly, by showing that the passage fit into the larger context of John 8. Baxter also read the story with sensitivity to the issue of gender, and noticed the double standard of the male accusers: only the woman caught in adultery was condemned, nothing is heard of the man who was with her. Butler also noted this double standard, calling it a key issue of the story for her day.

Barton's age-appropriate commentary takes the form of a letter addressed to children. She did not comment on each verse, but summarized the story with her young audience in mind. The commentaries by Cornwallis and Wheeler follow the standard format of the genre, though they divide the text differently: while Cornwallis commented on thought units within a chapter, Wheeler commented on every verse. They both addressed the interpretive issues relevant to their readers who lacked access to scholarly resources. Both cited the opinions of scholars on issues raised in the story. Baxter took a more homiletical tone in her commentary on John; she preached to her readers.

These excerpts on the adulterous women include fewer obviously feminine reflections on the text than most other sections in this volume. Barton, Cornwallis, and Wheeler reflected at length on the conscience. Baxter, by contrast, was concerned that her readers not continue to condemn themselves when Jesus did not condemn them. Sarah Tooley's interview with Josephine Butler contains the most obviously feminine and feminist reflections. Only three of the five authors collected here noted the double standard used to condemn only the woman caught in adultery and not the man; these women were published in the final two decades of the nineteenth century.

LUCY BARTON (1808–1903)

Heart Searching

Lucy Barton was an author of children's books and collaborator in the publication of a selection of her father's letters and poems. She was born into a Quaker family in Woodbridge, England. After her mother died in childbirth, her father, Bernard Barton, became a bank clerk and poet, publishing eight volumes of verse and a number of occasional pieces of poetry. He encouraged his daughter, who worked as a governess, to pursue writing. Father and daughter worked together on a number of writing projects. A death-bed promise to her father resulted in her failed marriage to a family friend, the writer Edward Fitzgerald. Barton's works on the Bible include *Bible Letters for Children*, 1831; *The Gospel History of our Lord and Saviour Jesus Christ*, 1837; *Natural History of the Holy Land, and Other Places Mentioned in the Bible*, 1856; *The Life of Christ: A Gospel History for the Use of Children*, 1857.[5]

The extract below is taken from *The Gospel History of our Lord and Saviour Jesus Christ*. This book built on the success of Barton's earlier volume on the Old Testament, *Bible Letters*. Barton's *Gospel History* was one of many Scripture histories written during this period which set out to present a coherent harmonized history of Jesus' life and ministry. Barton personalized her age-appropriate history for children by using a series of letters to tell the story. Reviewers regarded Barton's history as the best of its kind for children and young persons, and praised "its clear and simple narrative."[6]

In the letter that addresses the story of the adulterous woman, Barton used material from Luke 10 and John 7 to put the story into context. She did not mention the nature of the woman's crime in John 8, but invited readers into the story asking them to reflect on their own responses to hearing about wicked people. She contrasted the usual human response of despising or even hating the wicked with Jesus' response of pity and sorrow. She encouraged her readers to emulate Jesus rather than the scribes and Pharisees. Barton implicitly challenged the commonplace assumption that sexual sin was more displeasing than other kinds of sin.

5. Biography from Marion Ann Taylor and Heather E. Weir, eds., *Let Her Speak for Herself: Nineteenth-Century Women Writing on Women in Genesis* (Waco, TX: Baylor University Press, 2006), 29–30.

6. Review of Lucy Barton's *The Gospel History of our Lord and Saviour Jesus Christ*, in *Tait's Edinburgh Magazine*, vol. 21, 1837, 62. See also the review in *The Literary Gazette and Journal of Belles Lettres, Arts, Sciences, & c.* (W. A. Scripps, 1837), 835.

LETTER XXV.

You know that the Saviour had chosen twelve men as his disciples, to be with him wherever he went. And at this time he sent out seventy others, who were to go two and two before him, into every city and place, to teach and to preach in his name. They were to heal the sick, [Luke 10:1–9] and to do all those acts of love which they had learned from the example of their Divine Master.

He then sent the twelve to a feast which was to be held at Jerusalem; Jesus himself went in secret, and did not shew himself to the people at first,—for there was much talk of him. Some said that he was a good man; others, that he deceived the people. Once or twice he was graciously pleased to come into the temple, where many, when they heard his words, believed on him; others would have taken him up. But the officers, whom the chief priests and people had sent for that purpose, said, "Never man spake like this man" [John 7:1–52].

Dear children, when you hear of people who have been very wicked, who have taken what does not belong to them, or have not told the truth, or who may even have been so very wicked as to kill a fellow-creature, do you not feel in your hearts that you are a great deal better than they are? And, instead of feeling pity and sorrow for them, do you not despise, and almost hate them? But I am going to shew you that our blessed Saviour did not feel thus. And remember, that if we are really led and taught by his Spirit, we shall learn more and more to act like him.

One morning early, when Jesus was sitting in the temple teaching the people, the Scribes and Pharisees brought unto him a woman who had been guilty of a crime which the Jews punished with death. But they were not sorry for her. They did not pity her, and bring her to Jesus, that he might teach her how sinful she had been, and pardon her. Oh, no; they were proud and hard-hearted. They cared nothing about the woman or her sin. But they wished to make the people dislike Jesus; and they thought that if he condemned her to die, the Romans would be angry; and if he spared her life, they knew the people would think he had broken the law of Moses. They did not remember that they were speaking to him who had given the law to Moses, but said, "Moses commanded that such should be stoned: what sayest thou?"

Jesus stooped down, and with his finger wrote on the ground as though he heard them not. They still kept on asking. At length he lifted up himself, and said unto them, "He that is without sin among you, let him first cast a stone at her." They were not prepared for this. Highly as they thought of themselves, the voice of conscience would be heard; and not one of them dared take up the stone. They went out one by one, beginning at the eldest, and left Jesus alone with the woman. When he had lifted up himself, and saw none of them, he said, "Woman, where are those thine accusers? hath no man condemned thee?" She said, "No man, Lord." And Jesus said unto her, "Neither do I condemn thee; go, and sin no more."

Now, we cannot for a moment think that the pure and holy Jesus did not feel the guilt of this poor woman much more strongly than her sinful accusers. Yet they had been ready and willing to make the most of it. But, perhaps, he who knows what is in a man, [1 Chron. 28:9] saw that she was sorry for what she had done; and her sin was not more displeasing in the sight of Jesus than the secret sins of those proud men who had brought her before him. Let us, then; dear children, instead of thinking harshly of others who may seem to be more wicked than we are willing to think ourselves, search our own hearts; and we shall soon feel that it is of God's mercy that we have been kept from falling [Ps. 94:18].

Source: Lucy Barton, *The Gospel History of our Lord and Saviour Jesus Christ* (London: W. Tweedie, 1837), 136–39.

MARY CORNWALLIS (1758–1836)

We Behold the Woman

Mary Cornwallis was the author of a four-volume commentary on the Bible, entitled *Observations, Critical, Explanatory, and Practical on the Canonical Scriptures.*[7] She was married to Rev. William Cornwallis, who served as the Anglican priest to the parish of Elham and Wittersham in Kent for more than fifty years. The Cornwallises had two daughters. The elder married

---

7. A sketch of Mary Cornwallis's life is found in the introduction to her *Observations, Critical, Explanatory, and Practical on the Canonical Scriptures,* 2nd ed. (London: Baldwin, Cradock, & Joy, 1820). For a full treatment of Cornwallis's work as an interpreter of the Bible see Marion Ann Taylor, "Mary Cornwallis: Voice of a Mother," in *Recovering Nineteenth-Century Women Interpreters of the Bible,* ed. Christiana de Groot and Marion Ann Taylor (Atlanta: Society of Biblical Literature, 2007), 31–44. See also Marion Ann Taylor, "Cornwallis, Mary (1758–1836)," in *Handbook of Women Biblical Interpreters,* ed. Marion Ann Taylor and Agnes Choi (Grand Rapids, : Baker Academic, 2012), 142–45.

James Trimmer, the son of author and educator Sarah Trimmer,[8] and died after their son was born. The younger daughter, Caroline Frances Cornwallis (1786–1858), became a well-known writer, scholar, feminist, and social advocate who began her professional writing career by helping her mother complete her Bible commentary.

Mary Cornwallis's four-volume commentary on the Bible was first published in 1817, with a second edition printed in 1820. Cornwallis wrote her commentary over a long period of time. The project began as the notes she took her from a variety of scholarly works, including commentaries. She revised her notes as she taught her own daughters, then her young grandson, James Trimmer. After the tragic death of her grandson, Cornwallis published her copious teaching notes, using the proceeds to endow a free primary school in his memory. Cornwallis's commentary follows the standard form of commentaries. She commented on individual chapters of Scripture, drawing on the expertise of scholars to help her explain difficult words and ideas, and probe theological and practical significance. She synthesized the work of scholars and theologians, fusing these with her own motherly reflections and opinions on the text.

Cornwallis commented on the story of the adulterous woman in its entirety. She suggested that the brevity of the account invites the imagination to fill in details. She recommended readers visualize the drama of the scene that included not only "the confident intruders pushing their way through the multitude," but also the confused woman, her accusers, and curious onlookers. Cornwallis was especially interested in the woman's inner life, suggesting that she remained behind when her accusers left because she was penitent.

[John] CHAPTER 8:1–11.

Whether the woman brought before Jesus in the temple was only betrothed, as some have thought, or actually married, is a matter of very little importance; because she was in either case amenable to the laws for breach of chastity, and death was the penalty attached to it. It should be remembered that the power of inflicting capital punishment was taken from the Jews, and lodged in the hands of governors appointed by the Romans, as clearly appears in the proceedings which took place after the apprehension of Jesus: had he therefore taken upon himself undue authority, he would have incurred the resentment of that power,

8. For a biography of Sarah Trimmer, see "Blessed Humility" in the chapter on Mary.

no less than that of the Sanhedrin; and if he declined any cognizance of such an offence, it might be represented to his disadvantage as a prophet, and one claiming Divine affinity. The crafty Pharisees therefore probably thought that they had at last placed him in a situation from which he could not extricate himself; and that his life or fame must be implicated. The imagination is sensibly struck with a scene described by the apostle in such few words. We behold the confident intruders pushing their way through the multitude, who were listening to the instructive precepts of Jesus, and dragging with them the wretched offender. We behold her placed in the midst, sunk in confusion and dismay: her eager accusers not only proclaiming her crime, but the law of Moses respecting it; and the wondering people collected to hear the issue of this novelty. The disregard paid by Jesus to the objects before Him must have surprised and mortified them: his tracing characters on the pavement probably excited both curiosity and awe in the multitude: for the actions of prophets were still considered as signs:* his silence, however, had one evident effect; it compelled the Scribes and Pharisees to reiterate their demands, and to expose their uncharitable zeal by their importunity. When Jesus raised himself up, and began to speak with his wonted grace and dignity, we can but conclude that triumph was visible in their eyes; short-lived indeed, as that of the wicked usually is, and to be succeeded by the deepest disgrace and mortification. The sentence was such an one as mortals may admire, but the wisest among them could not have devised; and we may conclude by the sequel, that conscience was permitted to enforce it with more than common severity. Dr. Bragge on the subject, says, 'However men may affect to despise all laws of God and man, there is a law within them, written upon their hearts by the finger of their Creator, which, one time or other, they will be forced to attend to, and which will fix their guilt home upon them. And CONSCIENCE, which is God's vicegerent in the soul, when roused by some awakening accident, some moving, well-applied discourse, or pain, or sickness, or affliction, will then do its office impartially, and become both *witness, judge,* and *executioner*.'[9] This most true and judicious assertion was wonderfully exemplified in the case before us; and we now behold the woman, conscience-smitten also, deserted by her accusers, and fixed as it were on the spot. That she was penitent, there is every reason to suppose by this very circumstance; for, had she been bold in sin, she would have taken advantage of the opportunity Jesus

9. Francis Bragge (1664–1728), the Anglican Vicar of Hitchin in Hertfordshire, published widely on Scripture and other related subjects. Cornwallis quotes his practical discourses on the parables as well as work on the miracles in her comments on the gospels.

*See [John] Chap. 2:13.

afforded, by apparent preoccupation, to make her escape with the rest. In the mildness of Christ's behaviour to the woman, some have found occasion for censure, as if he had not expressed sufficient indignation at her crime: indeed there have been persons sufficiently profane to assert, that he sanctioned her offence by saying, "Neither do I condemn thee:" but the word here used relates to a condemnation rather penal than moral; and in the words, "Sin no more," Jesus sufficiently shows that he meant neither to encourage, nor to justify her offence.

Source: Mary Cornwallis, *Observations, Critical, Explanatory, and Practical on the Canonical Scriptures*, 2nd ed. (London: Baldwin, Cradock, & Joy, 1820), 4:171–73.

CHARLOTTE BICKERSTETH WHEELER (1818–1884)

Who Could Invent It?

Charlotte Bickersteth Wheeler was an Anglican author and educator. She was born in London to Rev. John Cooper and Mary Anna Bickersteth and married her father's curate, John Blucher Wheeler in Cheshire. The couple had six children; their eldest son had special needs, which required specialized care in an institution. Wheeler ran a girls' school in Croydon with the help of two of her daughters. She authored a number of books, including memoirs of her parents, a book on creation and the flood, devotional works, and a popular commentary on the four gospels.[10]

Our Master's Footsteps; or, Bible Class Notes for Thoughtful Girls (1883) began as the detailed notes on the gospels written over a period of fifteen years for a Bible class for educated girls in their teens. Wheeler revised her notes as she worked with different classes of girls, making full use of the Revised Version of the New Testament published in 1881. She commented on each verse of the biblical text separately, explaining what was difficult or unclear and suggesting its spiritual significance.

Wheeler drew her readers into the story found in John 8 by asking them to picture the scene which she painted in fuller colors than the biblical narrator. Wheeler added an imagined moment at the end of the story in which the

---

10. See Wheeler's memoir of her mother, *Memorials of a Beloved Mother: Being a Sketch of the Life of Mrs. Cooper* (London: Wertheim and Macintosh, 1853).

woman worshipped Jesus. Wheeler theorized that if this penitent moment had been included in the text, some early copyists might have left the story in their manuscripts. She concluded that it was easy to explain why some copyists might have dropped the story, then argued that it must be authentic because "who could invent it?"

[John] CHAPTER 8.

1. THIS verse clearly belongs to Chapter 7. The Mount of Olives is a mile to the east of Jerusalem; Gethsemane and Bethany were very near. David went weeping up Mount Olivet (2 Sam. 15:30). It was on this mountain that Christ wept over Jerusalem, which appears like a map spread out before it, from a spot two thirds up the hill (Luke 19:41, 42). Christ often passed the night there (Luke 21:37).

2. On previous occasions, Christ met the people in the Temple early in the day. Let us, too, seek Him early in the morning, ere the day's work sets in!

3, 4. It was hatred of Christ, not hatred of sin, that actuated them: He had foiled them on the previous day, so now they try another plan. It is right to bring a poor sinner to Jesus, but in this case the vile motive marred it utterly, though a good motive would not palliate a sin.

5. The custom of stoning such offenders had passed away; probably they had no power to do it. The harsh sentence, 'Stone her' would have been strangely unlike One so pitiful to sinners, and would have seemed like stepping out of His province and usurping civil authority. They must have felt sure that He would not say *that*; but 'Spare her' would have suited them equally well, as enabling them to say that He disobeyed Moses and countenanced sin.

6. He was sitting when they came to Him, and at this point He stooped down and wrote on the ground. What He wrote, or why He did so, we are not told; perhaps it was to show aversion to entering on the subject.

7. 'Continued asking Him,' *i.e.* pressed for an answer. 'He lifted up Himself'; doubtless this time His glance took in each one of them: the miserable, despairing woman, her life trembling in the balance, and everything that makes life a blessing blighted, blasted, gone; and the cunning, malignant faces of the accusers to whom the sin was nothing, the opportunity of at last outwitting Christ everything. Listen to His answer: 'He that is without sin,' etc. Of course this does not mean literally sinless, for all

have sinned; but each man's conscience knew to what Christ referred, and spoke in a still small voice, more appalling than thunder, 'Thou art not the man to stone her.' The 'stone' means the first stone, which was always cast by a witness or accuser, as a signal that by-standers should cast other stones, till the victim lay dead beneath them.

8. Evidently this second stooping down was to give them the opportunity of slinking away without meeting His eye.

9. Mighty power of conscience! What *is* conscience? Every part of our complex nature is fallen—the will most, the conscience least. Yet, though this inner monitor can never be wholly silenced, as we see in the case of these wicked men, it is often blinded, lulled into false peace, or so perverted that men call evil good and good evil. You may, however, be absolutely sure of this; nothing which conscience denounces can be right *for you*; do not argue with conscience—let its first protest suffice. Picture the group going out one by one, shame and conscious guilt written on their foreheads, 'beginning at the eldest,' the deviser perhaps of this foiled project; all felt that the trap they had laid for Christ had entangled themselves. The woman might have followed them; there was nothing to hinder it, unless some Divine attraction detained her. St. Augustine says, 'Two things were left alone together—misery and mercy.'

10. And now the last footstep died away, and He spoke to her, as she stood trembling, and astonished at the skill with which He had dispersed her accusers, and saved her from a terrible death, had their power sufficed to inflict it.

11. Christ was far from saying that she did not deserve condemnation; He merely left the matter as it was; He did not say 'Thy sins are forgiven,' far less did He bid her 'Go in peace.' He simply said, 'Go, and sin no more.' How one longs to know whether she threw herself at His feet, to thank Him for His wondrous mercy, and to entreat His pardon; surely she must have done. This whole narrative is wanting in some of the earliest MSS.; it seems to have been purposely omitted, under the impression that Christ could not have acted with such tenderness to one who expressed no penitence, but probably we do not know all that passed. In any case a copyist could easily omit this story, but who could invent it? Few of His works of love bear more manifestly the stamp of *Christ*.

Source: Charlotte Bickersteth Wheeler, *Our Master's Footsteps; or, Bible Class Notes for Thoughtful Girls* (London: Elliot Stock, 1883), 329–31.

Elizabeth Baxter (1837–1926)

....

Where Is the Man?

Elizabeth Baxter was an English preacher, evangelist, teacher, and author of some forty books and a great number of smaller booklets, tracts, and expositions. She wrote weekly Sunday School lessons published in her husband's successful paper, *The Christian Herald*.[11] Several of her books can properly be called commentaries, including her book on the gospel of John.

Baxter's commentary on the gospel of John does not follow the more traditional format used by Cornwallis and Wheeler. She focused less on individual verses or thought units and more on the story of the adulterous woman and its present placement in the gospel. She tied the story into the larger narrative context of the series of seven disputes with the Jews at the Feast of Tabernacles and Jesus' self-identification as the light and life of the world in John 8:12. Baxter's contextual reading implicitly critiqued the bracketing of John 7:53–8:11 in the Revised Version. Baxter moved seamlessly from exposition to application and characteristically preached the text's message to her readers.

Of the women excerpted in this chapter, only Baxter raised issues related to the accused woman's rights.[12] She drew attention to "the unjust and unequal standards by which men and women are judged in this world," in contrast to God's impartiality in the law, which mandated the stoning of both partners.

Go And Sin No More.

John 8:1–12.

NONE could touch Jesus until His hour was come, so the disappointed scribes and Pharisees went every man "unto his own house," and Jesus was still at large; none of the officers or of the people had been found proof against His

---

11. For more information on Baxter, see "A Woman with a Vocation," in the chapter on Anna and "The Gospel Preacher," in the chapter on the Samaritan woman.

12. Baxter was not the only women to note the double standard displayed in this story; one other woman who did so was Mary Deverell (fl. 1774–1797). Deverell wrote sympathetically about the woman in John 8 in her sermon "Mercy," addressing male bias or "vile partiality" on the part of the accusers as they make no mention of the adulterous man. For more on Deverell, see Joni Sancken, "Deverell, Mary," in *Handbook of Women Biblical Interpreters*, ed. Marion Ann Taylor and Agnes Choi (Grand Rapids: Baker, 2012), 159–62.

words, for they were "with Power" (Luke 4:32). Jesus was at large—still in a position to bless; but the scribes and Pharisees left no stone unturned to bring Him under condemnation. The following morning, they caused an interruption to His teaching by dragging into the midst of His audience a poor unhappy woman, who had been taken in the very act of grievous sin—that of unfaithfulness to her husband. Another had been her partner in sin, but he was not dragged before the public, and no question was raised as to whether *he* should suffer the penalty of the law, although they knew that it was written, "The adulterer and the adulteress shall surely be put to death" (Lev. 20:10). God's Word is not responsible for the unjust and unequal standards by which men and women are judged in this world. God is STRICTLY IMPARTIAL.

They said, "Moses in the law commanded us that such should be stoned: but what sayest Thou?" Their words imply that they thought Jesus would differ from Moses. They thought to catch Him in a trap. If He should say that the poor woman must suffer the penalty of the law, then, where would be His reputation for love and gentleness? He would lose all His popularity. If, on the contrary, He should decide the other way, they would, at last, have a just ground for the accusation that He taught contrary to Moses. They thought to have Him this time,—they saw no way of escape for Him. Little did they expect the reception which their question met with. At once He paused in His teaching: but, instead of answering them, He wrote with His finger on the ground. He who was "of purer eyes than to behold evil" [Hab. 1:13] turned away from the relation of the details of sin. But they were urgent, and continued asking Him, so He raised Himself, and answered, "He that is without sin among you, let him first cast a stone at her." She must be dealt with according to the law, she must be stoned: but WHO SHOULD BE THE EXECUTIONER?

Again He turned away, and with His finger wrote upon the ground. Truly, "never man spake like this Man" [John 7:46]. His hearers were silenced; the Word had judged them: the oldest man of the company led the way from the presence of Him whose Word had searched and found him out; and then, one after another, the whole of those who had condemned her filed out, and "Jesus was left alone, and the woman standing in the midst." Alone with Jesus! Alone with Him who, of all that company, had a right to execute upon her the sentence of death which the law pronounced, and which He could never make light of! "Woman," He said, "where are those thine accusers? Hath no man condemned thee?" She answered, "No man, Lord," but attempted no self-justification, and pleaded for no mercy from Him who had her life, for time and eternity, in His hands; and He said what no other man on earth and no angel in heaven would have dared to say, "Neither do I condemn thee. Go, and sin no more." "Is Christ the minister of sin?" (Gal. 2:17). Does He teach us to make more light of sin than did His Father under the law? "God forbid." Jesus, the Saviour, did not condemn this sinful woman, because, for her sake, He Himself was condemned. He was made sin for her, though He "knew no sin" (2 Cor. 5:21). He was "made a curse for" her, to redeem her "from the curse of the law;" [Gal. 3:13] and thus had He, and He alone, A RIGHT TO PRONOUCE PARDON.

Jesus came, not "to condemn the world, but that the world through Him might be saved" (John 3:17)—the world whether the morally upright, like Nathaniel, Saul of Tarsus and Cornelius (John 1:47; Acts 22:3; 23:1; 10:1, 2), or shameless, open sinners, like the Samaritan woman, [John 4:3–42] the woman of whom we have just spoken, and Mary Magdalene, out of whom He cast seven devils [Mark 16:9]. Where *He* says, "Neither do I condemn thee," because our iniquities are laid on Him, He also says, with equal authority, and equal power, "Go, and sin no more." He has as much power to keep us from sinning as He has to pardon us for our past sins. He has redeemed us, soul and body, and we have a right to go free. O, if those who are under the power of any fleshly lust, whether drunkenness, gluttony, or uncleanness, could but believe that every member of their bodies, as well as every power of their souls, has been redeemed, and is capable of being holy unto the Lord, as a part of the temple of the Holy Ghost [1 Cor. 6:19–20]—then, self-despair, the self-despair which often seizes this class of sinners, would come to an end. Satan crushes them by saying, 'Your appetites are yours by birth, *you* cannot help them; they are sinful, but then *you* cannot control them; you are under the curse, and there is no help for it.' O, how blessed is God's Word, "Christ hath redeemed us from the curse of the law; being made a curse for us" [Gal. 3:13–14]. He has redeemed, not our souls only, but our bodies, our appetites, our desires, our whole spiritual, moral and physical man, from sin, and from all impossibility. Glory to His name! He has made eating and drinking, so long as it is under His control, holy, for He ate and drank habitually here on earth. He has made marriage, so long as He controls it, holy; by His presence at the marriage of Cana in Galilee [John 2:1]. He has made our natural love of the beautiful, so long as He rules it, holy, by His talk about the lilies of the field [Matt. 5:28]. All which Satan has used in our human nature to develop the germs of sin, Christ has redeemed to be an instrument of righteousness, a vehicle for the life of Jesus, and for the working of the Holy Ghost. The man born blind (John 9) was born so "*that* the works of God might be made manifest in him." If our nature had not fallen so low, the glory of God in the glorious redemption which Christ has wrought, could not have been so great.

"Neither do I condemn thee." 'Yes, I know that; but I CANNOT FORGIVE

MYSELF,' say some. Dear reader, this proceeds more from mortified pride than from real humility. To be angry with yourself shows that you have expected something from yourself, and have been disappointed. A friend remarked the other day, 'While we are condemning ourselves, we are in an atmosphere of condemnation, and are ready to condemn everyone else as well.' One of the surest fruits of our accepting to the full the forgiveness of God is that we forgive ourselves and accept that command which is with power, "Go, and sin no more."

When Jesus re-commenced His teaching, He said, "I am the Light of the world" [John 8:12]. What light He had shed on that poor woman! She came out of the thick darkness of a life blasted by her own sin, a family life broken up, the sentence of death upon her for soul and body, and the bitter thought that he who had equally sinned with her went, as far as human judgment went, scot free, perhaps walked in the streets with large phylacteries and an added breadth to the border of his garment. She could look to no blessing in the future in family life, no possible reparation, no place of repentance. But a bright, broad, glorious light had shone in. Instead of the stones which were her due, and a public execution, with the curses of her husband and child ringing in her ears, she, who had deserved it all, had heard the Son of God say to her, "Neither do I condemn thee," and, joy of joys, "Go; and sin no more." Here was hope beyond all expectation, A NEW LIFE AND A BETTER WAS OPENING before her, not for time only, but for eternity. "I am the Light of the world, he that followeth Me shall not walk in darkness, but shall have the light of life" [John 8:12]. It is Satan's plan, when we are saved, or when we are sanctified, to bring some darkness over our souls. He tries, in some way or other, to make the Word of God to seem to be at issue with our experience, and then turns round with his old question, "Hath God said?" [Gen. 3:1] insinuating that, after all, God does not keep His Word. There is but one way to meet him, and that is, to follow Jesus, in the dark or in the light, when we understand, and when we do not understand; then we shall come out into the light some time. We may start on a railway journey when the rain is falling in torrents, and the thunder rolling over-head, but we sit still and are borne along, and, by-and-by, we have been carried right through the storm, and out on to the other side. And just so, if we continue following Jesus, does He carry us through any time of darkness, right out into the light. We may come into darkness, but cannot "*abide*" in it, when we follow Him. Looking into our selves is more productive of darkness than any other thing. Light is not inherent in any man, all light comes from without, we are naturally without light, "Ye were sometimes darkness, but now are ye light in the Lord" (Eph. 5:8). As we follow Jesus, we see ourselves, as well as others, from His point of view, we see circumstances as He sees them, and O, how, different they look. In His light, we see all things subject to Him, we see sin, Satan, the world, the flesh, all overcome, we see constant victory, because He has gained it, and whatever He does, is "forever." And seeing all this, how can we abide in the darkness of sin, or of self-condemnation, or of despair? How can we abide in the darkness of ignorance, or of fear, when His glorious light shines in? Thank God, He lights us from sinning to a life in which, just as we quite and for ever yield ourselves up to Him, we are kept by His abiding power. It is a life of joy and liberty, in which "Neither do I condemn thee" is our theme of praise, and "Go; and sin no more" our joyful warrant and power for a life in which we walk in the light of His countenance and know that we please Him. "Blessed is the people that know the joyful sound; they shall walk, O Lord, in the light of Thy countenance. In Thy name shall they rejoice all the day: and in Thy righteousness shall they be exalted. For Thou art the glory of their strength" (Ps. 89:15–17).

Source: Elizabeth Baxter, *The Living Word in the Gospel of John* (London: Christian Herald, 1887), 79–85.

JOSEPHINE BUTLER (1828–1906)

The Sex Bias of the Commentators

Josephine Butler was a social activist, lecturer, and prolific author of pamphlets, essays, and books.[13] Her parents, John Grey and Hannah Annette Grey, were Anglican advocates for abolition and other social justice concerns. Her husband, George Butler, an Anglican priest and educator, supported his wife's call for changes in Britain's prostitution laws as well as her advocacy for women's education, employment, and rights to legal justice.[14]

---

13. Amanda Benckhuysen, "Butler, Josephine Elizabeth Grey (1828–1906)," in Taylor and Choi, *Handbook of Women Biblical Interpreters*, 104–5. See also Timothy Larsen, "Evangelical Anglicans: Josephine Butler and the Word of God," in *A People of One Book: The Bible and the Victorians* (Oxford: Oxford University Press, 2011), 219–46; Helen Mathers, *Patron Saint of Prostitutes: Josephine Butler and a Victorian Scandal* (Gloucester: The History Press, 2014).

14. Butler led the Ladies' National Association for the Repeal of the Contagious Diseases Acts. English Parliament enacted The Contagious Disease Act in 1864, and amended and extended this law by acts passed in 1866 and 1869. Butler and her associates argued that the laws discriminated against women, as the legislation contained no sanctions against men.

All of Josephine Butler's work and writing grew out of her strong sense of a prophetic call to listen and to proclaim God's word.

Butler published many works on the Bible. Stories from both the Old and New Testaments became the platforms from which she called her readers to reform their own lives as well as the structures of society. This particular selection comes from an interview conducted by journalist Sarah Tooley entitled "The Sex Bias of the Commentators."[15] In the interview, which reflects Butler's mature thoughts on Scripture, Butler spoke at length on her perceptions of the ways men and men's understanding of the world had shaped biblical studies. She was aware of the contemporary scholarly debates over the authenticity of the story of the adulterous woman. Butler supported her own position with the views of the Cambridge scholar Frederic William Farrar, who believed that the "real moral and meaning [of the story of the adulterous woman] are too transcendent to admit of its having been originally invented, or interpolated without adequate authority into the sacred text."[16]

The Sex Bias of the Commentators

In answer to the query whether the revision of the New Testament afforded in her judgment evidences of sex bias, Mrs. Butler said:—

"I cannot help thinking that the dispute concerning the authenticity of the eighth chapter of St. John is due to the feeling natural to the masculine mind that Christ's act of emancipation of the woman sinner would be a dangerous precedent for women. Men would say this is dangerous teaching; we shall have women thinking that they can sin and not be punished. You will see a marginal reference, in the revised version, that many of the ancient authorities omit verses 8–11 from the chapter, so the revisers have placed the wonderful story of Christ and the woman taken in adultery in parentheses. But, as Dr. Farrar[17] so beauti-

---

15. Tooley was a journalist working at the end of the nineteenth century. Her interviews and writings are documented and discussed in *Women in Journalism at the Fin de Siècle: Making a Name for Herself*, ed. F. Elizabeth Gray (New York: Palgrave Macmillan, 2012).

16. Frederic William Farrar, *Life of Christ* (London: Cassell, Petter & Galpin, 1874), vol. 2, 73–74. Farrar was an Anglican priest, teacher, and author.

17. Farrar includes a chapter on John 8 in his *Life of Christ*. He states clearly that there is "no shadow of a doubt that the incident really happened, even if the form in which it is preserved to us is by no means indisputably genuine." He summarizes at length the arguments for and against the genuineness of the story and proposes possible early sources for the story in the Gospel of the Hebrews or even the ground document of the synoptic gospels (vol. 2, 61–62).

fully says, when criticising the objection raised to the authenticity of the story, how can any one dispute the divine origin of this Scripture? No man writing out of his own heart could possibly have imagined such a position as that taken up by Christ in pronouncing a standard of absolute morality for both sexes. It was so foreign to the practice and belief of the Jews at that time.

"How Christ must have horrified the Jews in their self-righteousness when he said: 'He that is without sin among you, let him first cast a stone at her.' Christ condemned each of those men by His insinuation. What a sublime mingling there is, too, in his attitude of severity and tenderness.

"It is one of the most wonderful stories in the Bible, and how greatly we still need the application of its teaching? It is the woman whose sin is dragged to the light of day. 'Master,' said those Scribes and Pharisees, 'this woman hath been taken in adultery,' and wildly they clamoured for her to be stoned. But what of the man, her fellow-sinner, do they bring him to be stoned, also? Oh no; then, as now, it was the woman who must pay. It is strange that people today, should be asking whether sexual morality is equally binding upon woman and man, when we have the teaching of Christ so clearly defined in this incident."

Source: Sarah A. Tooley, "The Sex Bias of the Commentators: An Interview with Mrs. Josephine Butler," *The Humanitarian* V, no. 6 (December 1894): 418–19.

STUDY QUESTIONS

1. How do these commentators make the adulterous woman accessible or understandable to their audiences? How effective is their portrayal?
2. Lucy Barton writes about the adulterous woman for children. How did Barton attempt to make the story understandable for children? Did she succeed? Are there portions of Scripture that are deemed too "adult" for children? How and why is that determined?
3. How did the commentators explain the marking of this passage as disputed in the Revised Version of the Bible? How did they resolve the textual issue? Are their resolutions plausible? Why or why not?
4. Compare and contrast how these commentators attempted to explain Jewish and Roman laws concerning adultery. Why do you think these commentators thought it was important to explain the socio-historical context to their audiences? Is it still considered important to understand the socio-historical context of the biblical text? Why or why not?
5. What theological presuppositions concerning the character and attributes of God do these commentators explicitly (or implicitly) assume?

8

Mary Magdalene: Receiving the Text

Introduction

Mary Magdalene has intrigued interpreters of the gospels throughout history. Who was this woman to excite such interest? Mary of Magdala was a Galilean disciple who, after seven demons were exorcised from her, joined the women who travelled with Jesus (Luke 8:1–3). Along with these women who cared for Jesus, she witnessed the crucifixion (Matt. 27:55–56; Mark 15:40–41; John 19:25) and burial of Jesus (Matt. 27:61; Mark 15:47). Mary Magdalene went with the women to visit the tomb, and so was among the first to witness the resurrection (Matt. 28:1–10; Mark 16:1–8 also 16:9–11; Luke 24:1–11; John 20:1–18).

The incidents listed here are the only places Mary Magdalene's name is found in the canonical gospels. Her prominence among the followers of Jesus can be inferred from the position of her name as the first in many of the lists of women in the gospels, and the number of times she is named. Her extended personal encounter with the risen Jesus (John 20) lends further weight to this inference. An early interpretive tradition identified her with the unnamed penitent woman in Luke 7. Similarities between the story of the penitent woman's washing of Jesus' feet in Luke 7, and other stories of women anointing Jesus with ointment from an alabaster jar (Matt. 26 and Mark 14) and the identification of the woman in Simon the Leper's house as Mary of Bethany (John 12) then led to the identification of Mary Magdalene and Mary of Bethany. The conflation of these figures was given considerable weight in the late sixth century when Pope Gregory I preached on Luke 7 and identified the woman in that passage as Mary Magdalene.[1] The sin of the

---

1. See "Homily 33" in Gregory the Great, *Homilies on the Gospels*, trans. Dom David Hurst (Kalamazoo, MI: Cistercian Publications, 1990), 268–79.

penitent woman of Luke 7 was assumed to be prostitution, thus completing Mary Magdalene's traditional portrait.

The gospel narratives that name Mary Magdalene cluster around the death and resurrection of Jesus. Interpreters dealt with the differences between the gospel narratives of the first Easter morning in different ways. Most attempted some kind of harmonization of the accounts. Of more interest than the varying accounts of the events of that morning, however, was the clear identification of Mary Magdalene as one of the first people to see and speak with the risen Jesus. Given the traditional identification of Mary Magdalene as a reformed prostitute, what did her prominence at the resurrection mean?

Women who wrote on Mary Magdalene in the nineteenth century engaged the question of her identity, her prominence in the resurrection narratives, and the minor (for them) issue of the apparent differences between the gospel stories. The power of the tradition surrounding Mary Magdalene as it was expressed in art, literature, and history was acknowledged, but not always accepted. Clara Balfour, though not excerpted here, was one example of a clear voice calling attention to the way "public institutions for penitent women have been very erroneously called by the name of one, whose life, as far as the gospel narrative unfolds it, was pure and spotless."[2] Most of the women excerpted in this chapter assessed her character differently. They distinguished between Mary Magdalene and Mary of Bethany, but they let the tradition of the penitent woman being Mary Magdalene stand. This tradition was too powerful to challenge, and it provided them with an opportunity to discuss Christian forgiveness and acceptance of all, even the most sinful. Anna Jameson, Harriet Beecher Stowe, and Elizabeth Rundle Charles explicitly engaged the reception history of Mary Magdalene in art, literature, and liturgy.

The first two excerpts in this chapter, by Jameson and Stowe, are reception history and reflect on the influence of tradition on contemporary understandings of Mary Magdalene. The next three excerpts, by Charlotte Bickersteth Wheeler, Elizabeth Baxter, and Elizabeth Cady Stanton, are commentaries on John 20, the extended post-resurrection encounter of Jesus and Mary Magdalene. Wheeler's and Baxter's treatments of the story display their hermeneutic of faith as opposed to Stanton's writing which displays her hermeneutic of suspicion. The final two works are educational, one for

---

2. Clara Lucas Balfour, *Women of Scripture* (London: Houlston & Stoneman, 1847), 320.

youth by Amelia Gillespie Smyth and a devotional for adults by Elizabeth Rundle Charles.

All the excerpted authors blend both traditional and contemporary scholarship to sort out the complex issues regarding Mary Magdalene's identity and significance. They did not always agree in their conclusions, but they used similar methods. They used other biblical texts, their own life experiences, and knowledge of the values and customs of the Middle East to fill out her character, giving her emotional depth. They treated Mary Magdalene as much more than an historical artifact; they recognized her significance in the Christian story and explored her ongoing importance for women and men. They invited their audiences to think with them about difficult interpretive issues, and to be transformed spiritually and vocationally by the lessons of Mary Magdalene's life.

ANNA JAMESON (1794–1860)

....

Mythic Magdalene

Anna Brownell Jameson was a writer of travel books, fiction, and essays on art and literature.[3] The daughter of the Irish miniature artist, Denis Brownell Murphy and his English wife, Johanna, she was born in Dublin and raised in England where she was educated by a governess until the age of eleven or twelve. She worked for a number of years as a governess, marrying Robert Sympson Jameson in 1825. Their marriage was unhappy and childless. Anna spent time traveling in Canada in 1836–37 as Robert was the attorney general of Upper Canada. Jameson's major work *Sacred and Legendary Art* was published after she had permanently separated from her husband and returned to England.

Sacred and Legendary Art (1848) consists of two volumes on the legends of Christian history. The first volume contains "legends of the Angels and Archangels, evangelists, the Apostles, the Doctors of the Church, and St Mary Magdalene." The second volume contains legends of "the Patron Saints, the

---

3. Nancy Calvert-Koyzis, "Jameson, Anna Brownell (1794–1860)," in *Handbook of Women Biblical Interpreters*, ed. Marion Ann Taylor and Agnes Choi (Grand Rapids: Baker Academic, 2012), 289–92.

Martyrs, the early Bishops, The Hermits, and the Warrior Saints of Christendom." Two other works in the series on sacred and legendary art followed: *Legends of the Monastic Orders* (1850), and *Legends of the Madonna* (1852). Jameson's stated purpose in writing these works was to assist people in understanding Western European medieval art. After a general introduction to symbols used in the art works, Jameson described the figures commonly represented in art, and the legends on which the artists based their representations. The stories of St. Mary Magdalene begin the final section of volume 1.

The excerpt below is the first, rather lengthy, paragraph of an eight-page recounting of the legends of St. Mary Magdalene. Jameson continued for thirty-one more pages on art featuring Mary Magdalene. Because Jameson was recounting the legends which gave rise to works of art, she was not concerned to resolve debates around Mary Magdalene's identity. Her extensive research into the tradition history of Mary Magdalene is evident in the one paragraph excerpted below. Jameson argued that the weight of tradition lent a reality to the stories of St. Mary Magdalene that could not be replaced by the results of historical research. Jameson found the traditional Magdalene a hopeful figure, and presented her as such to her readers.

St. Mary Magdalene

Lat. Sancta Maria Magdalena. Ital. Santa Maria Maddalena. Fr. La Madeleine. La Sainte Demoiselle pécheresse. (July 22, A.D. 68.)
Patroness of Provence, of Marseilles, and of frail and penitent women.

Of all the personages who figure in history, in poetry, in art, Mary Magdalene is at once the most unreal and the most real:—the most *unreal*, if we attempt to fix her identity, which has been a subject of dispute for ages; the most *real*, if we consider her as having been, for ages, recognised and accepted in every Christian heart as the impersonation of the penitent sinner absolved through faith and love. In this, her mythic character, she has been surrounded by associations which have become fixed in the imagination, and which no reasoning, no array of facts, can dispel. This is not the place to enter into disputed points of biblical criticism; they are quite beside our present purpose. Whether Mary Magdalene, 'out of whom Jesus cast seven devils,' Mary of Bethany, and the 'woman who was a sinner,' be, as some authorities assert, three distinct persons, or, as others affirm, one and the same individual under different designations, remains a question open to dispute, nothing having been demonstrated on either side, from Scripture or from tradition; and I cannot presume even to give an opinion where doctors—and doctors of the Church, too—disagree; Origen and St. Chrysostom taking one side of the question, St. Clement and St. Gregory the other. Fleury, after citing the opinions of both sides, thus beautifully sums up the whole question:—'Il importe de ne pas croire témérairement ce que l'Evangile ne dit point, et de ne pas mettre la religion à suivre aveuglement toutes les opinions populaires: *la foi est trop precieuse pour la prodiguer ainsi*; mais la charité l'est encore plus; et ce qui est le plus important, c'est d'éviter les disputes qui peuvent l'altérer tant soit peu.'[4] And this is most true;—in his time the fast hold which the Magdalene had taken of the affections of the people was not to be shaken by theological researches and doubts. Here critical accuracy was nothing less than profanation and scepticism, and to have attacked the sanctity of the Blessed Mary Magdalene would have embittered and alienated many kindly and many believing spirits. It is difficult to treat of Mary Magdalene; and this difficulty would be increased infinitely if it were absolutely necessary to enter on the much-vexed question of her scriptural character and identity; one thing only appears certain,—that such a person, whatever might have been her veritable appellation, did exist. The woman who, under the name of Mary Magdalene,—whether that name be rightfully or wrongfully bestowed,— stands before us sanctified in the imagination and in the faith of the people in her combined character of Sinner and of Saint, as the first-fruits of Christian penitence,—is a reality, and not a fiction. Even if we would, we cannot do away with the associations inseparably connected with her name and her image. Of all those to whom much has been forgiven, she was the first; of all the tears since ruefully shed at the foot of the cross of suffering, hers were the first; of all the hopes which the Resurrection has since diffused through nations and generations of men, hers were the first. To her sorrowful image how many have looked up through tears, and blessed the pardoning grace of which she was the symbol—or rather the impersonation! Of the female saints, some were the chosen patrons of certain virtues—others of certain vocations; but the accepted and glorified penitent threw her mantle over all, and more especially over those of her own sex who, having gone astray,

4. Quote from Claude Fleury, "Opinion on the Three Marys," in *Nouveaux Opuscules* (Paris, 1807), 194. "It is important not to believe imprudently what the Gospel does not say and not to have religion blindly follow all popular opinions: faith is too precious to be given away in this manner; but charity is even more [precious]; and what is most important is to avoid disputes which may alter it even in the slightest." (Translation thanks to Sean A. Otto.)

were recalled from error and from shame, and laid down their wrongs, their sorrows, and their sins in trembling humility at the feet of the Redeemer.

Source: Anna Jameson, *Sacred and Legendary Art*, vol. 1 (London: Longman, Brown, Green & Longmans, 1848), 343–44.

HARRIET BEECHER STOWE (1811–1896)

Redeemed Penitent

Harriet Beecher Stowe was an author, abolitionist, and sophisticated interpreter of Scripture.[5] Her prose writings on the Bible, *Woman in Sacred History* (1873) and *Footsteps of the Master* (1878), are particularly fine examples of her eclectic hermeneutical approach, which effectively blended the resources of the male theological academy and church with insights and questions honed in a woman's world.

Stowe's success as a writer provided her with opportunities to travel and view the world's greatest paintings. She included 25 chromolithographs of famous paintings of women by such great European artists as Raphael, Batoni, and Boulanger in *Women in Sacred History*. Jameson and Stowe were both interested in art as an interpretive medium. While Jameson discussed as many works of art on a subject as she could, Stowe used particular paintings as starting points for her discussion of select women of the Bible.

The excerpt below comes from Stowe's essay on Mary Magdalene in *Women in Sacred History*. In this essay, she engaged both biblical scholarship and the history of interpretation in art as well as literature.[6] She used Batoni's elegant, calm, pure Magdalene as a platform for a discussion of woman's nature, and the issues of sexual double standards in ancient and modern life. While Stowe accepted the traditional identification of the unnamed women in Luke 7 as Mary Magdalene and the tradition of her as an

---

5. For more information on Stowe see "It's All about Power" in the chapter on Herodias and Salome.

6. While Stowe blends the biblical tradition and reception history in her treatment of Mary Magdalene, she has two chapters on the Blessed Virgin Mary, one on the mythical Mary of tradition history and one on the Mary of the gospels.

enthusiastic preacher, she did not follow the tradition that identified Mary of Bethany with Mary Magdalene. She drew on the work of biblical scholars to further her understanding of the nature of demon possession. Her parallels between Jesus and Socrates, and her placement of the story of Mary Magdalene alongside Goethe's *Faust* show the breadth of her thought and reading.

Mary Magdalene

ONE of the most splendid ornaments of the Dresden Gallery is the Magdalen of Batoni.[7]

The subject has been a favorite among artists, and one sees, in a tour of the various collections of Europe, Magdalens by every painter, in every conceivable style. By far the greater part of them deal only with the material aspects of the subject. The exquisite pathos of the story, the passionate anguish and despair of the penitent, the refinement and dignity of Divine tenderness, are often lost sight of in mere physical accessories. Many artists seem to have seen in the subject only a chance to paint a voluptuously beautiful woman in tears. Titian[8] appears to have felt in this wonderful story nothing but the beauty of the woman's hair, and gives us a picture of the most glorious tresses that heart could conceive, perfectly veiling and clothing a very commonplace weeping woman. Correggio[9] made of the study only a charming effect of light and shade and color. A fat, pretty, comfortable little body lying on the ground reading, is about the whole that he sees in the subject.

Batoni, on the contrary, seems, by some strange inspiration, to set before us one of the highest, noblest class of women, a creature so calm, so high, so pure, that we ask involuntarily, How could such a woman ever have fallen? The answer is ready. There is a class of women who fall through what is highest in them, through the noblest capability of a human being,—utter self-sacrificing love. True, we cannot flatter ourselves that these instances are universal, but they do exist. Many women fall through the weakness of self-indulgent passion, many from love of luxury, many from vanity and pride, too many from the mere coercion of hard necessity; but among the sad, unblest crowd there is a class who are the victims of a

7. Pompeo Girolamo Batoni (1708–1778) was an Italian painter. His Magdalene is a full-length figure lying on the ground, her hands clasped and her hair fallen on her shoulders.

8. Titian (1488/9–1576) was an Italian painter in the Venetian school.

9. Antonio Allegri da Correggio (1489–1534) was an important painter of the Parma school of the Italian Renaissance.

power of self-forgetting love, which is one of the most angelic capabilities of our nature.

We have shown all along that in the dispensation which prepared the way for the great Messiah and the Christian Era, woman was especially cared for. In all that pertained to the spiritual and immortal nature she was placed on an equality with man,—she could be the vehicle of the prophetic inspiration; as mother she was equally with man enthroned queen of the family; and her sins against chastity were treated precisely as those of man,—as the sin, not of sex, but of a personal moral agent.

The Christian Era, unfolding out of the Mosaic like a rare flower from a carefully cultured stock, brought, in a still higher degree, salvation to woman. The son of Mary was the protector of woman, and one of the earliest and most decided steps in his ministry was his practical and authoritative assertion of the principle, that fallen woman is as capable of restoration through penitence as fallen man, and that repentance should do for a fallen woman whatever it might do for fallen man.

The history of the woman taken in adultery [John 8:1–11] shows how completely that spirit of injustice to woman, which still shows itself in our modern life, had taken possession of the Jewish aristocracy. We hear no word of the guilty man who was her partner in crime; we see around Jesus a crowd clamoring for the deadly sentence of the Mosaic law on the woman. Jesus, by one lightning stroke of penetrative omniscience, rouses the dead sense of shame in the accusers, and sends them humbled from his presence, while the sinful woman is saved for a better future.

The absolute divinity of Jesus, the height at which he stood above all men, is nowhere so shown as in what he dared and did for woman, and the godlike consciousness of power with which he did it. It was at a critical period in his ministry, when all eyes were fixed on him in keen inquiry, when many of the respectable classes were yet trembling in the balance whether to accept his claims or no, that Jesus in the calmest and most majestic manner took ground that the sins of a fallen woman were like any other sins, and that repentant love entitled to equal forgiveness. The story so wonderful can be told only in the words of the sacred narrative.

[Here Stowe inserted Luke 7:36–50 in full.]

Nothing can be added to the pathos and solemn dignity of this story, in which our Lord assumed with tranquil majesty the rights to supreme love possessed by the Creator, and his sovereign power to forgive sins and dispense favors. The repentant Magdalene became henceforth one of the characteristic figures in the history of the Christian Church. Mary Magdalene became eventually a prominent figure in the mythic legends of the medieval mythology. A long history of missionary labors and enthusiastic preaching of the gospel in distant regions of the earth is ascribed to her. Churches arose that bore her name, hymns were addressed to her. Even the reforming Savonarola[10] addresses one of his spiritual canticles to St. Mary Magdalene. The various pictures of her which occur in every part of Europe are a proof of the interest which these legends inspired. The most of them are wild and poetic, and exhibit a striking contrast to the concise brevity and simplicity of the New Testament story.

The mythic legends make up a romance in which Mary the sister of Martha and Mary Magdalene the sinner are oddly considered as the same person. It is sufficient to read the chapter in St. John which gives an account of the raising of Lazarus, to perceive that such a confusion is absurd [John 11:1–44]. Mary and Martha there appear as belonging to a family in good standing, to which many flocked with expressions of condolence and respect in time of affliction. And afterwards, in that grateful feast made for the restoration of their brother, we read that so many flocked to the house that the jealousy of the chief priests was excited. All these incidents, representing a family of respectability, are entirely inconsistent with any such supposition. But while we repudiate this extravagance of the tradition, there does seem ground for identifying the Mary Magdalene, who was one of the most devoted followers of our Lord, with the forgiven sinner of this narrative. We read of a company of women who followed Jesus and ministered to him. In the eighth chapter of Luke he is said to be accompanied by "certain women which had been healed of evil spirits and infirmities," among whom is mentioned "Mary called Magdalene," as having been a victim of demoniacal possession. Some women of rank and fortune also are mentioned as members of the same company: "Joanna the wife of Chusa, Herod's steward, and Susanna, and many others who ministered to him of their substance." A modern commentator thinks it improbable that Mary Magdalene could be identified with the "sinner" spoken of by St. Luke, because women of standing like Joanna and Susanna would not have received one of her class to their company. We ask why not? If Jesus had received her, had forgiven and saved her; if he acknowledged previously her grateful ministrations,— is it likely that they would reject her? It was the very peculiarity and glory of the new kingdom that it had a better future for sinners, and for sinful woman as well as sinful man. Jesus did not

---

10. Girolamo Savonarola (1452–1498) was a Dominican friar who preached against the moral corruption of clergy.

hesitate to say to the proud and prejudiced religious aristocracy of his day, "The publicans and harlots go into the kingdom of heaven before you" [Matt. 21:31]. We cannot doubt that the loving Christian women who ministered to Jesus received this penitent sister as a soul absolved and purified by the sovereign word of their Lord, and henceforth there was for her a full scope for that ardent, self-devoting power of her nature which had been her ruin, and was now to become her salvation.

Some commentators seem to think that the dreadful demoniacal possession which was spoken of in Mary Magdalene proves her not to have been identical with the woman of St. Luke. But on the contrary, it would seem exactly to account for actions of a strange and unaccountable wickedness, for a notoriety in crime that went far to lead the Pharisees to feel that her very touch was pollution. The story is symbolic of what is too often seen in the fall of woman. A noble and beautiful nature wrecked through inconsiderate prodigality of love, deceived, betrayed, ruined, often drifts like a shipwrecked bark into the power of evil spirits. Rage, despair, revenge, cruelty, take possession of the crushed ruin that should have been the home of the sweetest affections. We are not told when or where the healing word was spoken that drove the cruel fiends from Mary's soul. Perhaps before she entered the halls of the Pharisee, while listening to the preaching of Jesus, the madness and despair had left her. We can believe that in his higher moods virtue went from him, and there was around him a holy and cleansing atmosphere from which all evil fled away,—a serene and healing purity which calmed the throbbing fever of passion and gave the soul once more the image of its better self.

We see in the manner in which Mary found her way to the feet of Jesus the directness and vehemence, the uncalculating self-sacrifice and self-abandon, of one of those natures which, when they move, move with a rush of undivided impulse; which, when they love, trust all, believe all, and are ready to sacrifice all. As once she had lost herself in this self-abandonment, so now at the feet of her God she gains all by the same power of self-surrender.

We do not meet Mary Magdalene again till we find her at the foot of the Cross, sharing the last anguish of our Lord and his mother. We find her watching the sepulcher, preparing sweet spices for embalming. In the dim gray of the resurrection morning she is there again, only to find the sepulcher open and the beloved form gone. Everything in this last scene is in consistency with the idea of the passionate self-devotion of a nature whose sole life is in its love. The disciples, when they found not the body, went away; but Mary stood without at the sepulcher weeping, and as she wept she stooped down and looked into the sepulcher. The angels said to her, "Woman, why weepest thou? She answered, Because they have taken away my Lord, and I know not where they have laid him." She then turns and sees through her tears dimly the form of a man standing there. "Jesus saith unto her, Woman, why weepest thou? whom seekest thou? She, supposing him to be the gardener, saith unto him, Sir, if thou have borne him hence, tell me where thou hast laid him, and I will go and take him away. Jesus saith unto her, Mary! She turned herself and said unto him, Rabboni,—Master!"

In all this we see the characteristic devotion and energy of her who loved much because she was forgiven much. It was the peculiarity of Jesus that he saw the precious capability of every nature, even in the very dust of defilement. The power of devoted love is the crown-jewel of the soul, and Jesus had the eye to see where it lay trampled in the mire, and the strong hand to bring it forth purified and brightened. It is the deepest malignity of Satan to degrade and ruin souls through love. It is the glory of Christ, through love, to redeem and restore.

In the history of Christ as a teacher, it is remarkable, that, while he was an object of enthusiastic devotion to so many women, while a band of them followed his preaching and ministered to his wants and those of his disciples, yet there was about him something so entirely unworldly, so sacredly high and pure, that even the very suggestion of scandal in this regard is not to be found in the bitterest vituperations of his enemies of the first two centuries.

If we compare Jesus with Socrates, the moral teacher most frequently spoken of as approaching him, we shall see a wonderful contrast. Socrates associated with courtesans, without passion and without reproof, in a spirit of half-sarcastic, philosophic tolerance. No quickening of the soul of woman, no call to a higher life, came from him. Jesus is stern and grave in his teachings of personal purity, severe in his requirements. He was as intolerant to sin as he was merciful to penitence. He did not extenuate the sins he forgave. He declared the sins of Mary to be many, in the same breath that he pronounced her pardon. He said to the adulterous woman whom he protected, "Go, sin no more" [John 8:11]. The penitents who joined the company of his disciples were so raised above their former selves, that, instead of being the shame, they were the glory of the new kingdom. St. Paul says to the first Christians, speaking of the adulterous and impure, "Such were some of you, but ye are washed, but ye are sanctified, but ye are justified in the name of the Lord Jesus, and by the Spirit of God" [1 Cor. 6:11].

The tradition of the Church that Mary Magdalene was an enthusiastic preacher of Jesus seems in keeping with all we know of the strength and fervor of her character. Such love must find expression, and we are told that when the first persecution scattered the little church at Jerusalem, "they that were scattered went everywhere, preaching the word" [Acts 8:4]. Some of the most effective preaching of Christ is that of those who testify in their own person of a great salvation. "He can save to the uttermost, for he has saved ME," [Heb. 7:25] is a testimony that often goes more straight to the heart than all the arguments of learning. Christianity had this peculiarity over all other systems, that it not only forgave the past, but made of its bitter experiences a healing medicine; so that those who had sinned deepest might have therefrom a greater redeeming power. "When thou art converted, strengthen thy brethren," [Luke 22:32] was the watchword of the penitent.

The wonderful mind of Goethe[11] has seized upon and embodied this peculiarity of Christianity in his great poem of Faust. The first part shows the Devil making of the sweetest and noblest affection of the confiding Margaret a cruel poison to corrupt both body and soul. We see her driven to crime, remorse, shame, despair,—all human forms and forces of society united to condemn her, when with a last cry she stretches her poor hands to heaven and says, "Judgment of God, I commend myself to you"; and then falls a voice from heaven, "She is judged; she is saved."

In the second part we see the world-worn, weary Faust passing through the classic mythology, vainly seeking rest and finding none; he seeks rest in a life of benevolence to man, but fiends of darkness conflict with his best aspirations, and dog his steps through life, and in his dying hour gather round to seize his soul and carry it to perdition. But around him is a shining band. Mary the mother of Jesus, with a company of purified penitents, encircle him, and his soul passes, in infantine weakness, to the guardian arms of Margaret,—once a lost and ruined woman, now a strong and pitiful angel,—who, like a tender mother, leads the new-born soul to look upon the glories of heaven, while angel-voices sing of the victory of good over evil:—

"All that is transient
Is but a parable;
The unattainable
Here is made real.
The indescribable
Here is accomplished;

11. Johann Wolfgang von Goethe was a German writer, artist, scientist, and mathematician. His tragic play *Faust* has two parts, the first published in 1808 and the second in 1832.

The eternal womanly
Draws us upward and onward."[12]

Source: Harriet Beecher Stowe, *Woman in Sacred History* (New York: J. B. Ford and Company, 1873), 207–18.

CHARLOTTE BICKERSTETH WHEELER (1818–1884)

Carry the Glad Tidings

Charlotte Bickersteth Wheeler was an English author, educator, mother and Anglican clergy spouse.[13] She authored a number of books, including *Our Master's Footsteps*, a 400-page commentary for women on the four gospels that grew out of her teaching ministry over a period of fifteen years.

In *Our Master's Footsteps*, Wheeler explained words and customs that might be unclear, harmonized the gospel stories, and probed the spiritual significance of the texts under discussion. She explored connecting scriptural themes and texts; for example, she identified Mary and Jesus with the woman and her lover in Song of Songs 3:3. Wheeler made use of the theological resources at her disposal.[14] She also used material from the other gospels and from other parts of Scripture as commentary on the gospel of John. She tried to bring narrative coherence to the story, explaining, for example, why Mary took so long to recognize Jesus.

Wheeler shifted to a more subjective approach when she moved from an analysis of the biblical text to its application to the spiritual lives of her readers. She identified with the feelings of biblical figures and used them as a bridge to connect her readers to the text. When the text did not flesh out

---

12. This is taken from the closing lines of the Chorus Mysticus in *Faust*.

13. For more biographical information on Wheeler, see "Who could Invent It?" in the chapter on the Adulterous woman.

14. In the introduction to her commentary, Wheeler states her indebtedness to Edward Greswell's *Harmonia Evangelica*, and D. Brown and A. R. Fausset, *Critical and Explanatory Pocket Bible* (1863). Her explanation of the meaning of "the gardener" as "overseer of the garden," for example, compares to Adam Clark's similar comments on the expression in his commentary on the gospel of John.

the feelings, inner thoughts, or motives, she imaginatively supplied them for readers. Wheeler's comments on the significance of the disciples' calling Jesus Lord instead of brother demonstrate how her social location as a middle-class woman influenced her reading. Wheeler's anti-Catholic and perhaps female musings as to why the Virgin Mary did not see the risen Christ also illustrate how her context shaped her reading of texts.

[John] CHAPTER 20

3–8. Mary Magdalene ran with her imperfect knowledge of the circumstances to Peter and John, who hurried to the sepulchre, John, the younger, arriving first, then Peter, and probably last came Mary. Very minute are John's details, telling how, though he arrived first, Peter was the first to enter, and describing the position and orderly arrangement of the linen in which the Body had been wrapped. 'Linen cloths' should not be understood here to mean apparel. Doubtless the angels folded them, and the fact of their being left there shows the absurdity of the lie that He had been removed by the disciples. Moreover, their being so neatly arranged was evidence that no thieves had carried Him away; they would have been in too much haste and fear of detection. John saw and believed; in other words, he believed *because* of what he saw, not because he remembered or understood the promise of the resurrection. What a glorious moment it must have been when he *did* remember and understood! They do not appear to have seen the angels, though the women saw them (Luke 24:12).

10. Went away perplexed; perhaps dismayed.

11. Loving Mary! weeping over that which, in another moment, would fill her with joy unspeakable. How often we weep over disguised blessings, and feel overwhelmed with care and trouble! and our desolate hearts say, 'All those things are against me,' when all the while they are working together for our good [Rom. 8:28]—dovetailing in the most wonderful manner; and perhaps the next turn in God's Providence makes all plain. Oh! to *trust* while He keeps us waiting! there is where we all fail so sadly.

12. At last she gazes through her tears into the empty grave; but *was* it empty? Ah, no! two white-robed messengers from the world of light are seated there, waiting with words of gentle rebuke for her grief. The other women had been 'affrighted' at the vision (see Mark 16:5, and Luke 24:6); but Mary, full of the longing to recover the lost Body of her Lord,

had no room in her heart for fear; no inclination to think of *herself* at all. One strong emotion excludes for the time all others.

13. It is as though she said, 'How can I help weeping when they have taken away my Lord?'

14, 15. Then, hoping for no comfort, waiting for no answer, from them, she turned desolately away, and saw Jesus, but without recognising Him. So Jacob might have seen Joseph, the desire of his eyes, in Egypt, had he accompanied his sons on their journeys to buy food, without recognising in his glory the son whom he mourned as dead. Afraid, it may be, of startling her with too sudden an appearance, He seems to have made Himself known gradually. Doubtless something in His words or manner, or some familiar tone in His voice, was all unconsciously to herself preparing her for the revelation which was to follow. Jesus asks the same question that the angels had asked. She was so intent on seeing her dear Lord's dead Body, that she could not realise, or even imagine, that her Living Lord stood visibly before her. 'The gardener' probably means 'overseer of the garden.' 'If thou hast borne Him hence.' She does not *name* Him; in the wide world there was for her but *One*. See Canticles 3:3.[15] She pauses not to answer His question, in her anxiety to ask. 'I will take Him away.' How she was to accomplish it she never thought; intense affection feels equal to superhuman effort, and sometimes achieves what is next to impossible, as when the Swiss mother scaled a crag deemed inaccessible, and saved her child from the eagle's nest.

16. And now her 'sorrow was turned into joy.' One word, her own name, brought her to full consciousness of her Saviour's actual presence. 'Woman,' just like 'Sir,' was a distant though respectful title. Now the loved Voice speaks the familiar 'Mary'; it is enough, she turns and says, 'My Master!' In all *deep* emotion words are few; the heart's speech is eloquent, the lips are all but silent. She had all she wanted now. It is often in a single word or two of Scripture, strongly carried home to the heart, that the Holy Spirit makes Christ known to us. Oh! pray for His most blessed teaching!

17. Doubtless she was clasping His knees, or bathing His pierced feet with happy thankful tears, and *that* was not the work she was to do. She must carry her good tidings to the rest, and add the glorious words, 'I ascend,'

---

15. Canticles is more commonly called Song of Songs or Song of Solomon. Song of Songs 3:3: "The watchmen that go about the city found me: to whom I said, Saw ye him whom my soul loveth?"

etc. Wondrous news indeed! They had only recently understood that He was to die; they did not understand His promised resurrection; of His ascension they had probably no idea whatever, though He had said so plainly, 'I go to prepare a place for you' (John 14:2). Notice the words, 'My brethren.' He might well have said, My faithless followers, My forsakers. First they were His servants; then His disciples; just before His death they were His friends, but now His *brethren* (Heb. 2:11, 17). Yet we should reverently note that not one of them ever seems to have called Him 'Brother'; they call Him 'Lord,' or 'my Lord, and my God.' Infinite condescension on His side leads to no presumption or forwardness on theirs.

18. For minuter details see Mark 16:10, 11. Possibly the reason why the Virgin Mary was to *hear* of the resurrection ere she saw Him, was to spare her the overpowering shock of so intense a joy. Moreover, any *special* honour done her in being the first to welcome Him, would only have been used as a plea for the superstitious veneration of the Romanists. For the next recorded event of this most marvellous day we must turn to Luke 24:13–35, the memorable walk to Emmaus.

Source: Charlotte Bickersteth Wheeler, *Our Master's Footsteps* (London: Elliot Stock, 1883), 400–403.

Elizabeth Baxter (1837–1926)

Apostle of the Resurrection

Elizabeth Baxter was a prolific British author, educator, and preacher. She wrote many commentaries, among them one on the Gospel of John (1887).[16]

Baxter's *The Living Word in the Gospel of John* contains no introduction, but her approach and rhetoric suggests that it grew out of her teaching ministry. Unlike Wheeler, Baxter commented on thought units rather than on individual chapters and verses. In her discussion of Jesus' resurrection in the first eighteen verses of John 20, Baxter discussed Mary Magdalene. She

---

16. For further biographical information on Baxter see "A Role Model for Female Ministry" in the chapter on Anna.

raised the question of her identity, giving some credence to the idea that Mary Magdalene and Mary of Bethany were one and the same. She also identified her as the woman out of whom seven demons were cast (Luke 8:2). Baxter found spiritual meaning in both the figural and literal senses of the text. In her figural reading, she interpreted Mary Madgalene as a type or figure of the believing Christian. Just as Mary waited at the tomb and then saw the risen Jesus, so believers should cling to what they know, and they will be taught more. In her literal reading of the text, Baxter underscored the importance of women's ministry as messengers and even apostles of the resurrection.

Jesus Risen.

John 20:1–18

Mary Magdalene and the other Mary, probably the mother of Jesus, sat without the sepulchre until the sabbath, when they rested according to the commandment (Luke 23:56). But one of them could not rest apart from Jesus. Mary Magdalene (if, as some suppose, she was the same as Mary of Bethany) had understood that Jesus should die, had anointed His body for the burying, and, no doubt, had more comprehension of the resurrection than had the rest of the disciples. No sooner was the Sabbath past, than, long before the day dawned, "while it was yet dark," she was at the sepulchre. She was the first to discover that the stone was rolled away, that the precaution of the chief priests had, some way, been in vain. The "watch" of Roman soldiers was on guard no longer, something, she knew not what, had happened. When God leads on His believing children to know something of the power of Christ's resurrection, they find themselves out in all their experiences and expectations. . . .

Mary ran to Peter and John; HER FIRST CONCEPTIONS WERE EARTHLY. "They have taken away the Lord out of the sepulchre, and we know not where they have laid Him." Did she suspect the soldiers of stealing His body? O why did she not believe His own words? Peter and John came to the sepulchre; John looked in, Peter went into the sepulchre. They saw His empty grave clothes, which the soldiers would not have left if they had taken the body away. Then John went in, "and he saw, and believed. For as yet they knew not the scripture, that He must rise again from the dead." Four distinct times He had taught them this precious truth (Mark 8:31; 9:9, 31; 10:34), yet "they understood none of these things: and this saying was hid from them, neither knew they the things which were spoken" (Luke 18:34). Then the two disciples went away—even John who had "believed," even Peter to whom it had been revealed that Jesus was "the Christ, the Son of the living God!" [Matt. 16:16]. But Mary did not go away. He whose body had lain in that sepulchre had been too much to the saved sinner out of whom He had cast seven devils, and His works and teaching had too much thrown the world into the shade for her to find any other point of interest. If Jesus were lost, then all was lost, and what certainty had she that the demons who once possessed her would not return? If she could not find Jesus living, she would not, at least, leave the spot where she had last seen Him. This is how Jesus risen is found by his disciples. Cling to all you know and you shall yet know more. Mary looked into the sepulchre, and she saw life there—not death, not emptiness, but life. True, it was not the life of Jesus, but it was heavenly life. Two angels were sitting there, and the grave of Jesus spoke to her through those angel voices, "Woman, why weepest thou?" It was the same old story—she had no other to tell—"Because they have taken away my Lord, and I know not where they have laid Him." But ANOTHER WAS ON THE SCENE whom she had not perceived, though He saw her. His voice repeated the angels' question, yet she was so unprepared to see Him living, that she recognised neither voice nor form. Her conceptions were still earthly, she was still accounting for things on human lines. She, supposing Him to be the gardener, saith unto Him, "Sir, if Thou have borne Him hence, tell me where Thou hast laid Him, and I will take Him away." She still hankered after the dead Christ, the experience of Him which she had had in the past. One word awoke her, "Mary." It was the old voice, and it spoke her name. In an instant the whole truth flashed across mind and heart. "She turned herself and saith unto Him, Rabboni; which is to say, Master." Yes, she yielded herself to the risen Christ, to be, to do, to suffer, as He would. When God has led His children to turn their backs once and for ever on a life of sin and worldliness, when, as far as they know, they are wholly yielded up to Him, and yet, in their nearest approaches to Jesus, they find their experience only what Mary found—an empty, unoccupied grave, whilst there is nowhere else to seek Jesus, what shall they do? Go away like Peter and John? or abide, by the last traces of Jesus? Surely the latter, the empty grave is the token to faith that Christ is risen. The conscious emptiness of our own hearts, so long as, like Mary, we seek to be satisfied with nothing short of Christ, only shows us that He is going to reveal Himself in power and glory as never heretofore. But are we, like Mary, abiding by the empty tomb with thoughts and words full of "my Lord," even when He seems to be taken away from us? Are we in the place of blessing?

"Jesus saith unto her, Touch Me not." He allowed the women who returned, shortly after, with Mary to the sepulchre to hold Him by the feet and worship Him (Matt. 28:9)—why should this privilege be denied to Mary? Jesus gives as His reason, "For I am not yet ascended unto My Father; but go to thy brethren, and say unto them, I ascend unto My Father and your Father, unto My God and your God." It was as though He had said, 'Mary, thou shalt have a privilege of love far greater than to embrace My feet. Be thou THE APOSTLE OF THE RESURRECTION. Tell those whom I, the risen, and soon the ascended Son of God, am not ashamed to call brethren, that I am going to resume My place of power in heaven, with My Father.' He had another message to send by the other women—they should tell His brethren to go before Him into Galilee (Matt. 28:10), But Mary learned more of the heavenly glory of Jesus than was given to the others to know. To her, heaven and earth, God and man, were bound together as never before; a new world was open to her—Jesus risen was God, the Lord of heaven "manifest in the flesh." and yet her Saviour, her Lord, her friend!

Source: Elizabeth Baxter, *The Living Word in the Gospel of John* (London: Christian Herald, 1887), 205–9.

ELIZABETH CADY STANTON (1815–1902)

Gullible Woman

Elizabeth Cady Stanton was a lecturer, writer, and leading activist in the abolitionist and women's rights movements in America. She was born to Judge Daniel Cady and his wife Margaret in Johnston, New York.[17] Following her schooling, she read law at her father's office and became interested in women's legal status. She married abolitionist Henry Brewer Stanton in 1840 and they had seven children. Stanton and Lucretia Mott convened the first women's rights convention in 1848 in Seneca Falls, New York. Stanton worked tirelessly for women's rights throughout her life. In 1895, she published the first volume of *The Woman's Bible*, which excerpted and

---

17. Priscilla Pope-Levinson, "Stanton, Elizabeth Cady (1815–1902)," in Taylor and Choi, *Handbook*, 469–73.

commented on sections of the Pentateuch, which she and members of her revising committee felt were oppressive to women. In the preface to the second volume (1898), Stanton declared that the Bible had been "made a fetich [sic] . . . long enough," arguing that it be read critically like any other book. She advocated "accepting the good and rejecting the evil it teaches."[18]

Stanton's brief comments on John 20 focus on the association of women and the supernatural. She called attention to the different way women and men experienced the resurrection, and criticized John's portrayal of women as gullible and ready to believe miracles. Unlike any of the other authors excerpted in this chapter, Stanton found little encouragement in the representation of women in John 20. She did not comment on Jesus' directives to Mary that interpreters like Baxter understood to elevate Mary Magdalene as the Apostle of the Resurrection. Like Jameson and Stowe, Stanton interpreted the Bible with a confidence that allowed her to challenge scholarly consensus. Stanton's independence, however, is more striking as she challenged the wisdom of male commentators, adapting instead a female-centered ideologically-driven approach to reading the Bible.

Comments on John 20:1–18

Mary appears to have arrived at the sepulchre before any of the other women, and conversed with Jesus. Though the disciples, in visiting the tomb, saw nothing but cast-off clothes, yet Mary sees and talks with angels and with Jesus. As usual, the woman is always most ready to believe miracles and fables, however extravagant and though beyond all human comprehension. Several women purposed to be at the tomb at sunrise to embalm the body.

The men who visited the tomb saw no visions; but all the women saw Jesus and the angels, though the men, who went to the tomb twice, saw nothing. Mary arrived at the tomb before light, and waited for the other women; but seeing some one approaching, she supposed he was the person employed by Joseph to take care of the garden, so asked him what had been done to him. Though speaking to a supposed stranger, she did not mention any name. Jesus then called her by name; and his voice and his address made

18. Elizabeth Cady Stanton, "Preface to Part II," *The Woman's Bible Part II: Comments on The Old and New Testaments from Joshua to Revelation* (Boston: Northeastern University Press, 1898), 8.

him known to her. Filled with joy and amazement, she called him "Rabboni," which signifies, "teacher." Jesus said unto her, "Touch me not."

This finishes the consideration of the four Gospels—the direct recorded words of Jesus upon the question of purity; and all further references should harmonize, in spirit, with his teachings, and should be so interpreted, without regard to contrary assertions by learned but unwise commentators. E. C. S.

Source: Elizabeth Cady Stanton, *The Woman's Bible Part II: Comments on The Old and New Testaments from Joshua to Revelation* (Boston: Northeastern University Press, 1898), 142–43.

Amelia Gillespie Smyth (1788–1876)

Harmonizing Magdalene

Amelia Gillespie Smyth was a Scottish author of stories and books for children and adults. She was born in Vienna where her father, Sir Robert Murray Keith, was a diplomat. At twenty, she married Robert Gillespie, a major in the County Militia and a Deputy Lieutenant who assumed the name Smyth as his wife was the heiress of Gibleston. Amelia Smyth was a member of the Scottish Episcopal Church before moving to England after her husband's death in 1855. Smyth wrote short stories as well as works on history and Scripture.[19] Her series of books on the Old and New Testaments for pre-adolescent and adolescent children were published over a period of six years as *Mornings with Mama, or Dialogues on Scripture for Young Persons*.

In *Mornings with Mama*, Smyth adopted the genre of catechetical writing, casting her interpretive work as a series of conversations between Mama and her child, Mary. Smyth's lessons were not confined to a study of Jesus' life and ministry. Other related lessons on ancient customs and the nature of Scripture, including a discussion of the nature of prophecy and gospel harmonies, were included as sidebars. She expected that her readers were

---

19. She published a book on Olympia Morata (1526–55) whose life and writings she found an inspiration to women in 1836. She edited her father's memoirs and correspondence and the memoirs of Queen Carolina Matilda of Denmark (1849).

already familiar with the Scriptures. Her lessons were intended to draw them into a deeper study of the texts. When Mary expresses bewilderment about Old Testament prophecy, for example, Mama suggests that Mary consult Alexander Keith's work on the fulfillment of prophecy.[20]

Smyth anticipated the questions that careful readers of Scripture would have in their reading of the gospel accounts of Mary Magdalene. Thus Mary's observation regarding the similarities between the story of the sinner who anointed Jesus in Luke 7 and the anointing of Jesus by Mary of Bethany in John 12 generated Mother's arguments for the distinctiveness of the two accounts. It also prompted a discussion of the story's middle-eastern cultural, social, and historical contexts that illuminated the text's literal sense. In this dialogue, Smyth portrayed Mary as an expert, as she had read about customs of the ancient Middle East and seen pictures of how they lounged when eating. Smyth had Mother move the discussion to the spiritual sense of the text as she probed the spiritual application of the story to Mary.

From Morning Fifteenth, Series One and Morning Twentieth, Series Two

Lessons on Luke 7–8:4 and John 19:38–42, Matthew 27:55–28:15, and John 20:1–19

MARY. He sat down to meat at a Pharisee's, who invited Him; and a woman, who had been a sinner, anointed Him with precious ointment, and washed his feet with her tears. Mama, I thought this had happened at Bethany, and that Mary, the sister of Lazarus did it.

MAMA. A similar occurrence certainly took place there, a few day[s] previous to our Lord's crucifixion, at the house of "Simon the leper;" and from the general resemblance in the features of both, and the host on the present occasion being also addressed by the name of "Simon," some confusion has not unnaturally taken place [Matt. 26:6–14; Mark 14:3–9; John 12:1–9]. But there are, when minutely scrutinized, differences sufficient in the particulars to distinguish the two events from each other, as completely as they were separated by time and distance.

---

20. Alexander Keith, *Evidence of the truth of the Christian religion: derived from the literal fulfilment of prophecy, particularly as illustrated by the history of the Jews, and by the discoveries of recent travellers*, 8th ed. (Edinburgh: Waugh and Innes, 1832).

The entertainment, or "supper," at Bethany, is said to have been "made" expressly for our Lord; probably in joint token of gratitude from the family of the risen Lazarus (for Martha served at it, and her brother was present), and one of the many "lepers" whom his benevolent interposition had restored to society. Now, the invitation mentioned in our chapter is supposed simply to refer to that general and ostentatious hospitality which the richer Jews were wont to exercise (when the duties of the Sabbath were over) towards their poorer brethren. And that no special honour to our blessed Lord was even implied in it, is apparent from the omission by the supercilious host of the customary salutation to a guest, as well as the refreshments of oil for the head and water for the feet. These, by the grateful humility of a converted transgressor, were supplied in a manner so unprecedented and so altogether foreign to our usages, that it may be well to inquire whether you fully understand the circumstances of it.

Mary. I used to be much puzzled how a poor sinner could get admittance to a rich man's feast, till I read somewhere that entertainments in the East were open to every body, even beggars. And since I have seen Scripture pictures, I understand better the way in which persons lay when eating,—along couches, so that every man's head (like John's) was opposite to another's "bosom," and his feet stretched out behind, so that anyone could get at them without disturbing him.

Mama. I see, by the accuracy of your description, that you really comprehend those peculiarities of Eastern manners, so necessary to a clear understanding of the letter of Scripture; and happy shall I be if your spiritual application of our Lord's touching parable proves that He has indeed had "something to say" in it to your young heart, and that by "loving much" you testify your sense of having had "much forgiven."

To enter deeply into this, to all most interesting, subject, what was the cause to which our Lord ascribes the want of common courtesy, and of the "love" by which it should have been dictated, in his proud entertainer?

Mary. He did not think he owed Christ any thing, or at least very little.

Mama. Alas why did the humble penitent think no honour—no, not royal ointment—too high for Christ, and no personal humiliation too deep to testify her sense of benefits received from Him?

Mary. Because she knew she had been a great sinner, and owed our Lord every thing.

Mama. Mary, let us never forget that our "sins," like hers, have been "many;" that if open profligacy (excused in some measure by ignorance) marked her previous life, ours—ay, the shortest one ever yet enjoyed by an

234

accountable creature—is stained by a daily amount of actual transgression, and yet more criminal forgetfulness of God, of which the "five hundred pence" [Luke 7:41] owed by the forgiven debtor here, or the "ten thousand talents" [Matt. 18:24] remitted to the merciless servant in another parable, afford equally inadequate representations.

Nay, could we even persuade ourselves, like the haughty Simon, that our debt of guilt was indeed of small amount, who is it, Mary, that "makes us thus to differ"? And would not the duty of "loving much" be tenfold enhanced if, indeed, by the aid of "Him through whom we can do all things," [Phil. 4:13] we had been preserved from our evil tendencies, and those bitter fruits of sin whence flowed the remorseful, though salutary, tears of Mary? As ransomed penitents, we may learn from "publicans and sinners" the duty of "loving much;" but were we sinless as angels, *they* might teach us the nobler lesson of daily gratitude for the boon; of gratitude to "Him that sitteth on the throne, and to the Lamb for ever and ever" [Rev. 5:13].

But by what gracious assurances was the "love" so conspicuous in the behaviour of the "woman who was a sinner" signally rewarded?

MARY. "Thy sins are forgiven; thy faith hath saved thee; go in peace."

MAMA. Peace, indeed; such as she alone, who had writhed under the burden of unexpiated guilt, and whose tortured frame had been the receptacle of yet guiltier spirits, could adequately appreciate. And truly might our Lord say in reference to it, "Not as the world giveth, give I unto thee" [John 14:27].

But how did the terms of the boon itself, and the style, suited only to the lips of the Son of God, in which it was announced, arouse the ire of the haughty bystanders?

MARY. They "began to say within themselves, 'Who is this that forgiveth sins also?'" But as if answering their thoughts, and reproving them, our Lord told her again that her faith had saved her; that very "faith" which, He says, "He had not found in Israel."

MAMA. Except in those few "Israelites indeed," who stood out in happy contrast from an unbelieving and impenitent nation.

But we must borrow from the succeeding chapter some practical proofs that the faith ascribed to Mary did not evaporate in vows and tears. What is said of her, and others similarly disposed, in its first three verses?

MARY. That when Christ "went through every city and village, preaching and showing the glad tidings of the kingdom of God," certain women which had been healed of evil spirits and infirmities, "Mary" among them ("out of whom went seven devils"), "ministered to Him of their substance."

MAMA. Are you aware whence she derived that surname of "Magdalene," which she has honoured by making it to this day synonymous with "penitent"?

MARY. I never thought of it, because two names are so common among the Jews.

MAMA. She received it, as many among them did, from her birth-place, a town called "Magdala," the "coasts" of which are elsewhere mentioned in the Gospel. But what more nearly concerns us is, the application of her worldly "substance" to the best and worthiest of purposes, in the earthly sustenance of her heavenly Benefactor. Who united with her in this meritorious work?

MARY. "Joanna, the wife of Chuza, Herod's steward." I *hope*, Mama, this really was the nobleman's wife whose son Christ so compassionately healed.

MAMA. We have the authority of tradition, at least, for thus considering her. But of "Susanna," her coadjutress in the pious office, we know nothing, save that her "record is on high," and that her "works do follow her."

. . .

[MAMA] When did the anxious female disciples of our Lord return to complete their funeral rites?

MARY. All the Evangelists agree that it was on the "first day of the week" (our Sunday, you know). John says, "while it was yet dark," and Matthew, "as it began to dawn." There is no material difference among them; but still, Mama, I dare say you could make it all clearer.

MAMA. To do so has employed the skill of abler persons, and many have bent their energies to the task (no very easy one) of harmonising, as it is called, into one continuous whole, the consistent, yet at first sight various, Gospel narratives. Taking as a guide (for the order of events) one of the ablest of these harmonists, we shall find little difficulty in tracing the steps of the different companies of pilgrims led by devoted affection to the tomb of their departed Master, or, according to the tenor of the angelic invitation, to "come and see where the Lord lay."

But to justify the use of that expression in the past tense, we must set out with the fact which, it is obvious from the remarks of the astonished women, had preceded the arrival of any of them at the sepulchre. What miraculous occurrence do we find recorded in the second verse of the twenty-eighth chapter of St. Matthew?

MARY. That there was a great earthquake, and the angel of the Lord descended from heaven, and came and rolled back the stone from the door and sat upon it. "His countenance was like lightning, and his raiment white as snow, and for fear of him the keepers did shake, and became as dead men." Nobody seems to have witnessed this but them, Mama; for the women coming along were perplexed "who should roll the stone away, for it was *very great*;" and lo, when they came, it was gone already.

MAMA. Did this unexpected facility at once afford them satisfaction?

MARY. No; Mary Magdalene who saw it first, never doubted "some enemy" had done it; and came running back to Peter and John, and said, "They have taken away the Lord out of the sepulchre, and we know not where they have laid Him."

MAMA The conclusion, though erroneous, was a natural one. But while she was absent how was it, in the case of her companions, removed?

MARY. The angel "answered and said unto them, Fear not ye, for I know that ye seek Jesus who was crucified. He is not here, for He is risen. Come, see the place where the Lord lay." This is all plain, Mama. But St. Luke speaks of "*two* men in shining garments."

MAMA. It is generally supposed that, as the first interview with the *one* angel evidently took place *without* (as he was sitting *on the stone* at the door), on his inviting them in to see where the Lord had "been laid," the vision of the other "young man sitting on the right side, clothed in a long white garment," met their eye, and *then* it is added, they were "affrighted."

But how greatly must their alarm have been alleviated, when kindly reminded by both heavenly messengers of their Lord's own predictions of his death, and resurrection on the *third day*; and desired to go "quickly," and communicate the joyful fact to the disciples, whom they were to warn of his going *before them* into Galilee.

In the mean time, when the women ("Mary the mother of James, and Salome," Mary Magdalene not having as yet returned) had left the sepulchre, the guards, recovering from their trance, and no longer beholding the angels (perhaps mercifully withdrawn for the purpose), "went into the city," and reported to the chief priests the wonderful events which, if generally circulated, would have so materially raised the fame and strengthened the cause of Jesus. They resorted therefore to the expedient of bribing the soldiers, and promising them impunity in the military crime of slumbering on their post; forgetting that, if really asleep, they ceased to be credible witnesses of any thing which might have occurred during their slumbers.

What next occurred at the sepulchre?

MARY. Peter and John came running to it on the report of Mary Magdalene, but not having met the other women, else they would have known better what had happened.

MAMA. Are you aware why so much stress is laid upon the "linen clothes" and "napkin" being left "lying in order" in the tomb?

MARY. No, Mama, unless as a proof that no one had carried away the body; else surely they would have taken the grave "clothes" with it.

MAMA. Precisely; and therefore it is added, when Peter and John had seen this, they "believed" though as yet ignorant or forgetful of the Scripture testimony that He "must rise from the dead," they "returned unto their own home."

Mary Magdalene, however, in the mean time came back to the tomb, and "stood weeping" without; until, stooping to look in, she again saw the angels. Still prepossessed with the idea of some hostile interference, she replies to their query of "Woman, why weepest thou?"—"Because they have taken my Lord away, and I know not where they have laid Him,"—words expressive of devoted though misjudging attachment. While yet speaking, Christ Himself stood unrecognised before her; and repeating the question, she ("supposing Him to be the gardener") said, "Sir, if Thou have borne Him hence, tell me where Thou hast laid Him, and I will take Him away." Would to God, Mary, that we, and all who say unto Jesus, "Lord, Lord," felt or showed half as much zeal for the honour and service of a risen and glorified Master as this poor bewildered woman testified for the recovery and decent disposal of his inanimate remains!

Truly was our Lord's testimony to her affectionate anticipation of his funeral honours—*"she hath done it for my burial"*—verified by the alacrity with which she came, *before day*, to perform the last melancholy duties, and her deep disappointment when defrauded, as she thought, of the opportunity of so doing. Proportionable must have been her joy, when at length made aware, by the repetition in his own wonted tones of benignant familiarity of the single word "Mary," that it was indeed He whom she sought that stood before her. How did she, on recognising, address Him?

MARY. "Rabboni, which is to say, Master."

MAMA. Nor "master" simply but my *great* Rabbi or Master,—an adjunct most natural on witnessing the extent of power manifested in rising from the dead.

MARY. Why did our Lord say, "Touch Me not" (when, I suppose, she had fallen at his feet), *for* I am not yet ascended unto my Father"?

MAMA. It should rather perhaps have been rendered, "Detain Me not now, for the time of my ascension is not yet." But "go to my *brethren*, and say unto them, I ascend unto my Father and your Father, unto my God and your God."

MARY. Mama, these are most beautiful words. His calling them "brethren" (after they had all forsaken Him), and speaking of God as their common "Father," must have affected them beyond description.

MAMA. Yes, my dear, when on the testimony of their own senses they at length saw and "believed." But was this the case on the report either of Mary or of the other women who also met Jesus?

MARY. Oh, no; "their words seemed unto them as an idle tale, and they believed them not."

MAMA. So rooted, in short, was their incredulity and "slowness of heart to believe" even what would have been the most welcome of tidings, as to compel the most bigoted enemies of their Master's cause to acquit them of any fabricated plan for propagating a belief which they could not themselves be persuaded, even by the testimony of an eye-witness, to adopt.

Let us not, my dear, while blaming and wondering at a conduct at variance even with the usual proneness of human nature to give credit to what coincides with its own wishes, be insensible to its value to ourselves, in stamping with unquestionable authenticity the relation of the most stupendous fact in all the Gospel history, and on which, as on some mighty pivot, the Christian's hope of a kindred immortality must ever be suspended.

Source: Amelia Gillespie Smyth, *Children's Bible Stories: Being Conversations on the New Testament* (Philadelphia: Porter & Coates, 1883), 152–55, 487–91.[21]

ELIZABETH RUNDLE CHARLES (1828–1896)

Hidden Depths

Elizabeth Rundle Charles was a prolific author of poetry, spiritual and devotional reflections, and commentaries.[22] A gifted linguist, Charles also translated a variety of German and Latin works including an old Latin hymn on

---

21. Originally published in Amelia Gillespie Smyth, *Mornings with Mama, or Dialogues on Scripture for Young Persons* (Edinburgh: W. Blackwood, 1830–36).

22. For a fuller discussion of Charles, see "Communion and Sacrifice" in the chapter on Mary and "Traveling to Tyre" in the chapter on a woman of Canaan. For more on her interpretive methods, see Marion Ann Taylor, "Elizabeth Rundle Charles: Translating the Letter of Scripture into Life," in *Recovering Nineteenth-Century Women Interpreters of the Bible*, ed. Christiana de Groot and Marion Ann Taylor (Atlanta: Society of Biblical Literature, 2007), 149–63.

Mary Magdalene still sung in churches today.[23] In 1888, Charles published *By Thy Glorious Resurrection and Ascension: Easter Thoughts*, a collection of six reflections on the events of Easter, beginning with Jesus' death and burial and ending with his ascension. She concluded her book with a collection of her poems on the same subject. The second poem in the collection, entitled "'Mary' and 'Rabboni,'" is included here.

Charles's thoughts on the resurrection combined careful exegesis and devotional reflection. She quite consciously lifted Scripture's veil to expose the hidden parts of the story, using a variety of interpretive methods to fill in the gaps. Like Smyth, Jameson, and Stowe, Charles portrayed Magdalene as a fallen woman. Unlike many of her contemporaries, however, Charles refused to be drawn into schemes of harmonizing the differences in the gospels, a task she likened to "trying to make a perfect picture out of the fragments of an ancient mosaic of which some pieces are lost."[24] In addition to using classic interpretive techniques, she drew on her own experiences of travel and personal loss, her cultural and social assumptions, and her profound knowledge of both Scripture and liturgy to fill in the blanks of the story and probe its spiritual significance. Like Baxter, Charles explored the significance of Jesus' choice of Mary Magdalene to announce the resurrection. Charles's poem on the tender post-resurrection meeting of Mary and Jesus displays her remarkable ability to lift the veil on the silences of Scripture.

Appearances to One Only

The questionings about those four days of Lazarus, those three days between the Crucifixion and Easter, are answered not by details about the unseen world, but by the Resurrection; not by expansions of the meaning of the "Paradise," but by fuller revelation of the "with Me."

The whole significance of the Resurrection, morally and spiritually, is enshrined in the words "Behold . . . that *it is I Myself.*" No "phantom," no being changed and glorified into another nature than yours; no mere phase or aspect of God; no mere manifestation of an impersonal universal life: "It is I *Myself*," come back to you yourselves, "My brothers." Individual immor-

23. The Latin hymn on Mary Magdalene that Charles translated is "Lift Your Voice Rejoicing Mary."

24. Elizabeth Rundle Charles, *Ecce Ancilla Domini: Mary, the Mother of Our Lord: Studies in the Christian Ideal of Womanhood* (London: SPCK, 1894), 53.

tality, personal identity, ensured, as the one central reality of the universe, the condition and basis of Reason and Love, and therefore of the essential being of God and man. *"It is I Myself," "ye need not look for another."*

The two incidents of Easter Day which meet us first are the two manifestations to one disciple alone—to Mary Magdalene and to Peter.

The morning had come at last. The rest from work of the Sabbath Day, so loyally observed by hearts that could not rest, whose restless anguish the cessation from outward work could only intensify, was over. The dawn of the new day had come, or rather was coming, not with the slow gradual deepening of the sunrise glow as in our northern lands, but treading close on the darkness.

"Very early in the morning, while it was yet dark, Mary Magdalene came to the sepulchre."

There is something most beautiful in the association of the Resurrection not only with the Spring of every year, but with the morning of every day. As we feel the approach of this morning, of this Sun which burns with the full glow of day from the first moment of His shining, the "great stone is rolled away" from the sepulchre of our hearts. We arise and live.

But it was not so that first Easter Morning with the Magdalene. She came, not with songs, but with blinding tears; not with offerings to the living, but with embalming spices for the dead; to render to the mortal remains the last services of immortal love, but without a ray of hope.

The rolling away of the stone rolls away none of the load from her heart; the emptiness of the sepulchre only makes the void of her desolation deeper. The shining vision of the white-robed angels brings her no light, scarcely awakens her interest; their announcement of the Resurrection does not seem to penetrate her heart at all. All she seems to comprehend is that she is to go and "tell the disciples *and Peter*," that they had taken away her Lord. Some strange emphasis in the most tender and gracious individuality of that message to Peter seems to have penetrated through the bewilderment of her grief.

The "other women" who brought the spices and heard the angel's message (St. Mark says) "fled affrighted from the sepulchre; for they trembled and were amazed: neither said they anything to any man; for they were afraid."

We do not read that Mary Magdalene was troubled or affrighted. She had nothing worse to fear. Her desolation had reached a depth to which fear could not descend. The fact that the Lord was dead, that His very grave was robbed and empty, absorbed her altogether. The message that He was risen and living, and going before them into Galilee, her own Galilee, made no impression on her at all.

241

She uses still the pathetic passive words, not "He has gone" but "they have taken," "they have laid." She only understands what she has lost, and what she has to do; that the Lord was "taken away," and that she had to tell Peter. And this she did, with the eager haste, not of fear, but of love.

"She *runneth* and telleth Peter."

It need not detain us now to harmonise the details of the narratives. Perhaps they can be made to fit together as they are. The study will always have its interest. Certainly they would be found to fit, if we had all the missing pieces. But in all attempts to harmonise Revelation and Science, the facts of the physical and of the spiritual world, the lessons of our own little lives, or the details of these Gospel histories, perhaps the greatest mistakes are made by trying to harmonise too impatiently, and so fitting in the mosaic wrong, and marring, or narrowing the design.

At all events, just now, what we want to do is to grasp the meaning of this one story.

Who was this Mary of Magdala, this woman to whom, of all the bewildered world, of all the expectant Church, the Desire of all nations, the Saviour of all men, "when He was risen early, the first day of the week, appeared first?"

St. Mark, who tells us this of her, says only, "out of whom He cast seven devils." St. Luke tells us the same, and adds that many other women went with the Lord and His disciples, as He made His progress throughout the cities and villages; women "who had been healed of evil spirits and infirmities," and among them some of wealth and standing, such as Joanna the wife of Chuza, Herod's steward, "who ministered unto Him of their substance."

All the Evangelists also record that this Mary of Magdala stood with the Mother of our Lord and St. John beside the Cross, and that she was among those who watched when Joseph of Arimathæa and Nicodemus "laid Him in the sepulchre and rolled the great stone to the door."

This is all that the Gospels positively and unquestionably tell us of her by this name, evidently well-known, of the Magdalene.

That she had been among the possessed, is recorded, a woman surely, of a powerful nature, with the terrible as well as the glorious possibilities of a strong character; "seven devils" would scarcely have been detached to do the work which might have been achieved by one. Whatever Mary Magdalene had been, she was no weak demonstrative creature, of easy tears and hysterical emotions (however the redeeming strength of the Master and the great spaces of the Church may find room and work even for the feeblest of such). Everything about her shows another type of womanhood, strong to

242

endure as well as to dare; to control emotion, when that was the service love demanded, as well as to feel. Otherwise she could never have kept day by day in that ministering company, among the Founders, walking along the rough roads and mountain paths, listening to the Divine teaching, and taking her woman's part of ministering to the earthly wants of all; and certainly she could never have been at the Cross.

When the Twelve, or at least eleven of the Twelve, had forsaken and fled, and one had denied, she was at the Cross, saying nothing. "When it was yet dark," after the "three days," she was awake, watching for the morning she had been waiting for to dawn. The morning she had been waiting for, patient and hopeless; but how little did she know what a morning for her and for the world!

This is all that is told us of Mary Magdalene by that name before the interview of that Easter Morning. The rest of her traditional history has grown out of identifying her story with other stories in the Gospels.

A general though not universal tradition in the Western Church has woven into one the stories of "the woman who was a sinner," of Mary of Bethany, and of Mary Magdalene.

The Eastern Church, on the other hand, recognizes these narratives as records of three different women.*

Our own Church, originally accepting the Western tradition which identifies the Magdalene with "the woman who was a sinner," and appointing a great festival with an especial Collect sanctioning this belief, finally abolished the Collect, and placed her name among the minor Saints, thus losing for us the general celebration of a most significant festival.

But still, popular language continues the tradition, so that the name of the Magdalene is the expression of Christian hope for the most fallen, of the great Christian truth that the Church, like her Lord, admits of no outcast class, or creature, in the world. And whatever conclusion may be reached as to the gathering of the three narratives into one, there can be no doubt that as the Blessed Mother of our Lord stands before Christendom as a type of the grace that keeps "without spot and blameless," the Magdalene also abides with us for ever as a type of the grace which restores, as the witness

---

*In the Greek Church she is honoured as the "equal of the Apostles" (Blunt, Annotated Prayer Book), as the first witness of the Resurrection, and is thought to have spent the close of her life at Ephesus with the Blessed Mother and St. John.

The Latin tradition also represents her as among the noblest of fallen creatures, moving masses of people to Christianity in the cities of Provence, where she died, and borne daily by angels to heaven in rapturous communion.

for ever that those who have fallen to the lowest depths may rise to the most glorious heights of love and service; may stand with the Mother beside the Cross; may be chosen—the last first—to see the risen Lord first and alone at the sepulchre, and be sent as His first messenger on the highest missions to the Church and the world.

But it is not with any debated questions that we have now to do. Our attention is fixed at present only and, entirely on that first appearance to Mary Magdalene on the Resurrection Morning.

She had gone, running swiftly on her errand, to Peter and John. She had returned with them to the sepulchre. John, reaching it first, had looked in; Peter had gone in. But they had found only darkness and emptiness, and the traces of order and care in the folded graveclothes. Then they had departed.

"But Mary remained without the sepulchre;" and now we are told she was weeping. She had watched the last dying look and movement, listened to the last words, faithfully watched as He was laid to rest, seen the sepulchre safely closed. That morning she had given her message, yet we hear of no weeping, though when she came to the disciples they mourned and wept. But now the last possible service had been rendered; there was nothing else to do; now there was time for tears. The grave was empty; there was no use for her spices. Yet still she remained. The empty sepulchre where her Lord had been laid was the most sacred place left in the world for her.

She "stood;" not prostrate in the abandonment of grief. "She stood without at the sepulchre weeping; and as she wept, she stooped down and looked into the sepulchre."

It was no longer empty, or dark. Two angels in white were there illumining the darkness; "the one at the head, the other at the feet, where the Body of Jesus had lain." But the radiant heavenly presences seem to have brought no light to her heart. They do not seem even to have surprised her. Perhaps she had seen them before, that morning, with the other women. At all events they were nothing to her. Her heart was filled with one Presence, and its loss. She was looking, not for soothing consolations, or for rapturous experiences, or heavenly illuminations; but for Jesus only, for Him she had lost.

And, we must not forget, she was looking not for the living but for the dead.

When the angels spoke to her *it* was apparently in wonder at her continued grief. They knew, and they had told her, that all cause for weeping was over. Their question has wonder if not reproach in it.

"Woman, why weepest thou?" They do not repeat the glad news they had given before. And still, uncomforted by *voice* or vision, she goes back to her old passive words, her old lament over the dead.

Again she says, in the same words as to Peter and John, only changing the "we" for the "my" (as if not recognising any communion in sorrow with those radiant strangers), "Because they have taken away my Lord, and I know not where they have laid Him."

And then, turning herself back, away from the sepulchre and the angels towards the open world and the dawning light without, "she saw Jesus standing." He was actually there, "and she knew Him not."

Not only to the angels, to HIMSELF, to His visible Presence, her grief, her grief at losing Him blinded her. The dead Christ in the sepulchre of her heart hid from her the living. And this also, in the spiritual life, in the life of Christendom, is it not again and again repeated?

Even His voice, the most unchangeable and characteristic sign of individuality, the one thing by which we recognise each other without question, His own living voice speaking to her did not wake her from her dream.

To His question she answers, as to the angels', with her old lament over the helpless passive dead whom she sought, still without a ray of hope, except that perhaps she might have found the one who had stolen away the treasure she was seeking. "Supposing Him to be the gardener," apparently thinking His enemies grudged the sacred Body even the shelter of the tomb, she said, "Sir, if thou have borne Him hence, tell me where thou hast laid Him, and I will take Him away."

She is quite out of the region of weight and measure, of balancing her forces against her passionate purpose.

But once more we are in His presence; once more the words of life are here; the penetrating questions which search the heart and reveal its wants to itself; the questions which become answers in the consciences and hearts they touch; the sayings, so intensely individual, as if spoken only to the one who hears them, so universal throughout the ages for every soul that needs them.

"Woman," He says, as to His Mother at the Cross—not first "Mary," but "Woman," as if speaking through her to all womanhood for ever—"Woman, why weepest thou?" The question of the angels, the only question to be asked by sympathy, even angelic, which cannot bring Himself, the Divine and human Friend, to the sufferer.

"*Why Weepest thou?*" He says, to all the womanhood to which through all generations so large a share of the tears of the world must fall. It echoes softly down the centuries again and again to every woman's heart.

At that question the angels stopped. He followed it with a second question, which was to answer the first.

"Whom seekest thou?"

The weeping is for a loss; for a lost treasure which is being *sought*; which is sought that it may be found.

She is seeking; let her ask herself what is the lost treasure she is seeking. Not *"What* seekest thou?" He says, but *"Whom."*

Not for any "what," any thing, any impersonal delight; not for any mere memory; not even for any restoration of the dearest past; not even for the dead Body of her Lord is she really seeking, is the real thirst of her heart.

Not in the sepulchre, in the past, do we find those we have laid in the sepulchre; but "turning back" from the sepulchre to the wide world of life, to the morning, do we find them.

And, always, all humanity, whatever it may dream, *is* seeking a Person, to be adored, to respond to adoration, to be served. If in some moments of bewilderment it abandons Personality, unconsciously it begins to delude itself with personifications. The "Nature" by which God is, for the time, hidden, becomes a creature beloved and worshipped and idolised with a playful fondness, "reverenced" and "adored" with a worshipping wonder. The Humanity no longer rooted and fulfilled in the Son of Man is embodied in its greatest examples, is tenderly ministered to in its lowest falls, is more or less personified as one sublime Being to be contemplated, loved, and devotedly served, though without hope of response to the aspiration or of recognition of the service.

And when, for each one of us, that second question of our Lord's answers the first, and we learn at last that we are weeping because in the depths of our hearts we are needing, seeking, thirsting for nothing less, none else than this risen, living Jesus, Son of God, Son and Saviour of man; then *He is there*; we recognise Him at last, His face and His voice; and all questions are solved for us, or begin to be solved, in the joy of His perpetual Presence.

He said unto her, "Mary."

"She turned herself" entirely at last from the darkness of the grave to Him, "and said unto Him, Rabboni."

The "I" and "thou," absolutely individual, as if (as with St. Peter afterwards) no one else in the world had ever heard one detail of the interview, one syllable of the words spoken; yet renewed at one time, in one mode or another, between everyone of that great multitude no man can number and their Lord. "He calleth His own sheep by name, and leadeth them out" [John 10:3].

The "Rabboni"—"my Master"—the most reverent form, it is said, of the title; but essentially also "*my* Master;" not merely Master and Teacher of all the disciples, but "mine."

It is one of the few instances, always so significant, in which the actual word is given. Also it is said to be in her own Galilean dialect; her speech bewrayeth [sic] her. "Rabbouni"* which gives a most expressive touch of nature, the heart and tongue falling, in crises of life or death, in moments of intense feeling, into the familiar speech of childhood; "Rabbouni," from the lips of the Galilean Magdalene to Him Who was also "of Galilee."

No impassioned exuberance of expression, nor, as with Thomas, any new utterance of wondering worship; simply the old familiar title, the usual calm and reverent address of the disciples; yet indeed, from her lips, at that moment implying everything—adoration, subjection, service, every longing satisfied, every faculty absorbed: "My Master," Lord of my whole life, of my whole being, Lord of me.

For the heart needs duty as much as love; the will needs rule as much as freedom. Or, to speak more truly, without dividing ourselves metaphysically into sections, *we*, mind and heart and will, crave and demand and *have* the living Lord of our whole being. Christianity, for us as well as for the Magdalene, enkindles every emotion of our hearts, commands every portion of our complex nature; for it combines the tender loyalty to a sacred memory—to a love which was proved and sealed by death—with the joyful activity of service to One Who is living, and commanding and teaching us "all the days" to the end of the world.

And then (whatever adoring movement on her part the words are meant to answer), follows on His part a *negation*, a denial—"*Touch Me not.*" Strange and startling words, one would imagine, from His lips, always full of invitations to draw near, of welcomes to the most fallen, of the "Hither to Me," of the unreproving "She has not ceased to kiss My feet."

Of old He was wont to fulfil His words of healing by the healing touch to those men shrank from most; to recognise and single out with honour the touch of faith which had drawn the healing virtue from Him. But now, "*Touch Me not*" He said; and however that saying may chill or surprise us, it seems not for a moment to have chilled or perplexed the Magdalene.

It seems as if the great truth must have flashed on her at once that this Resurrection was something altogether quite new in the world: not like the coming back of the young damsel, darling of her household, to be fed and cherished again by her father and mother [Luke 8:40–56]; not like the giv-

*[B. F.] Westcott, *Gospel of St. John*. [(London: J. Murray, 1882).]

ing back of the son to the widowed mother at Nain [Luke 7:11–15]; not like the coming forth of Lazarus to the sisters of Bethany to be the brother once more in the home, to sit with them again at the welcoming table, and listen with Mary and be served by Martha as of old [John 11:1–44]; no mere coming back to our human homes to live and die again. Altogether new was this Resurrection; not an interruption of the long triumph of Death, but a triumph over Death for ever; not a break in the old, but a beginning of the new; not a flash in the night, but a new morning, morning of the new day, the first day of a new Creation. Not as one wrenched for a few years from the grave did He come back, but as a Conqueror and Fountain of new life for all, the "Firstborn from the dead" [Col. 1:18], "Firstborn among many brethren" [Rom. 8:29] of a new humanity, through all its generations new created and conquering in Him.

We must remember that the disciples, and probably Mary Magdalene herself, had seen resurrections, had seen the dead come back to life before, at His summons. What she had to learn was that this Resurrection of the Lord was *not* like those former resurrections, *not* a coming back to the old familiar life on earth, but the rising to a higher life, and thus raising all with Him.

It was indeed *"Mary"* and *"Rabbouni;"* but it was also *"Touch Me Not."* The message with which she was sent to the disciples was not "I *am risen,"* but "I *ascend."* "Touch me not; for I am not yet ascended to My Father: but go to My brethren, and say to them, I ascend unto My Father and your Father, and to my God and your God."

As "Firstborn from the dead" He speaks to her; as "the Firstborn among many brethren" He sends her to the disciples with that first Easter message.

With what a Divine quietness the narrative flows on:

"Mary Magdalene came and told the disciples that she had seen the Lord, and that He had spoken these things unto her."

That is the simple record of the first note of that great peal of victory which has never since ceased throughout the ages; of the ushering in of that new life which began the new Creation for the whole world.

One other interview alone with one other disciple is recorded. We are three times told it occurred, by three different narrators, though of the interview itself we are told nothing.

In St. Mark's history the message of the angels to the women was, "Tell His disciples *and Peter,"* of which the emphasis seems so to have rested on the "Peter," that to him at once Mary Magdalene, who only took the message, went.

St. John tells us, "Then she runneth and cometh to Simon Peter."

In St. Luke's narrative we are told that when the two came back from "the breaking of the bread" and the opening of their eyes at Emmaus, on the morning of Easter Day, "they found the Eleven gathered together, and those that were with them, saying, "The Lord is risen indeed, and hath appeared unto Simon."

And St. Paul, years afterwards, gathering up the various proofs of the Resurrection through the manifestations of the Risen Lord, writes, "He was seen of Cephas."

That interview was between the Master and the disciple, and remains absolutely hidden from us. Not a syllable breaks the sacred silence that veils that meeting. Not a word tells us of the look from the Risen Saviour which followed that other look, when the Lord turned and looked on Peter, and Peter went out and wept bitterly.

Thank God for the reticences and the silences of the Holy Scriptures; that whatever our poor biographies may dare to intrude into and profane, the Divine story recognises that there are depths never to be unveiled to any but the soul that has fathomed them and God.

No record is given us of the first meeting of the Risen Lord with His Mother; of the words which in the Resurrection followed the last proof of tender filial care from the dying lips, "Behold thy mother;" "Woman, behold thy son."

No record is given us of the first meeting between the Apostle who denied and the Lord who forgave. But thank God also that we are told three times, that as the very first announcement of the Resurrection was entrusted to a woman once raised from depths of degradation and misery, so also the very first message to any human creature by name was sent to him who, to himself at all events, must have seemed to deserve it least, to the heart that in its shame and repentance must have needed it most of all.

Source: Elizabeth Rundle Charles, *By Thy Glorious Resurrection and Ascension* (London: SPCK, 1888), 28–49.

"Mary" and "Rabboni"

"Jesus saith unto her, Mary. She turned herself, and saith unto Him, Rabboni; which is to say, Master."

A moment since a sepulcher
    Was all the world she cared to own,
An empty tomb, vain balms and myrrh,
    Tears with no heart to shed them on.

And now the living Lord was there,
    Immortal, glorious, yet the same;
The voice the fiends once fled in fear
    Now spake the old familiar name.

No language could that bliss have told;
    She had no words the joy to greet;
She said but "Master!" as of old,
    And rested silent at His feet.

Yet all Heaven's choirs could scarce entwine
    A music more profound and sweet
Than when, as from His heart to thine,
    Thus "Mary" and "Rabboni" meet.

Source: Elizabeth Rundle Charles, *By Thy Glorious Resurrection and Ascension*, 139.

STUDY QUESTIONS

1. How do these commentators fill in the gaps or silences in Mary Magdalene's story? Are these attempts to complete the story convincing? Why or why not?

2. What are the different ways Mary Magdalene has been portrayed in books, plays, musicals, or movies? How does this tradition compare with the gospel texts? How does it influence the interpretations of Mary Magdalene in the nineteenth century and today?

3. How did the nineteenth-century writers deal with the extra-biblical tradition surrounding Mary Magdalene in their readings of her story?

4. How do these commentators harmonize the various gospel texts about Mary Magdalene? Which harmonizing attempts are most convincing?

5. How do the commentators challenge the predominant nineteenth-century readings of the story of Mary Magdalene? How are the various challenges similar? How are they different?

6. What key theological concepts and issues do the nineteenth-century writers address in their discussion of Mary Magdalene? Would these same theological concepts and issues be pivotal in a current discussion of Mary Magdalene? Why or why not?

Epilogue

Women have different reactions to discovering the history of women's work on the Bible. In Anna Carter Florence's book *Preaching as Testimony* she describes her anger at discovering a tradition of women preachers.

> It struck me as a personal affront that I had never known these women existed, never heard their stories, never believed I was a part of any tradition, never known the truth about the preaching women I came from. Clearly, my very identity had been compromised and possibly stunted: *If only I had known, surely I would be a different person! I would be braver, stronger, wiser, more self-assured! I would be a better person and a better preacher!*[1]

Florence's response reflects that of many women in the theological disciplines upon discovering that women did theological work for centuries. The tradition of the women represented in this book who preached, who studied and interpreted Scripture, who thought theologically, who taught, and who provided leadership in the Church is a vital part of the history of the Church and the academic theological disciplines. In forgetting women of the past, we have lost an indispensable part of our heritage. In remembering them, in listening to them, we gain witnesses who will continue to speak into our future.

---

1. Anna Carter Florence, *Preaching as Testimony* (Louisville: Westminster John Knox Press, 2007), 111.

Selected Bibliography of Nineteenth-Century Women's Writings on the Gospels

Adams, Hannah. *Letters on the Gospels.* Cambridge, MA: Hilliard & Metcalf, 1824.

Alden, Isabella Macdonald ("Pansy"). *Stories and Pictures from the New Testament.* Boston: D. Lothrop, 1889.

Alexander, Cecil Frances. *Poems.* London: MacMillan, 1896.

Ashton, Sophia Goodrich. *The Mothers of the Bible.* Boston: J. P. Jewett & Co., 1855.

Balfour, Clara Lucas. *Women of Scripture.* London: Houlston and Stoneman, 1847; 2nd ed., 1850.

Barton, Lucy. *Natural History of the Holy Land, and Other Places Mentioned in the Bible.* London: T. Allman & Son, 1856.

———. *The Gospel History of our Lord and Saviour Jesus Christ.* London: W. Tweedie, 1837.

Baxter, Elizabeth. *The Living Word in the Gospel of St. John.* London: Christian Herald, 1887.

———. *The Women in the Word.* 2nd edition. London: Christian Herald, 1897.

Beck, Mary E. *Bible Readings on Bible Women: Illustrated by Incidents in Daily Life.* London: S. W. Partridge & Co., 1892.

Boddington, Gracilla. *A Practical Commentary on the Gospel of St. Matthew, in Simple and Familiar Language.* London: J. Nisbet and Co., 1861.

———. *A Practical Commentary on the Gospel of St. Mark, in Simple and Familiar Language.* London: J. Nisbet and Co., 1863.

———. *A Practical Commentary on the Gospel of St. Luke, in Simple and Familiar Language.* London: J. Nisbet and Co., 1869.

———. *A Practical Commentary on the Gospel of St. John, in Simple and Familiar Language.* London: J. Nisbet and Co., 1870.

Cappe, Catherine. *A Connected History of the Life and Divine Mission of Jesus Christ: as Recorded in the Narratives of the Four Evangelists.* York: T. Wilson and Sons, 1809.

Charles, Elizabeth Rundle. *Ecce Ancilla Domini: Mary the Mother of Our Lord; Studies in the Christian Ideal of Womanhood.* London: Society for Promoting Christian Knowledge, 1894.

————. *"By Thy Glorious Resurrection and Ascension": Easter Thoughts.* London: Society for Promoting Christian Knowledge, 1888.

————. *Mary, the Handmaid of the Lord.* London, 1854.

————. *Sketches of the Women of Christendom: Dedicated to the Women of India.* London: Society for Promoting Christian Knowledge, 1880.

————. *Wanderings over Bible Lands and Seas.* London: T. Nelson and Sons, 1862; New Edition, 1887.

————. *The Women of the Gospels: The Three Wakings, and Other Poems.* New York: M. W. Dodd, 1867.

Clere, Mrs. *The Apostles of Jesus.* London: Hatchard & Co., 1867.

Copley, Esther. *A Brief View of Sacred History from the Creation of the World to the Destruction of Jerusalem by the Romans.* London: William Darton and Son, 1831.

————. *Scripture Biography: Comprehending All the Names Mentioned in the Old and New Testaments.* London: Fisher, Fisher, and Jackson, 1835.

Corner, Julia. *The Picture Nursery Sunday-Book.* London: Dean & Son, 1852.

Cornwallis, Mary. *Observations, Critical, Explanatory, and Practical, on the Canonical Scriptures.* 4 vols. London: Baldwin, Cradock, and Joy, 1817; 2nd ed., 1820.

Cutts, Mary. *The Autobiography of a Clock, and Other Poems.* Boston, 1852.

Dibdin, Emily. *Outline Lessons on Women of the Bible.* London: Church of England Sunday School Institute, 1893.

Donaldson, Mrs. *Home Duties for Wives and Mothers, Illustrated by Women of Scripture.* London: William Hunt and Co., 1882.

Dyer, Winnifred M. *The Holy One: Poems on Gospel Incidents.* Boston: Advent Christian Publication Society, [19--].

Ellet, Mrs. *Family Pictures from the Bible.* London, 1849.

G., M. *Women Like Ourselves: Short Addresses for Mother's Meetings, Bible Classes, Etc.* London: Society for Promoting Christian Knowledge, 1893.

Gilman, Caroline Howard. *Verses of a Lifetime.* Boston: James Munroe and Company, 1849.

Gould, Hannah Flagg. *Hymns and Other Poems for Children.* New York: Allen Brothers, 1869.

————. *New Poems.* Boston, 1850.

————. *Poems.* Boston, 1832.

Graves, Elisabeth A. *Commentary on the Gospel According to St. John.* Liverpool: Henry Young & Sons, 1904.

Hale, Sarah Josepha. *Woman's Record; or, Sketches of All Distinguished Women from the Creation to A.D. 1854.* New York: Harper & Brothers, 1855.

Hanaford, Phebe A. *Daughters of America: or, Women of the Century.* Boston: B. B. Russell, 1883.

Houghton, Louise Seymour. *The Bible in Picture and Story.* New York: American Tract Society, 1889.

————. *The Life of the Lord Jesus: An Aid to the Study of the Gospel History of Jesus Christ.* Boston: Bible Study Publishing Company, 1895.

Jameson, Anna. *Sacred and Legendary Art*. London: Printed for Longman, Brown, Green, and Longmans, 1848.

———. *Legends of the Madonna: as represented in the fine arts, forming the third series of Sacred and legendary art*. London: Longmans, Brown and Longmans, 1852.

Jameson, Anna, and Elizabeth Eastlake. *The History of Our Lord: As Exemplifed in Works of Art, With That of His Types, St John the Baptist, and Other Persons of the Old and New Testament*. London: Longman, Green, Longman, Roberts, and Green, 1864.

King, Frances Elizabeth. *Female Scripture Characters; Exemplifying Female Virtues*. London: F. C. & J. Rivington, 1813.

Lady. *Children Invited to Christ*. New York: American Tract Society, c. 1849.

Latimer, Faith [Mrs. John A. Miller]. *From Bethlehem to Calvary*. New York: Nelson & Phillips, 1876.

Locker, Hannah Jane. *Bible Readings from the Gospels for Mothers' Meetings, Etc*. London: Religious Tract Society, 1877.

Mackenzie, Mary Jane. *Lectures on Miracles, Selected from the New Testament*. London, 1823.

Martyn, Sarah Towne Smith. *Women of the Bible*. New York: American Tract Society, 1868.

McFadyen, Nina L. *Stories from the Life of the Wonderful*. Los Angeles, 1897.

Menken, Adah Isaacs. *Infelicia*. Philadelphia, 1868.

Mortimer, Favell Lee. *Light in the Dwelling: or, A Harmony of the Four Gospels; with Very Short and Simple Remarks, Adapted to Reading at Family Prayers, and Arranged in 365 Sections, for Every Day of the Year*. London: J. Hatchard and Son, 1846.

———. *The Peep of Day; or, A Series of the Earliest Religious Instruction the Infant Mind is Capable of Receiving*. London: J. Hatchard and Son, 1833.

Nightingale, Florence. *Suggestions for Thought to the Searchers after Truth among the Artizans of England*. London: George E. Eyre and William Spottiswoode, 1860.

Norval, Leigh. *Women of the Bible: Sketches of All the Prominent Female Characters in the Old and the New Testament*. Nashville: Publishing House of the M. E. Church, South, Sunday-School Department, 1889.

Oliphant, Margaret. *Jerusalem, the Holy City: Its History and Hope*. London: Macmillan, 1891.

Palmer, Ellen. *The Fishermen of Galilee, or, Sunday Talks with Papa*. Edinburgh: William P. Nimmo, 1875.

Palmer, Henrietta Lee. *Home Life in the Bible*. Edited by J. W. Palmer. Boston: J. R. Osgood and Co., 1881.

Pansy [Mrs. G. R. Alden], *Stories & Pictures from the New Testament*. Boston: Lothrop, 1893.

Phelps, Elizabeth Stuart. *The Story of Jesus Christ: An Interpretation*. Boston and New York: Houghton, Mifflin, 1897.

Pridham, Caroline. *Little Elsie's Book of Bible Animals*. 2nd ed. London: A. S. Rouse, 1895.

Proctor, Adelaide Anne. *Legends and Lyrics: Together with a Chaplet of Verses*. London: G. Routledge & Sons, c. 1905.

Richmond, E. J. *Woman, First and Last: And What she has Done*. New York: Phillips & Hunt, 1887.

Rossetti, Christina. *The Complete Poems of Christina Rossetti*. Edited with textual notes and introductions by R. W. Crump. Baton Rouge, LA: Louisiana State University Press, 1979.

Sandys, Lucy. *Child Life in Bible Times*. London: Arthur H. Stockwell, 1908.

SchimmelPenninck, Mary Anne. *Biblical Fragments*. 2 vols. London: Ogle, Duncan, & Co., 1821.

Seldon, Almira, *Effusions of the Heart, Contained in a Number of Original Poetical Pieces on Various Subjects*. Bennington, VT: printed by Darius Clark, 1820.

Sheriffe, Sarah. *The Practical Study of Scripture: Recommended and Illustrated by Reflections on Some of the Most Remarkable Events, and Discourses, Recorded in the Old and New Testament: Intended to Assist Every Reader of the Bible, in Making a Profitable Application of the Contents of that Sacred Volume: To which are Added Prayers Adapted to Each of the Foregoing Subjects*. London: Printed for Hatchard and Son, 1823.

Sigourney, Lydia, *Daily Counselor*. Hartford: Brown and Gross, 1859.

Sinclair, Catherine. *Popish Legends or Bible Truths*. London: Longman, Brown, Green, and Longmans, 1852.

Smith, Mary Ann. *The Holy Women of Old: Seventeen Lessons*. Edinburgh: John Anderson, 1897.

Smyth, Amelia Gillespie. *Mornings with Mama, or Dialogues on Scripture for Young Persons*. Edinburgh: W. Blackwood, 1830–36. American Edition. *Children's Bible Stories: Being Conversations on the New Testament*. Philadelphia: Porter & Coates, 1883.

Stanton, Elizabeth Cady, ed. *The Woman's Bible, Part II: Joshua to Revelation*. Boston: Northeastern University Press, 1898.

Sterling Clark, M. B. *Questions on the Harmony of the Gospels*. New York: Pott & Amery, 1868.

Stowe, Harriet Beecher. *Woman in Sacred History: A Series of Sketches Drawn from Scriptural, Historical, and Legendary Sources*. New York: J. B. Ford and Company, 1873.

———. *Footsteps of the Master*. New York: J. B. Ford & Company, 1877.

Stretton, Hesba. *The Wonderful Life*. London: Henry S. King & Co., 1875.

Trimmer, Sarah. *A Help to the Unlearned in the Study of the Holy Scriptures: Being an Attempt to Explain the Bible in a Familiar Way, Adapted to the Common Apprehensions, and according to the Opinions of Approved Commentators*. London: Rivington, 1805.

Tynan, Katherine. *Poems*. London: Lawrence & Bullen, 1901.

Wheeler, Charlotte Bickersteth. *Our Master's Footsteps: or, Bible Class Notes for Thoughtful Girls*. London: Elliot Stock, 1883.

White, Ellen G. *Bible Biographies: New Testament*. Compiled by Walter T. Rea. Pomono, CA: n.p., n.d.

———. *Christ's Object Lessons*. Oakland, CA: Pacific Press Publishing Co., c. 1900.

Witter, Mary L. T. *Angels*. Glasgow: William Asher, 1900.

———. *The Edomites: Their History as Gathered from the Holy Scriptures*. Halifax, N. S.: S. Selden, 1888.

Woosnam, Etty. *The Women of the Bible: New Testament*. London: S. W. Partridge, 1885.

Wordsworth, Elizabeth. *Illustrations of the Creed*. London: Rivington's, 1889.

Wright, Julia McNair. *Saints and Sinners of the Bible*. Philadelphia: Ziegler & McCurdy, 1872.

Younghusband, Frances. *The Story of Our Lord*. London: Longmans, Green, and Co., 1887.

Bibliography

Primary Sources

Alexander, Cecil Frances. *Hymns for Little Children*. London, 1848. 66th edition London: Masters, 1887.

Balfour, Clara Lucas. *Women of Scripture*. London: Houlston and Stoneman, 1847.

———. "The Virgin Mary." In *Women of the Old and New Testaments*, ed. Rev. H. Hastings Weld, 176–98. Philadelphia: Lindsay & Blakiston, 1848.

Barton, Lucy. *The Gospel History of our Lord and Saviour Jesus Christ*. London: W. Tweedie, 1837.

Baxter, Elizabeth. *The Living Word in the Gospel of St. John*. London: Christian Herald, 1887.

———. *The Women in the Word*. 2nd ed. London: Christian Herald, 1897.

Beck, Mary E. *Bible Readings on Bible Women*. London: S. W. Partridge, 1892.

Black, Margaret. *Woman's Daily Text Book: Homely Lessons from Women's Lives, Old and New Testament*. J. Paisley and R. Parlane, n.d.

Boddington, Gracilla. *A Practical Commentary on the Gospel of St. Luke, in Simple and Familiar Language*. London: J. Nisbet and Co., 1869.

Charles, Elizabeth Rundle. *Wanderings over Bible Lands and Seas*. London: T. Nelson and Sons, 1862.

———. *"By Thy Glorious Resurrection and Ascension": Easter Thoughts*. London: Society for Promoting Christian Knowledge, 1888.

———. *Ecce Ancilla Domini: Mary the Mother of Our Lord; Studies in the Christian Ideal of Womanhood*. London: Society for Promoting Christian Knowledge, 1894.

Cornwallis, Mary. *Observations, Critical, Explanatory, and Practical, on the Canonical Scriptures*. 4 vols. London: Baldwin, Cradock, and Joy, 1817; 2nd ed., 1820.

Copley, Esther Hewlett. *Scripture Biography: Comprehending All the Names Mentioned in the Old and New Testaments*. London: Fisher, Fisher & Jackson, 1835.

Donaldson, Mrs. *Home Duties for Wives and Mothers, Illustrated by Women of Scripture*. London: William Hunt, 1882.

G., M. *Women Like Ourselves: Short Addresses for Mother's Meetings, Bible Classes, Etc.* London: Society for Promoting Christian Knowledge, 1893.

Hale, Sarah. *Woman's Record; or, Sketches of all Distinguished Women, from the Creation to A.D. 1854.* New York: Harper & Brothers, 1855.

Jameson, Anna. *Sacred and Legendary Art.* London: Printed for Longman, Brown, Green, and Longmans, 1848.

Jameson, Anna. *Legends of the Madonna: as represented in the fine arts, forming the third series of Sacred and legendary art.* London: Longman, Brown, Green, and Longmans, 1852.

King, Frances Elizabeth. *Female Scripture Characters; Exemplifying Female Virtues.* London: F. C. & J. Rivington, 1813.

Locker, Hannah Jane. *Bible Readings from the Gospels for Mothers' Meetings, etc.* London: The Religious Tract Society, 1877.

More, Hannah. *Practical Piety; or, the Influence of the Religion of the Heart on the Conduct of Life.* London: T. Cadell, 1811.

Nightingale, Florence. *Florence Nightingale's Spiritual Journey: Biblical Annotations, Sermons and Journal Notes,* ed. Lynn McDonald, vol. 2 of *The Collected Works of Florence Nightingale.* Waterloo: Wilfred Laurier University Press, 2001.

Palmer, Phoebe. *Promise of the Father; or, A Neglected Speciality of the Last Days.* Boston: H. V. Degen, 1859.

Phelps, Elizabeth Stuart. *The Story of Jesus Christ: An Interpretation.* Boston and New York: Houghton, Mifflin, 1897.

Pridham, Caroline. *Little Elsie's Book of Bible Animals.* 2nd ed. London: A. S. Rouse, 1895; 3rd ed. London: A. S. Rouse, 1903.

Richmond, E. J. *Woman, First and Last: And What she has Done.* New York: Phillips & Hunt, 1887.

Sadlier, Mrs. J. *A New Catechism of Sacred History: Compiled from Authentic Sources for Catholic Schools.* Montreal: D. & J. Sadlier, 1875.

SchimmelPenninck, Mary Anne. *Biblical Fragments.* 2 vols. London: Ogle, Duncan, & Co., 1821.

Smith, Mary Ann. *The Holy Women of Old: Seventeen Lessons.* Edinburgh: John Anderson, 1897.

Smyth, Amelia Gillespie. *Mornings with Mama, or Dialogues on Scripture for Young Persons.* Edinburgh: W. Blackwood, 1830–36. American edition. *Children's Bible Stories: Being Conversations on the New Testament.* Philadelphia: Porter & Coates, 1883.

Stowe, Harriet Beecher. *Woman in Sacred History: A Series of Sketches Drawn from Scriptural, Historical, and Legendary Sources.* New York: J. B. Ford and Company, 1873.

Tooley, Sarah A. "The Sex Bias of the Commentators: An Interview with Mrs. Josephine Butler." *The Humanitarian* V, no. 6 (December 1894): 418–19.

Trimmer, Sarah. *A Help to the Unlearned in the Study of the Holy Scriptures: Being an Attempt to Explain the Bible in a Familiar Way, Adapted to the Common Apprehensions, and according to the Opinions of Approved Commentators.* London: Rivington, 1805.

Wheeler, Charlotte Bickersteth. *Our Master's Footsteps: or, Bible Class Notes for Thoughtful Girls.* London: Elliot Stock, 1883.

Bibliography

Wilson, Elizabeth. *A Scriptural View of Women's Rights and Duties in the Important Relations of Life.* Philadelphia: Wm S. Young, 1849.

Wordsworth, Elizabeth. *Illustrations of the Creed.* London: Rivingtons, 1889.

Secondary Sources

Prior to the Twentieth Century

Gregory the Great. *Homilies on the Gospels.* Trans. Dom David Hurst. Kalamazoo, MI: Cistercian Publications, 1990.

Byron, George Gordon, Lord. "The Giaur, a Fragment of a Turkish Tale." In *The Works of Lord Byron Complete in One Volume*, 3rd ed., 49–60. London: John Murray, 1837.

Clarke, Adam. "The Plan of Human Redemption." In *The Miscellaneous Works of Adam Clarke*, vol. 5., 57–81 London: T. Tegg, 1836.

Crashaw, Richard. "Epigrammata Sacra." In *Complete Works*, vol. 2, ed. Alexander Ballochgrosart, 97. London, 1862.

Farrar, Frederic William. *Life of Christ.* 2 vols. London: Cassell, Petter & Galpin, 1874.

Holmes, Oliver Wendell. *The Poet at the Breakfast Table.* Boston: James R. Osgood, 1872.

Jowett, Benjamin. *The Interpretation of Scripture and Other Essays.* London: George Routledge and Sons, Ltd., 1907.

Keith, Alexander. *Evidence of the truth of the Christian religion: derived from the literal fulfilment of prophecy, particularly as illustrated by the history of the Jews, and by the discoveries of recent travellers.* 8th ed. Edinburgh: Waugh and Innes, 1832.

Lawrence, Brother. *Practice of the Presence of God.* London: J. Masters, 1855.

Lewis, Sarah. *Woman's Mission*, 4th ed. London: John W. Parker, 1839.

Liddon, Henry Parry. *Sermons Preached Before the University of Oxford.* London: Rivingtons, 1869.

Mercier, Anne. *The Story of Salvation: Thoughts on the Historic Study of Scripture.* London: Rivingtons, 1887.

Moore, Henry. *The life of Mrs. Mary Fletcher: consort and relict of the Rev. John Fletcher, Vicar of Madeley, Salop, compiled from her journal, and other authentic documents.* London: Wesleyan Methodist Book Room, nd.

Mortimer, Favell Lee. *Light in the Dwelling: or, A Harmony of the Four Gospels; with Very Short and Simple Remarks , Adapted to Reading at Family Prayers, and Arranged in 365 Sections, for Every Day of the Year.* London: J. Hatchard and Son, 1846.

Owenson, Sydney, Lady Morgan. *Woman and Her Master.* London: Henry Colburn, 1840.

Patmore, Coventry. *The Angel of the House.* London: Macmillan, 1866.

Petrie, Mary Louisa Georgina. *Clews to Holy Writ or, the Chronological Scripture Cycle: A Scheme for Studying the Whole Bible in Its Historical Order During Three Years.* London: Hodder and Stoughton, 1893.

Prideaux, Humphrey. *The Old and New Testament Connected in the History of the Jews and Neighbouring Nations from the Declension of the Kingdoms of Israel and Judah to the Time of Christ*. 4 vols. London: R. Knaplock; J. Tonson, 1715–18.

Shipton, Anna. "The First Missionary." In *A Library of Religious Poetry: A collection of the best poems of all ages and tongues; With biographical and literary notes*, edited by Philip Schaff and Arthur Gilman, 228–29. New York: Dodd, Mead, and Company, 1881.

Spurgeon, Charles Haddon. *The Metropolitan Tabernacle Pulpit: Sermons Preached and Revised during the year 1865*. London: Passmore & Alabaster, 1866.

Westcott, B. F. *The Gospel According to St. John: The Authorized Version with Introduction and Notes*. London: J. Murray, 1882.

Wheeler, Charlotte Bickersteth. *Memorials of a Beloved Mother: Being a Sketch of the Life of Mrs. Cooper*. London: Wertheim and Macintosh, 1853.

Wordsworth, William. "London, 1802." In *Poems in Two Volumes*, vol. 1, 140. London: Longman, Hurst, et al., 1807.

Yonge, Charlotte M. *How to Teach the New Testament*. London: National Society's Depository, 1881.

Twentieth Century and Later

Anderson, Olive. "Women Preachers in Mid-Victorian Britain: Some Reflexions on Feminism, Popular Religion and Social Change." *The Historical Journal* 12.3 (1969): 467–84.

Baird, William. *History of New Testament Research*. 3 vols. Minneapolis: Fortress Press, 1992.

Bartholomew, Craig. "Theological Interpretation." In *The Oxford Encyclopedia of Biblical Interpretation*, ed. Steven McKenzie, vol. II, 387–96. Oxford: Oxford University Press, 2013.

Barton, John. *Holy Writings, Sacred Text: The Canon in Early Christianity*. Louisville: Westminster John Knox, 1997.

———. *The Cambridge Companion to Biblical Interpretation*. Cambridge: Cambridge University Press, 1998.

Bebbington, D. W. *Evangelicalism in Modern Britain: A History from the 1730s to the 1980s*. London: Unwin Hyman, 1989.

Boss, Sarah Jane, ed. *Mary: The Complete Resource*. London: Continuum, 2007.

Brekus, Catherine A. *Female Preaching in America: Strangers & Pilgrims 1740–1845*. Chapel Hill and London: The University of North Carolina Press, 1998.

Calvert-Koyzis, Nancy, and Heather E. Weir, eds. *Strangely Familiar: Protofeminist Interpretations of Patriarchal Biblical Texts*. Atlanta: Society of Biblical Literature, 2009.

———. *Breaking Boundaries: Female Biblical Interpreters Who Challenged the Status Quo*. London: T & T Clark, 2010.

Childs, Brevard S. *The New Testament as Canon: Introduction*. Philadelphia: Fortress, 1985.

Croy, N. Clayton. "Textual Criticism: New Testament." In *The Oxford Encyclopedia of Biblical Interpretation*, ed. Steven McKenzie, vol. II, 379–87. Oxford: Oxford University Press, 2013.

Bibliography

Davis, Elizabeth M. "Wisdom and Mercy Meet: Catharine McAuley's Interpretation of Scripture." In de Groot and Taylor, *Recovering Nineteenth-Century Women Interpreters of the Bible*, 63–80.

Degan, Mary Bertrand, ed. *Retreat Instructions of Mother Mary Catherine McAuley.* Westminster, MD: Newman, 1952.

De Groot, Christiana, and Marion Ann Taylor, eds. *Recovering Nineteenth-Century Women Interpreters of the Bible.* Symposium Series. Atlanta: Society of Biblical Literature, 2007.

Demers, Patricia. *Women as Interpreters of the Bible.* New York: Paulist Press, 1992.

Doern, Kirstin G. "Balfour, Clara Lucas." In *The Oxford Dictionary of National Biography*, 3: 514–15. 60 vols. Oxford: Oxford University Press, 2004.

Edwards, O. C., Jr. *A History of Preaching.* Nashville: Abingdon Press, 2004.

Eggen, Weil. "Jn 8:1–11, A Finger Writing Down the History: On Dialogues Beyond Canonicity." *Exchange* 27, no. 2 (1998): 98–120.

Farmer, David Hugh. *The Oxford Dictionary of Saints*, 4th ed. Oxford: Oxford University Press, 1997.

Florence, Anna Carter. *Preaching as Testimony.* Louisville: Westminster John Knox Press, 2007.

Goodacre, Mark. "Synoptic Problem." In *The Oxford Encyclopedia of Biblical Interpretation*, ed. Steven McKenzie, vol. II, 354–62. Oxford: Oxford University Press, 2013.

Gray, F. Elizabeth, ed. *Women in Journalism at the Fin de Siècle: Making a Name for Herself.* New York: Palgrave Macmillan, 2012.

Griffin, Susan M. *Anti-Catholicism and Nineteenth-Century Fiction.* Cambridge; New York: Cambridge University Press, 2004.

"Hale, Sarah Josepha (Buell)." In *American Authors 1600–1900: A Biographical Dictionary of American Literature*, ed. Stanley J. Kunitz and Howard Haycroft, 326. New York: The H. W. Wilson Company, 1938.

Harrisville, Roy A. "The Woman of Canaan: A Chapter in the History of Exegesis." *Interpretation* 20, no. 3 (1966): 274–87.

Hedrick, Joan D. *Harriet Beecher Stowe: A Life.* New York: Oxford University Press, 1994.

———. "'Peaceable Fruits': The Ministry of Harriet Beecher Stowe." *American Quarterly* 40, no. 3 (1998): 307–32.

Heimann, Mary. *Catholic Devotion in Victorian England.* Oxford: Oxford University Press, 1995.

Hogan, Lucy Lind. "Negotiating Personhood, Womanhood, and Spiritual Equality: Phoebe Palmer's Defense of the Preaching of Women." *American Transcendental Quarterly* 14, no. 3 (2000): 211–26.

Isenberg, Nancy. *Sex & Citizenship in Antebellum America.* Chapel Hill: University of North Carolina Press, 1998.

Kerfoot, Donna. "Etty Woosnam: A Woman of Wisdom and Conviction." In de Groot and Taylor, *Recovering Nineteenth-Century Women Interpreters of the Bible*, 217–31.

Kienzle, Beverly, and Pamela J. Walker, eds. *Women Preachers and Prophets Through Two Millennia of Christianity.* Berkeley and Los Angeles: University of California Press, 1998.

Kim, Eunjoo Mary. *Women Preaching: Theology and Practice Through the Ages*. Cleveland: Pilgrim Press, 2004.

Krueger, Christine L. *The Reader's Repentance: Women Preachers, Women Writers, and Nineteenth-Century Social Discourse*. Chicago: University of Chicago Press, 1992.

Larsen, Timothy. *Contested Christianity: The Political and Social Contexts of Victorian Theology*. Waco, TX: Baylor University Press, 2004.

———. *A People of One Book: The Bible and the Victorians*. Oxford: Oxford University Press, 2011.

Larson, Rebecca. *Daughters of Light: Quaker Women Preaching and Prophesying in the Colonies and Abroad 1700–1775*. New York: Knopf, 1999.

Lerner, Gerda. *The Creation of Feminist Consciousness*. Oxford: Oxford University Press, 1993.

Lewis, Agnes Smith. *Light on the Four Gospels from the Sinai Palimpsest*. London: William & Norgate, 1913.

Lindley, Susan Hill. *"You Have Stept Out of Your Place": A History of Women and Religion in America*. Louisville: Westminster John Knox Press, 1996.

Mathers, Helen. *Patron Saint of Prostitutes: Josephine Butler and a Victorian Scandal*. Gloucester: The History Press, 2014.

Michaels, J. Ramsey. "A Washington Bible Class: The Bloodless Piety of Gail Hamilton." In Calvert-Koysis and Weir, *Strangely Familiar*, 191–202.

Neill, Stephen, and Tom Wright. *The Interpretation of the New Testament 1861–1986*. Oxford: Oxford University Press, 1988.

Newsom, Carol A., Sharon H. Ringe, Jacqueline E. Lapsley, eds. *Women's Bible Commentary*. Twentieth-Anniversary Edition. Louisville: Westminster John Knox Press, 2012.

Osborn, Ronald E. *Folly of God: The Rise of Christian Preaching*, vol. 1, *A History of Christian Preaching*. St. Louis: Chalice, 1999.

Perrin, Nicholas. "Gospels." In *Dictionary for Theological Interpretation of the Bible*, ed. Kevin J. Vanhoozer, 264–68. Grand Rapids: Baker, 2005.

Rogers, Sherbrooke. *Sarah Josepha Hale: A New England Pioneer*. Grantham, NH: Tompson & Ruetter, 1985.

Roland, Christopher, and Ian Boxall. "Reception Criticism and Theory." In *The Oxford Encyclopedia of Biblical Interpretation*, ed. Steven McKenzie, vol. II, 206–15. Oxford: Oxford University Press, 2013.

Sales, Francis de. *Introduction to the Devout Life*. London: Rivington's, 1864.

Sancken, Joni. "Calling Forth More Witnesses: Claiming the Voices of Preachers Silenced by History." *Toronto Journal of Theology* 26, no. 1 (2010): 47–58.

Schroeder, Joy A. "Elizabeth Wilson, the Bible, and Legal Rights of Women in the Nineteenth Century." *Postscripts: The Journal of Sacred Texts and Contemporary Worlds* 5, no. 2 (2009): 219–32.

Schüssler Fiorenza, Elisabeth. *Bread Not Stone: The Challenge of Feminist Biblical Interpretation*. Boston: Beacon Press, 1984.

———. *In Memory of Her: A Feminist Theological Reconstruction of Christian Origins*. Lexington, NY: Crossroad, 1983.

Bibliography

Selvidge, Marla J. *Notorious Voices: Feminist Biblical Interpretation, 1500–1920*. New York: Continuum, 1996.

Stolpa, Jennifer M. "Preaching to the Clergy: Anne Brontë's *Agnes Grey* as a Treatise on Sermon Style and Delivery." *Victorian Literature and Culture* 31, no. 1 (2003): 225–40.

Styler, Rebecca. *Literary Theology by Women Writers of the Nineteenth Century*. Farnham, UK: Ashgate, 2010.

Taylor, Marion Ann. "Elizabeth Rundle Charles: Translating the Letter of Scripture into Life." In de Groot and Taylor, *Recovering Nineteenth-Century Women Interpreters of the Bible*, 149–63.

——. "Mary Cornwallis: Voice of a Mother." In de Groot and Taylor, *Recovering Nineteenth-Century Women Interpreters of the Bible*, 31–44.

——. "'Cold Hands Upon Our Threshold': Josephine Butler's Reading of the Story of the Levite's Concubine, Judges 19–21." In *The Bible as a Human Witness to Divine Revelation: Hearing the Word of God Through Historically Dissimilar Tradition*, ed. Randall Heskett and Brian Irwin, 259–73. London: T & T Clark, 2010.

——. "Women and Biblical Criticism in Nineteenth-Century England." In *The Bible and Women: An Encyclopedia of Exegesis and Cultural History*, vol. 8.2, edited by Ruth Albrecht and Michaela Sohn-Kronthaler. Atlanta: SBL Press, forthcoming.

Taylor, Marion Ann, and Agnes Choi, eds. *Handbook of Women Biblical Interpreters: A Historical and Biographical Guide*. Grand Rapids: Baker Academic, 2012.

Taylor, Marion Ann, and Heather E. Weir, eds. *Let Her Speak for Herself: Nineteenth-Century Women Writing on Women in Genesis*. Waco, TX: Baylor University Press, 2006.

Weir, Heather E. "Helping the Unlearned: Sarah Trimmer's Commentary on the Bible." In de Groot and Taylor, *Recovering Nineteenth-Century Women Interpreters of the Bible*, 19–30.

Welter, Barbara. "The Cult of True Womanhood: 1820–1860." *American Quarterly* 18 (1966): 151–74.

Wiseman, Nathaniel. *Elizabeth Baxter: Saint, Evangelist, Preacher, Teacher and Expositor*. London: The Christian Herald, 1928.

Wray Beal, Lissa M. "Mary Anne SchimmelPenninck: A Nineteenth-Century Woman as Psalm-Reader." In de Groot and Taylor, *Recovering Nineteenth-Century Women Interpreters of the Bible*, 81–98.

Zink-Sawyer, Beverly A. "From Preachers to Suffragists: Enlisting the Pulpit in the Early Movement for Woman's Rights." *American Transcendental Quarterly* 14.4 (2000): 193–209.

——. *From Preachers to Suffragists: Woman's Rights and Religious Conviction in the Lives of Three Nineteenth-Century American Clergywomen*. Louisville: Westminster John Knox Press, 2003.

Index of Names and Subjects

Literal sense of the biblical text, 23, 52, 53, 54, 55, 58, 108, 175, 228, 233. *See also* Biblical interpretation; Figural sense; Hermeneutics

Liturgy, 20, 27, 46, 49, 78, 107, 213, 240

Locker-Lampson, Hannah: life, 151; as preacher, 122, 124, 138, 151; on the Samaritan Woman at the Well, 151-52, 152-58

Love: of disciples to Jesus, 82, 99, 103, 109, 136; of God, 8, 70, 74, 98, 133, 219, 241; of Jesus, 78, 83, 84, 86, 97, 102, 104, 108, 110, 112-13, 115, 161, 187, 194, 205, 206; messages of, in gospel, 8, 11; of mother, 192; to neighbor, 20, 101, 102, 105; strong as death, 38; virtue of Martha of Bethany, 81, 83, 94, 96, 104, 110, 117; virtue of Mary of Bethany, 89, 91, 92, 94, 103, 118; virtue of Mary Magdalene, 215, 219, 222, 230, 235, 241-42, 243, 244; virtue of Mary, the mother of Jesus, 38, 60, 66, 67, 68, 73; virtue of women, 8-9, 21, 27, 68, 107, 111, 172, 218-19, 247

McAuley, Catherine: on Mary and Martha, 78; theological writer, 21

McFadyen, Nina L.: life, 93; on Mary and Martha of Bethany, 93-100; spiritual biography, 79-80, 93

Martha of Bethany, 14, 19, 77-120, 234, 248; character of, 78, 81, 84, 85, 88, 98, 102, 110; example of, 11, 22, 23, 101, 107; faith of, 78, 82, 88, 97, 116; fault of, 78, 79, 81-82, 84, 86, 96, 103-4, 110, 114-15; and hospitality, 22, 79, 81, 85, 94-95, 99, 110-11; service of, 14, 21, 83, 91, 114, 116; virtues of, 21, 78, 94, 104. *See also* Hospitality; Lazarus; Mary of Bethany

Mary of Bethany, 14, 19, 77-120, 233, 248; anointed Jesus, 83, 91-92, 99-100, 103, 109, 117; character of, 87, 89, 102, 91, 94, 102, 117; contemplative, 22, 78, 87, 89, 117; example of, 11, 22, 23, 107, 111, 112-113, 117; at feet of Jesus, 81, 85, 95, 102, 109-10, 117; identity of, 212, 220; piety of, 78, 86, 117; virtues of, 86-87. *See also*

Lazarus; Love; Martha of Bethany; Mary Magdalene

Mary Magdalene, 15, 109, 178, 207, 212-250; apostle of the resurrection, 230; in art, 218; character of, 212, 225-26, 229, 242; at cross, 221, 242; demon possession of, 220, 221, 235, 242; and *Faust*, 218, 223; hymn about, 240; identity of, 15, 212-13, 215-16, 217-18, 220-21, 228, 242-43; incredulity of, 231; preacher of Jesus, 149, 220, 222-23; a prostitute or harlot, 179, 212-13, 220, 221; significance of, 180, 213, 214, 220, 243-44; tradition around, 213, 215-216, 219-20; traveled with Jesus, 220, 235-36. *See also* Jesus, resurrection of; Love; Mary of Bethany

Mary, mother of Jesus, 14, 19, 25-76, 125, 127, 148, 165, 167, 223; addressed as "Woman", 23, 26, 36, 51-52, 52-59, 74, 243; appearance, 40, 41; contemplative, 22, 34, 36, 41, 74-75; and Cleopatra, 59, 60-61;at cross, 38, 242; example of, 21, 22, 23, 25-26, 27, 29, 47, 67-68, 75; faith, 31, 41-42, 47; feasts of, 62, 63, 65; Magnificat, 50, 57; post-resurrection, 39, 148, 225, 227; and Roman Catholic devotion, 25, 33n16, 47-48, 49; Scripture knowledge, 32, 41; silence of, 33, 70-71; tomb of hidden, 65; type of church, 23, 52, 55-59; virtues of 21, 22, 28, 32, 39, 41-42, 60-61, 66; at wedding of Cana, 36-37. *See also*, Angels, at annunciation; Elizabeth; Gabriel; Humility

Mary's gospel, 7-8

Masculine interpretation of scripture. *See* Gendered exegesis, "manly" approach

Mephibosheth, 186

Mercy, 33, 47, 50, 57, 98, 186, 188, 189, 192, 192, 204, 207; Sisters of, 21

Methodist, 122, 147, 149; women preaching, 122n6, 159

Miracles, 37, 53, 58, 87, 99, 167, 190, 231

Miriam, sister of Moses, 30, 55, 168, 169

Moravian church, 51

Moses, 65, 74, 206; law of, 198, 201, 203, 206, 219

Mothers: as book audience, 51, 155, 174,

Index of Scripture